Thinking as Anarchists

Ferro Piludu (1930–2011), founder of the Gruppo Artigiano Ricerche Visive of Rome, collaborated with the various editorial and cultural initiatives promoted by the GAF [Federated Anarchist Groups] from the early 1970s until his death. This poster was made for the Anarchist May 1st in 1977 and inspired the cover of this book.

Thinking as Anarchists

Selected Writings from *Volontà*

Edited by Giovanna Gioli and Hamish Kallin

EDINBURGH
University Press

Edinburgh University Press is one of the leading university presses in the UK. We publish academic books and journals in our selected subject areas across the humanities and social sciences, combining cutting-edge scholarship with high editorial and production values to produce academic works of lasting importance. For more information visit our website: edinburghuniversitypress.com

Edinburgh University Press Ltd
The Tun – Holyrood Road, 12(2f) Jackson's Entry, Edinburgh EH8 8PJ

Typeset in 10/14 Warnock Pro by
Cheshire Typesetting Ltd, Cuddington, Cheshire, and
printed and bound by CPI Group (UK) Ltd,
Croydon, CR0 4YY

A CIP record for this book is available from the British Library

ISBN 978 1 4744 8313 1 (hardback)
ISBN 978 1 4744 8315 5 (webready PDF)
ISBN 978 1 4744 8316 2 (epub)

Contents

Part III: The Imaginary Turned Upside Down

Part IV: The Pride in Being Anarchists

Acknowledgements

First and foremost, we would like to thank Rossella Di Leo, who as well as being one of the protagonists of this anthology has been an invaluable help from beginning to end, with an attention to detail, memory and enthusiasm that shines just as brightly as it did in 1984. Without her assistance, alongside the support of everyone at the Centro Studi Libertari, especially Sara Giulia Braun and Roberto Viganò, this project would have been impossible.

As part of the research for this book we were lucky enough to visit several veterans of Italian anarchism. Everyone we spoke to was unfalteringly enthusiastic and warmly welcoming. Franco Melandri was interviewed in the Forlì countryside, thanks to the hospitality of Rocco Ronchi and Cristina Patrizi; Antonio Senta welcomed us at the Anarchist Circle 'Camillo Berneri' in Bologna; Aurora Failla and the late Paolo Finzi at the *A/Rivista Anarchica* headquarters in Milan; Gianpiero Landi at the Biblioteca Libertaria Armando Borghi in Castel Bolognese. We are grateful for the grant from the University of Edinburgh School of Geosciences that allowed us to undertake that trip. We also acknowledge the financial support of the University of Edinburgh and Bath Spa University to cover the translation costs.

We would like to thank Peter Kravitz for bringing the original manuscript over to Scotland and keeping it safe; Jennie Renton for running such a wonderful bookshop; and both of them for recalling so vividly its journey to Edinburgh. Neal Ascherson was unfalteringly courteous and generous with his memory; Ian Jack enabled this link. John Clark not only wrote the preface but provided invaluable feedback on our introduction. Sincere thanks to our copy editor Cathy Falconer. Carol Macdonald at Edinburgh University Press was supportive throughout and ensured everything progressed as smoothly as possible.

Hamish Kallin would like to thank Calum Barnes, Francesca Ceola, Hannah-Luisa Cohen-Fuentes and his dad, Ivor Kallin, for introducing him to anarchism all those years ago.

Giovanna Gioli thanks Maria Rita, Ankita, Valerio and Anubi.

Editors' Note

The 'libertarian Tower of Babel' that was the International Anarchist gathering 'Venice 1984' brought together speakers and texts presented at the conference in multiple languages. These were then disseminated via anarchist journals, anthologies and pamphlets, and later made available online. The selection of contributions put together into the original *Thinking as Anarchists* manuscript (see Chapter 1) by the Centro Studi Libertari was originally translated from Italian by April Retter (Chapters 2, 4, 6, 7, 10 and 11) and from French (Chapter 5) by 'M. Le Disez'. A shortened and significantly revised English translation of Chapter 10 was published in *Our Generation* (Volume 19, No. 1) in 1987, and was reprinted in *Radical Papers 2* (Montreal: Black Rose Books, 1989). These translations were a fruit of militant passion and solidarity, and as such they were carried out prioritising timely dissemination over rigour and editorial concerns. Many years have passed, and we felt that the available translations were in need of philological work. Hence, what we present here is the outcome of a significant labour of retranslation carried out by Giovanna Gioli with the support of Hamish Kallin. Whilst versions and extracts of several of these chapters are available elsewhere, the translations offered here are substantially closer to the originals.

In collaboration with the Centro Studi Libertari, we decided to include some additional texts (Chapters 3, 8, 9 and 12) belonging to the decade stretching from 1984 to 1998, all but two of which (Chapters 8, 9) were originally published in *Volontà*. Chapter 3 was translated from the original French for this volume by Giovanna Gioli; the others from Italian by Richard Braude (8, 9) and Giovanna Gioli (12, 13). Chapter 8 was originally written for the international workshop 'Les Incendiaires de l'Imaginaire', held in Grenoble in March 1998.

It was then published in the collective volume *Les Incendiaires de l'Imaginaire* (Lyon: Atelier de création libertaire, 2000), and we reproduce it here in English for the first time as it links to Bertolo's other chapters in multiple ways, and especially so with the following chapter (9), which was originally published in *A/Rivista Anarchica* in 1983. Finally, Chapter 13, an important overview of the experience of *Volontà*, was written by Francesco Codello in Italian especially for this anthology in 2020.

In all the chapters, we have replaced quotations with English-published versions of the cited texts (where available) unless a specific meaning is lost in this process, and we indicate these exceptions. When English translations were not available, we have translated the quotations ourselves from the original language of the publication (Italian, French or German). Where possible, we cite the most recent English editions, as we wanted to prioritise making the texts accessible to an English-speaking audience.

Throughout the texts we present the author's footnotes using an iterative sequence of asterisks, *, **, ***, etc. Our comments, added for clarity or further explanation, are numbered [1], [2], [3], etc., so that the reader can easily distinguish between those footnotes added for this volume and those in the original texts.

Preface
John Clark

WHEN I HEARD about the project of publishing *Thinking as Anarchists*, I was delighted for many reasons. These reasons included my admiration and affinity for many of the contributors, the fact that the collection is not only an extremely valuable work but one that is long overdue, and, not least of all, because of the Edinburgh connection. As the editors explain, Edinburgh is in a fascinating way essential to the very existence of the book.

As it happens, Edinburgh played an important role in the emergence of my own connection with anarchism. In 1968, as a graduate student, I attended a Summer School at the University of Edinburgh. As I walked through the city centre each day, I passed a hippie selling *Anarchy* magazine (at the time, brilliantly edited by Colin Ward) on a street corner near the Old College. When I say a hippie, I mean the popular stereotype of a hippie: long hair, beard, beads, a robe down to the ground. *Anarchy*, I discovered, was his primary means of support.

I began stopping by regularly to talk about politics, and, of course, bought and read voraciously the two issues of *Anarchy* that appeared during my stay. They told of revolutionary events that were going on, not far away, in Paris. I was quite inspired both by *les événements* there and by *Anarchy*. When I finally got to Paris in August, it was all over, except for the inspiration. But that was a lot, so I decided that when I returned home to New Orleans, I would organise an anarchist group and order copies of *Anarchy* in bulk to help spread the word. So, I brought back from Edinburgh a certain utopian ideal, plus a dedication to the pursuit of this still rather vague and amorphous, albeit inspiring, ideal.

Sixteen years later, as I arrived in Venice, the nature of that ideal had become much more concrete. Over those years, I had devoted myself to the study of anarchist theory and practice, and in fact written three books on the subject. But, perhaps more importantly, I had also encountered, and become part of, a living tradition that was grappling with the problem of how to realise the ideal, to make possible a future of the greatest freedom and mutual fulfilment, not only for ourselves, but for the entire world.

Over that time, I had the good fortune of developing a strong connection with an extraordinary circle of European activist intellectuals who were at the centre of the project of envisioning the theoretical and practical future of anarchism that Venice symbolised. I call them a 'circle' but perhaps I should use the term *ensō* – the Japanese circular form that lacks the static perfection of the geometrical circle, but is more expressive, energetic and full of life.

The focal point of this circle or *ensō* was the Italians, whose work makes up the bulk of this book. Over the years, I came to know them through their extraordinary theoretical conferences ('Power and its Negation', 'Sexual Inequality', etc.), their outstanding publications such as *A/Rivista Anarchica* and *Volontà*, the indispensable work of their Centro Studi Libertari, and the impressive catalogue of their publishing house elèuthera, which has produced well over 400 books.

Officially entitled an 'Incontro internazionale anarchico', Venice was labelled in English a 'gathering'. Yet, it was much more than that. Perhaps it should have been called, paralleling the Italian, an 'encounter', to convey the idea that we came together to encounter, confront and come face to face with certain realities. For example, one another, our movement, our ideas, our practice, our history, our present and our possible futures. Venice might even merit the label 'Event', with all the implications of theoretical or historical momentousness that the term often conveys.

As Amedeo Bertolo explains in 'The Venice Connection', the gathering and its reverberations 'represent a fundamental "passage" in the life of the anarchist movement'. The challenge of Venice, he says, was to transform the promise of 1968, embodied in an incipient 'process of cultural change', into 'a true agent of social transformation'. It pointed toward the day when we can say that that promise had become a social-historical reality.

Furthermore, we came to Venice to think (as anarchists, of course) about what was expressed in the subtitle of the conference as the 'authoritarian tendencies' and the 'libertarian tensions' of contemporary society. By this is meant its Orwellian and post-Orwellian aspects, on the one hand, and, on the other, the forces of freedom and the communal powers that are waiting to be liberated, to burst through the shell of that old society.

We came to Venice to think as anarchists in the sense of building on what anarchism had been, but also in the sense of going beyond any 'arché', any static, dogmatic or uncritically accepted principle, even our own. Rather, as Amedeo Bertolo says, we came to 're-immerse' anarchism 'in the differing forms of reality'. So, as many of the Alter-Venetians later demonstrated (I think, for example, of Daniel Colson), we were confronted with the project of creating an 'anarchism with a difference'.

The texts collected in *Thinking as Anarchists* represent the efforts to work out this project. One can see in these chapters the grappling of their authors with concepts that are fundamental for the anarchist tradition. We might think of this as part of a movement from master-signifiers to a 'signification beyond mastery'. One such concept is the concept of power. Much of traditional anarchist discourse has been resolutely focused on power in the repressive sense in which power is a synonym for domination. Nevertheless, anarchist theorists have often distinguished carefully between 'power to' and 'power over', power in the service of liberation and power in the service of domination.

The idea of human creative powers and of power as generative, and not merely repressive, has been an important element of the history of political thought, as exemplified by Spinoza, Marx, Nietzsche, Foucault and many other theorists. And, of course, *pouvoir populaire* was a famous slogan of May '68, and 'power to the people' has been the rallying cry of many radical movements. Thus, it is important for anarchism to continue its development of a theory of liberatory powers. In this connection, Tomás Ibáñez points out usefully in his chapter that 'the most general' signification of 'power' is 'capacity to'. And Amedeo Bertolo emphasises the anarchistic connotations of power when he asserts that '"power to do, ability to do" (*poter fare*) . . . is an expression of extreme freedom'.

One can also see in these texts a progression toward a more explicit focus on domination as the ultimate object of anarchist critique. Rossella Di Leo's crucial chapter relates the anarchist project both to the *origins* of domination and also to the diverse *forms* of domination. While there has been a tendency in anarchism to focus on the state and capital as the privileged manifestations of domination, Di Leo points out the importance of patriarchy, the most ancient and, in some respects, the most deeply entrenched form of domination.

In the end, the anarchist critique is focused above all on the phenomenon of domination (and we might even say, in a left-Hegelian spirit, on the phenomenology of domination). Anarchists have recognised that there can be an 'authority of competence' that differs from arbitrary authority, there can be structural hierarchies that differ from dominating hierarchies, and, as noted, there can be a 'power to' that differs from any 'power over'. However, there can be no benign forms of domination. Nico Berti makes explicit the conclusion toward which the discourse of power and domination in these chapters ultimately points.

'To be epistemologically precise,' Berti says, 'human emancipation' means 'the elimination of domination'.

Anarchism is thus, at its core, about the historical dialectic between domination and freedom, as elaborated classically in Élisée Reclus's monumental 3,500-page *L'Homme et la Terre*. The anarchist historical narrative is about the quest for freedom in history, and about the struggle against domination as a constraint on this unfolding freedom. Amedeo Bertolo pinpoints quite clearly this focus of anarchism: 'The axiological base of anarchism, the "primary" value from which its theory and practice derive, is freedom.'

Though freedom is not the only positive reality for anarchists, it is the ultimate one. For example, as Francesco Codello astutely points out, 'anarchism encompasses democracy yet wants to overcome it'. Democracy, or popular self-determination, is a good, and it may even be seen as an element of freedom. However, freedom is a much larger reality that goes far beyond it.

In short, we are anarchists, those who seek to destroy all forms of domination, above all because we are libertarians, those who seek to realise the most expansive form of freedom. And this form consists of the greatest possible mutual flourishing of all human beings, of all beings on Earth, and of the living Earth itself. The anarchist conception of freedom, the most all-encompassing one in history, goes beyond Étienne Balibar's famous concept of *Égaliberté* to the broader and deeper concept of *Écoliberté*.

As I write, we are on the eve of the 150th anniversary of the Paris Commune. Élisée Reclus called 18 March 1871, the date of the founding of the Commune, 'the greatest date in French history' since 10 August 1789, the turning point of the French Revolution, the inauguration of the modern revolutionary era. These two historic dates, which helped give birth to the modern ideas of both Revolution and the Commune, loom over Paris 1968, over Venice 1984, and over us today.

The Paris Commune was the great inspiration for the idea that a revolutionised people could organise themselves into free communes, or political communities, practising radical direct democracy, but also going far beyond democracy. We see this more utopian, and more deeply anarchic, ideal beyond democracy in the radical imaginary of the Manifesto of Artists of the Commune, which declared, in a Fourierist mode, the need to create 'communal luxury', a life of beauty and abundance for all, and, in an internationalist mode, the need to establish 'the Universal Republic', the global free federation of free communes.

In a certain sense, our gathering in that Other Venice of 1984 can be seen as a prefiguration of, and perhaps even an 'encounter' with, the ideal of a world beyond all forms of domination, a world that is a community of free peoples and free communities. And this book can be seen as testimony to the importance of engaged thinking toward such an ideal.

March 2021, New Orleans

This book celebrates the lives of
Amedeo Bertolo (1941–2016)
Eduardo Colombo (1929–2018)
Roberto Ambrosoli (1942–2020)
Paolo Finzi (1951–2020)
David Graeber (1961–2020)

Part I: To Venice and Back

Roberto Ambrosoli (1941–2020) was a microbiologist and founding member of the Federated Anarchist Groups (GAF). In the second half of the 1960s he created the iconic character 'Anarchik, the enemy of the State', who can be seen in various poses throughout this book. Here he is sitting in a Venice gondola, one of the many images created for Venice 1984.

1 The Importance of Thinking as Anarchists

Hamish Kallin and Giovanna Gioli

> Proud to be anarchists and proud of our history, but mainly inquisitive about the world, conscious of problems, open to doubts and to challenges.
>
> Another Venice 1986: 7

MAIN POINT BOOKS in Edinburgh is a dreamy place. Endearingly chaotic in appearance, its wares are piled high. The proprietor, Jennie Renton (whose father fought with the International Brigades in defence of the Spanish Republic), is something of an under-the-radar heroine of Scottish cultural politics. Her work as editor, activist, writer and bookseller weaves an intricate social web between the nation's literary iconoclasts. It is fitting, therefore, that the rebirth of this project began there.

There are two of us editing this book. One speaks Italian, the other does not. This biographical snippet might feel unnecessary, but we believe it highlights the specific importance of this volume as an act of cultural and political translation. Back in 2014, the one who cannot speak Italian was a PhD student with a side-habit for picking up anarchist literature wherever he found it. And there it was: a neatly typed manuscript. A4 in size. Soft-bound, with thin cream pages. *Thinking as Anarchists: Selected Writings from Volontà* emblazoned modestly on the cover. £3 scribbled in pencil on the inside. As we later found out (thanks to Jennie's remarkable memory), it had made its way there via a left-libertarian conference in Amsterdam in the late 1980s. From there it was taken to Glasgow by the editor Peter Kravitz and, thirty years later, it formed part of his book collection sold on for posterity.

The one who cannot speak Italian duly parted with three pound coins and, manuscript underarm, walked home. With hindsight (and some embarrassment), he did not know who any of the authors were, but there was enough about this manuscript to intrigue and inspire. Finding it was fortuitous, for it contained a set of English translations that had never seen the light of day. At the time, this was just a hunch.

Skip forward a few years and the one who cannot speak Italian gained an Italian colleague. Politics sussed out not so subtly, the manuscript was safe to reveal to eyes that lit up: where did you find this? How is it here? What shall we do with it? To leave it languishing on a shelf in Edinburgh would be complicity with its obsolescence. We got in touch with the authors, trying to complete its journey into publication some thirty years later than initially intended. The result is a thoughtful and challenging record of a unique moment in anarchist history, rescued from obscurity or, more accurately, rescued from obscurity *in English*. In our meeting as editors, two lenses met; two views of anarchism that were conditioned first and foremost by language, highlighting the importance of *visibility* in a history all too often curated by what we can and cannot read. Anarchism has always had an international spirit (Anderson 2007), but the effort to hold on to that is obfuscated by the encroaching hegemony of English (especially but not only within academia).

This is a collection that plays three roles simultaneously: first, it attempts to capture the intellectual and political vitality of an international 'gathering' held in Venice in 1984; second, it offers a set of English-language translations from the Italian anarchist journal *Volontà* and its cultural milieu together for the first time; third, and as testament to the power of the thinking itself, the chapters still do what they were intended to do three decades ago, namely engage with key debates at the heart of what anarchism is, was and might be. It is the task of this introduction to guide the reader through those three roles, and to explain why they matter.

There was every chance, of course, that the material would feel dated, tired or simply irrelevant, and whilst there are undoubtedly moments where the contemporary anglophone reader may feel a little lost (which we seek to explain where necessary through footnotes), the central arguments remain remarkably salient. Who drives the 'locomotive of history' when both the idea and the material reality of the Worker (male, proletarian, organised, proud) ceases to exist? How should we theorise state power? How does misogyny relate to capitalism and the state? What does the economy look like in our utopias? These are just some of the questions that our contributors sought to address. To put it bluntly, we are still searching for answers to all these questions.

The material is clearly of interest to anglophone historians of anarchism, or twentieth-century radicalism more broadly. But the heart of this volume is not 'merely' historical, and its relevance cuts through time. To use Nico Berti's

Figure 1.1 The main poster for Venice 1984 was a reinvention of Enrico Baj's *Cagacazzo*, designed by Baj with Fabio Santin.

(Chapter 11) phrase about anarchism itself, these texts are certainly '*in* history and yet *against* history'. They are *in* history because they were published by a specific group of people in a specific context. It is one thing, however, to say that these texts bear the imprint of the 1980s, which they surely do – in the reconciliation with historical defeat, in the use of what would now be labelled 'poststructuralist' philosophy, in the grappling with the 'new masters' of individualised bureaucracy (Berti 2009), and so on – but it is a disservice to box these ideas solely into that context. In many ways, good anarchist thinking is always difficult to 'place', for it is as much about *ignoring* orthodoxies as intentionally overturning them, and in this sense the texts are *against* history just as much as they belong to it. Our interest in these essays lies in the way they approach some of the defining questions of contemporary social science/humanities scholarship from an angle that is rarely, if ever, published. How should we think of the state as a mode of power rather than a 'thing' without devolving 'power' only on to ourselves? How does authority get internalised by those who are subjected to the will of others? How should we explain the origins of patriarchy? These are not 'anarchist' questions per se, but answering them from a standpoint that refuses to fundamentally question, inter alia, state power, the institutionalisation of domination, the link between gendered oppression and authority itself, and so on, will always offer only partial answers. To the extent that all these questions intersect with so much of influential twentieth-century thought (Foucault, Baudrillard, Negri, Butler, the 'New Left' and so on), it is about time that we took seriously the anarchist contribution to these debates.

This introduction is split into five sections. In the first, we explain the significance of the Venice gathering in 1984. In the second, we introduce the role of *Volontà* as a vehicle for thinking through the central tenets of a renewed anarchism. In the third, we provide an overview of what we see as some of the most important ideas that emerge in this volume. In the fourth, we reflect on the transition to a 'new' anarchism and, finally, we end by asking what it might mean to 'think as anarchists' in the third decade of the twenty-first century.

An International Anarchist *Incontro*: Venice 1984

> How refreshing to be in a community where everyone took it for granted that all governments are disasters, all bosses, capitalists or commissars, are tyrants.
>
> Colin Ward (1984), reporting from Venice

Campo Santa Margherita is an elongated triangular square on Venice's central island, close to the university. Whilst it is now 'off the tourist trail' enough to have become a tourist attraction (Airbnb room overlooking the square? €100 a night), in September 1984 it was full of a very different kind of visitor. As many as 3,000 anarchists, from as far away as South Korea, New Zealand, Iran and Uruguay, gathered here to discuss the future of their shared ideal. The date was chosen as a nod to Orwell's fantasy of a totalitarian future; the word *incontro* (rendered somewhat ineffectually in English as 'gathering') was chosen over words such as 'congress' or 'conference' to indicate the open and horizontal nature of the event. While 'gathering' remains a workable translation, it is worth mentioning that the nuances of the word *incontro* are not exhausted by it. *Incontro* is in the first place an *encounter*, the act of meeting. It can signify a date too, but also an uncanny experience, with connotations that are warm, friendly, adventurous, even carnal. As D'Attilio (1985: 4) notes, the word was 'chosen to indicate a wider scope than just an intellectually or politically orientated meeting', with none of the 'Gospel-like overtones' that 'gathering' might imply in English. Not for the last time in this volume, something is slightly lost in translation, but we have done our best to signpost any particular slippages that we think are important (see Editors' Note).

Venice 1984 caught the international anarchist movement at a particularly fascinating juncture. In Italian there is a specific word to indicate this period, *riflusso*, which could be translated as the backwash left by the receding wave of political activism that characterised the 1960s and 1970s. It is to that period that the content of this book belongs (though in some ways, *riflusso* never ended). The material itself can be thought of as a very different kind of *riflusso*, as a counter-flow against the tide of individualism, consumerism and acquiescence that characterised the 1980s across the Western world. This was a period in which the hope of the '60s had faded and the tension of the '70s had waned. The shoots of poststructuralism were growing in the academy, whilst the fantasists (and fanatics) of neoliberalism were in the ascendance left, right and centre. The Soviet Union was utterly stagnant ideologically and economically (though few predicted its imminent collapse), and the organs of the political working class had come so close (in Italy of all places) and yet stood so far from truly 'storming heaven' (Wright 2002). As Bookchin put it (1985: 22):

Venice unfolded under the shadow of an eclipsing anarchist tradition of syndicalism and the hidden challenge of so-called 'new social movements' like
ecology, feminism, anti-militarism, communitarianism, and urban concepts of
what in England is called 'local socialism' and what I have designated for some
twelve years as 'libertarian municipalism.' The old working class 'paradigm'
of 'wage labor versus capital' is giving way in much of Western society to

new movements that cut across traditional class lines and strategies for social change.

The *incontro* itself was a remarkable event, not least because of the range of people it brought together. There were well-known names among them – 'Murray Bookchin was one of the most important people in Venice, and he seemed to know this,' recalls Paolo Finzi with a wry smile[1] – but what gave the gathering a truly historical importance was not its leading lights, but the array of different voices present. As Finzi was determined to tell us, there were anarchisms *not* represented in Venice – 'I found out later that a number of Italian anarchist groups had boycotted the conference as being too academic,' notes Benello (1985: 16) – but the event was still one of the most important meetings in the history of the ideal simply in terms of how many people it brought together of different opinions and from different parts of the world.

All of this was thanks to the astonishing efforts of the Milan-based anarchist collective at the Centro Studi Libertari/Giuseppe Pinelli Archive [Centre for Libertarian Studies] (hereafter CSL) in collaboration with the Centre International de Recherches sur l'Anarchisme (CIRA) of Geneva, Switzerland, and the Anarchos Institute of Montreal, Canada. We can hardly imagine how difficult it must have been for the CSL to obtain the permits to use two Venetian squares – Campo San Polo as well as the aforementioned Campo Santa Margherita – with the antagonism of the Communists sitting in the municipal council and the obvious opposition and moral condemnation of Christian Democracy. The permits were only granted four days before the *incontro* was due to begin on 26 September. The University of Venice School of Architecture (IUAV) was chosen as the site for the more formal conference-like proceedings, where the intellectual bricks to (re)build the edifice of anarchism were to be presented and discussed under the title 'Authoritarian tendencies and libertarian tensions in contemporary societies'.

The behind-the-scenes materials of the conference – letters and circulars in multiple languages, invites, permits, design sketches, financial records – are

---

[1] Paolo Finzi (1951–2020) was a key figure in the anarchist journal *A/Rivista Anarchica*, based near to the *Centro Studi Libertari* (CSL) in Milan since its inception in February 1971. This was the best-selling anarchist journal in Italy throughout his life, and it ceased publication with Finzi's suicide on 20 July 2020. We spoke to him at length in the summer of 2018 during a research trip to northern Italy, and the quotes used here are from that time. A number of tributes and obituaries (in multiple languages) to his memory can be found on various anarchist websites, and we remain humbled by his kindness, humour and dedication.

Figure 1.2 Enrico Baj (1924–2003) during the preparation of *Cagacazzo*, a figure of his *Apocalisse*.

equally fascinating and preserved in the CSL archive. So too are the myriad responses and messages of support from anarchist groups across the world. As part of our research for this project we visited the CSL in Milan, where they are engaged in an ongoing digitisation of many of the resources connected to Venice 1984 and *Volontà* more broadly.[2] The superb quality of the posters and panels (and even wine labels!) is the result of a sadly long-gone spirit of solidarity and camaraderie. Enrico Baj (1924–2003; see Fig 1.2), the 'neo-dadaist' 'pataphysicist' (Eco 1979: 14) artist, designed the main poster for Venice 1984 (see Fig. 1.1). Luigi Veronelli, noted gastronome, wine critic and lifelong anarchist, supplied wine for the conference (see Fig. 1.3), with around 3,000 bottles fuelling the discussions. Roberto Ambrosoli's notorious 'Anarchik' (an auto-ironic comic character born in the mid-1960s, representing the grumpy, 'vintage' neo-anarchist) could not miss the event either. The striking aesthetic quality of the *incontro* matched the renewed vigour of *Volontà*, where an attention to the design of the covers was part of a broader attitude towards anarchism itself: a new look that would attract attention and convey a freshness of thinking.

[2] See <https://centrostudilibertari.it/en/ven84-homepage-en> (last accessed 17 May 2021).

Figure 1.3 Luigi Veronelli (1926–2004) was one of the most important Italian oenologists. A Proudhonian anarchist, he has long collaborated with the CSL. At his own expense, he provided a huge amount of excellent wines for Venice 1984, including the famous *Bricco dell'Uccellone*, which proved to be essential to cover the expenses of the meeting.

Without a doubt, the conference itself was an immense achievement, and deserves further study from an historian's perspective, but as Amedeo Bertolo explains in Chapter 2, 'Venice' should not be read here as a signifier of a place or a time, but rather a moment in the history of anarchism, characterised by a desire to renew the ideal without disavowing its roots. Bertolo sees Venice as a 'passage', a transition, not because it was that *actual* passage, but rather a virtual transition, the disclosure of a problematic field that still pertains to our present almost four decades later. Venice was a portal, opening up a field of possibility that is far from being exhausted or overcome. This is why Bookchin's (1985: 23) words still apply: 'The conference is still going on, not in any metaphorical sense that it is a "living memory" but in the problematic sense that it posed crucial questions for anarchism that have yet to be fully explored and answered.'

Once the dust had settled after the gathering in Venice, a substantial effort was made to disseminate some of the ideas that had been discussed. The majority of the chapters herein were translated from Italian and French into English relatively quickly (see Editors' Note for details), and a manuscript was dutifully prepared. For reasons lost in time, it never saw the light of day. Only a few draft copies were printed, and the whereabouts of the others is unclear. The core of this book

Figure 1.4 Giuseppe Pinelli reproduced by Baj from his painting *The Funeral of the Anarchist Pinelli* (1972) and gifted to the Centro Studi Libertari/Giuseppe Pinelli Archive in 1986. On Baj and Pinelli see Pozzoni (2021).

(Chapters 2, 4, 5, 6, 7, 10 and 11) are taken from that manuscript, substantially retranslated for clarity. In conversation with Rossella Di Leo and the CSL (whose effort in helping us with this project has been immeasurable), we have added some material (Chapters 3, 8, 9 and 12) whose content closely chimes with the original manuscript. In addition, Francesco Codello's piece on the significance of *Volontà* (Chapter 13) was commissioned to help unfamiliar readers get to grips with the context. We cannot promise to convey the full array of ideas discussed at this 'libertarian Tower of Babel' (Centro Studi Libertari 1984: 1), but we offer a fuller glimpse of its importance than has ever been available in English before.

Volontà: A Workshop of Anarchist Ideas

If 'Venice' represents the spirit in which these papers were written, they are also united by their connection to the journal *Volontà* (1946–1996), where all but two were originally published.[3] The connection between the journal and the event is not coincidental, for the editorial group running the former were also the principal organising team behind the latter, a milieu attached to the CSL, which also hosts the Giuseppe Pinelli Archive in Milan.

The story of Giuseppe 'Pino' Pinelli (1928–1969; see Fig. 1.4), an anarchist who worked on the Italian railways, is key to understanding the genesis of the cultural and political atmosphere that gave birth to the materials presented in this anthology. On 12 December 1969, a bomb exploded at the National Bank of Agriculture in Milan's Piazza Fontana (see Lanza 2003). Sixteen people died, and eighty-eight were wounded. Two attacks were carried out in Rome as well, wounding eighteen people. Within minutes, the police were instructed 'to direct their attention towards investigating the anarchists' (Christie 1984: 52). One hundred and fifty were arrested within days, among them Rome-based dancer and poet Pietro Valpreda (who was acquitted in 1987 for lack of evidence) and Pinelli. Following two days of confinement at the police headquarters in Milan, at around midnight on 15 December his body plunged from the fourth-floor window of the office belonging to the police commissioner, Luigi Calabresi. Whether he was dead before he fell remains unknown. The morning after, Luciano Lanza received a phone call from his comrade Amedeo Bertolo: 'They threw Pinelli out the window. Let's all gather in front of the police headquarters . . . in order to silence

---

[3] Bertolo's 'The Subversive Imaginary' (Chapter 9) first appeared in *A/Rivista Anarchica* in 1981. Its twin-essay (Chapter 8), Bertolo's 'Utopian Function', was published in the French anthology *Les Incendiaires de l'Imaginaire*, Atelier de création libertaire, Lyon, 2000.

us up they will have to throw all of us from the window' (translated from Senta 2015: 210). As the historian Paul Ginsborg (1990: 333) explains,

> The official version of Pinelli's death was that he had committed suicide. In a press conference that same night the Milanese police chief, Marcello Guida, announced that Pinelli's alibi had proved false, and that he was 'gravely implicated in the organization of the massacre'. Six years later the courts ruled, on the contrary, that Pinelli had been innocent of any involvement in the crime. The truth about how he died has never been established.

Evidence which the police had chosen to ignore pointed not to the anarchists but to a neo-fascist group led by Franco Freda and Giovanni Ventura based in the Veneto region under the protection of Christian Democracy. As Toscano points out (2019: 1,107), Piazza Fontana is 'a transformative date in Italian political history' as it inaugurated the '"strategy of tension"[4] that saw the Italian deep state find common cause with (or insistently manipulate) a galaxy of far right and neo-fascist movements whose progeny are still holding confidently forth, for instance in that particularly effective collective political entrepreneur that is the Casa Pound movement'. The period spanning from 1969 to the late 1980s and its long wave of political terrorism, known in Italy as the 'years of lead'

---

[4] The expression 'strategy of tension' first appeared in a British newspaper (*The Observer*) on 14 December 1969. Ascherson, Davie and Cairncross (1969: 2) were reporting on the Piazza Fontana massacre, writing that: 'Nobody is crazy enough to blame President Saragat for the bombings. But the entire Left is saying today that his "strategy of tension" indirectly encouraged the far Right to go over to terrorism.' As Neal Ascherson recalls (personal communication), the Italian journalists were eager to use the phrase, but none of them would risk taking responsibility for setting it in ink, and so they 'all benevolently conspired to set me up with tales and gossip and analysis about Saragat's "Strategy of Tension"'. Having convinced Ascherson they were all going to use it, 'none of them wrote the story or pointed a finger at Saragat. Instead, they all sanctimoniously denounced the outrageous slander against Italy published in *The Observer* – and thus were able to go on to print the whole "disgraceful" text of what I had written.' The very same day, the passage was translated and commented on in *Unità*, the official newspaper of the Italian Communist Party (PCI), who were at pains to outsource responsibility under the headline 'The Observer attacks the Socialdemocrats' (President Saragat's party). The anger of the Italian government was safely directed at *The Observer*'s editors, and the expression was then free to enter the Italian political lexicon, rising to become a defining term of those years, as well as of a specific strategy globally. Half a century after the act, Ascherson recalls: 'You have to laugh. I do think there probably was such a Strategy. But I didn't discover it, not even the phrase. I was used, adeptly. And I don't resent it at all.'

(where *lead* is a reference to bullets), is an important historical and political subtext to the thoughts and experiences narrated in this book. It made the threat of the state (and its proximity to fascist organisations) acutely clear, and in the face of such orchestrated tension, to remain an anarchist required both a clarity of vision and conviction of the will.

The name *Volontà* (meaning 'Will') is more often associated with two earlier anarchist periodicals: *La Volontà* ('The Will'), Errico Malatesta's newspaper published in Ancona from 1911 to 1914, and *Pensiero e Volontà* ('Thought and Will'), published between 1924 and 1926, co-founded by Malatesta and Luigi Fabbri. A 'fortnightly journal of social studies and general culture' (as its subtitle put it), *Pensiero e Volontà* was closed after only two years of activity because of fascist laws limiting freedom of expression. In its brief but intense life it attracted many important collaborators, including Camillo Berneri. At the end of the dictatorship in 1946, Giovanna Caleffi (a prominent figure of the international anarchist movement and widow of Camillo Berneri, who had been killed in Barcelona in 1937 during the Spanish Civil War, see footnote p. 243) and Cesare Zaccaria founded the magazine *Volontà*. They took up the title that Errico Malatesta had given to his newspaper, but we should not overemphasise the affinities between the two publications.

As Turcato (2015) argues, the word 'will' carries specific weight, for it tells us something important about the evolving politics of Malatesta's anarchism, and anarchism in general. It emphasises the intentionality that radicalism requires, as an antidote to both the historical determinism of mainstream Marxism and Kropotkin's attempt at grounding anarchism in a 'scientific' account of timeless nature. The importance of this 'will' lies in its rejection of a teleological understanding of historical agency (we need to want to change the world, not wait for it to change of its own accord). It is in some ways an anarchist analogue to Rosa Luxemburg's famous declaration that the future presented a choice between socialism and barbarism, where, as Löwy (2013) notes, it is the notion of a *choice* that was perhaps most radical.[5] It is not for nothing, then, in those lonesome post-

---

[5] It is intriguing to reflect on Gramsci's (1977: 188) original use of that oft-quoted phrase 'pessimism of the intellect, optimism of the will', attributed to the French Stalinist Romain Rolland, which is, we want to suggest, not an appropriate comparison in the way that Luxemburg's notion of a *choice* is. Rolland's formulation, whilst seductively phrased, is deployed by Gramsci in an otherwise strikingly authoritarian way. It denotes a *unified* will, subservient to a mass that yearns to be embodied in the 'proletarian' state. Written just a year before the suppression of the Kronstadt uprisings, its indictment of the Italian anarchists for so foolishly warning of the threat inherent in state-obsessed forms of communism makes for bitter reading.

war years, when the Italian anarchist movement was heavily depleted by fascism, war and Stalinism, that this name seemed appropriate for a new journal. As a rallying point for a beleaguered movement, the reminder that 'history' needed to be made rather than received was captured in this grandiose little word. Bertolo (Chapter 8, p. 148) hints at this when he reminds us that 'anarchism – in coherence with its choice of freedom – does not believe in history's necessary and progressive unfolding but rather sees social change as a voluntary action'.

The experience of *Volontà* spanned 339 issues over half a century (1946 to 1996). This is a history that can be divided into three distinct phases. The first begins in 1946 with the founding of the journal and lasts until the death of Giovanna Caleffi in 1962, during which this was the most important anarchist journal in Italy. The second phase runs from 1962 to 1979 with a succession of various editors (Giuseppe Rose, Vincenzo Di Maria, Aurelio Chessa, Roberto Tronconi) without much editorial support. The journal was characterised by a telling quiescence during the hot years preceding and following May 1968. *Volontà* needed to change, or it would become irrelevant. It is only with the passage of the editorial office to Valdobbiadene (Treviso), under the responsibility of Francesco Codello, that the journal witnessed a cultural rebirth. In 1980 the editorial collective moved back to Milan and became a vibrant hub of anarchist thinking for over a decade. Codello (Chapter 13) provides an overview of the journal's evolution in more detail, written especially for this anthology.

The renaissance of *Volontà* in the 1980s coalesced around two important experiences. The first is the foundation, in 1976, of the CSL in Milan, which was largely driven by the Gruppi Anarchici Federati (GAF) [Federated Anarchist Groups] (for a history of the CSL see Balsamini 2021). The second is the international anarchist journal *Interrogations* (1974–1979), founded by Louis Mercier Vega. *Interrogations* published articles in four languages (French, Italian, Spanish and English), and Amedeo Bertolo, Rossella Di Leo, Luciano Lanza and Giampietro 'Nico' Berti were key figures on the Italian editorial team. The international experience of *Interrogations* certainly contributed to the consolidation of what would become the core editorial team and the 'galaxy' of *Volontà*. Eduardo Colombo, forced to flee his native Argentina for Paris in 1970, was also part of this galaxy, together with Tomás Ibáñez, who spent his youth in France after his parents fled to escape Franco's regime in Spain.

In 1978 the CSL and *Interrogations* co-organised the International Conference on the New Masters in Venice (see Berti 2009). The conference pivoted around the core belief that the capitalist-bourgeois order was destined to undergo a transformation due to the coming to power of a new techno-bureaucratic class that would replace the power of the old bourgeoisie. As Roberto Ambrosoli (translated from *I Nuovi Padroni* 1979: 8) put it, 'we are studying the new masters . . . not because they are merely an interesting social phenomenon, but because they are our enemies, ours and of those who, like us, fight for a society that has its cornerstones in equality and solidarity, not in power.' This urgent call for a more fundamental interrogation on the roots of domination (same Latin root as *dominus*, 'master') and its eradication from society informs the research of the *Volontà* group in the years between the 'New Masters' conference and Venice 1984. The chapters in this anthology weave together the voices of their authors in an incessant discussion on the nature of power (Bertolo, Colombo, Ibáñez), its relationship to freedom and equality (Berti), patriarchy (Di Leo) and with both the realms of the imaginary and the economic (Lanza and Bertolo) that centred around the idea of differentiating domination from power, thus strengthening and renewing the conceptual arsenal of anarchism. We address these themes in more detail below.

English-language accounts of Italian anarchism tend to focus on its heyday, roughly beginning with Bakunin's first visit in 1864 and ending with the rise of fascism in the 1920s (Pernicone 2009; Levy 1989; Di Paola 2017; Turcato 2015). There are good reasons for this, but the risk is that it leaves a hole in the historiography of anarchism, one that is fed intellectually (if inadvertently) by suggestions that the 1980s were a period in which 'interest in anarchism seemed to be waning' (Amster et al. 2009: 4) or that we can jump straight from something called 'classical anarchism' to postmodernity (Newman 2011) without stopping to refuel along the way. It also fails to understand the deeply international nature of the anarchist movement, and how its allegedly 'national' varieties are never a single national story (and rarely carried out in a single language!). Turcato's (2015) insistence that we reject the 'wave' model of anarchism – where it appears to flare up in one generation, disappear in the next, and flare up again a decade down the line with no continuity between the two – is especially important here. So too is his insistence that there is a geography to those waves that can be all too easily overlooked: if anarchism 'disappears' in one part of the world, then the first task should be to look further afield before asserting that the heartbeat has stopped.

Volontà in this period had no English-language equivalent. The British journal *Anarchy* (1961–1970), under the stewardship of Colin Ward (1987), was perhaps closest. Indeed, there was plenty of crossover, for Ward was another figure at the Venice gathering, and his writing was published in *Volontà* multiple times.[6] If the two journals shared an editorial aim (a desire to renew anar-

---

[6] Ward's 'Italian connection' is missing from English-language accounts of his life or his politics (e.g. Goodway 2006; Honeywell 2011), which can risk framing him as quintes-

chism, to reconnect it to 'everyday life' as a realm of struggle), in terms of style they are quite distinct. *Anarchy* was determinately pragmatic, wilfully direct in its prose; *Volontà* was far more theoretically and philosophically focused, far more avowedly intellectual. *Anarchy* pre-empted the insurrections of the late 1960s; *Volontà* tried to pick up the pieces. There is nothing inherently virtuous in theoretical complexity, however, and this is not to suggest that one was 'better' than the other: they are fascinating to consider alongside each other as complementary attempts to haul the anarchist idea out of the nineteenth century and into the collapsing embers of the twentieth. In this sense, they both point towards a contemporary anarchism that is in no way reducible (through either adoption or rejection) to the grand names of the nineteenth century. To draw further from Turcato (2015), one of the most frustrating and recurrent errors that historians (even sympathetic ones) commit when considering 'anarchism' is to see it as an unchanging (hence hopelessly antiquated) ideal, proscribing to anarchists the fate of the fatally certain – albeit perhaps morally laudable – idiot (a caricature Di Leo aptly dismantles in Chapter 12). As Clark (1984: 120) points out, far too many political theorists engage with 'an anarchism that has existed primarily as a fiction in the minds of its opponents', and we are more interested in the anarchism that existed in the minds of its proponents, and their minds certainly were not static. *Volontà* in the early 1980s, like *Anarchy* a decade before it, shatters so many of these fictions, and shows instead how anarchism was being concertedly reworked to reflect the world it confronted.

In recent years there has been a surge of interest in anarchism within the academy (for better or for worse), reflected in such initiatives as the Anarchist Studies Network, the *Anarchist Studies* journal, and the multiple scholarly books that have come out under academic publishers, a list to which we can add the present volume.[7] This means, arguably for the first time, that anarchism has an active academic current alongside its social current. The relation between the two raises issues regarding the sometimes fraught interaction between theory

---

sentially 'British' in a way that downplays his international links. This oversight seems entirely attributable to the language barrier.

[7] A full list of these titles is beyond our scope here, but to gain some sense of the blossoming of anarchist scholarly work, see the Contemporary Anarchist Studies series from Manchester University Press (with earlier volumes published by Bloomsbury/ Continuum), as well as recent contributions from Kinna (2016) and Ferretti (2018). It is also worth noting that many of the historical texts put out by anglophone anarchist publishers over recent years first saw the light of day as academic books at much higher prices (e.g. Di Paola 2017; Ealham 2010; Turcato 2015).

and praxis, similar to those debates that wracked the political conscience of earlier Marxists. Much of the surge in anarchist academia is historical in scope (which is not to detract from its importance) but, we want to suggest, the present volume is quite unusual in this regard. It is historical in both form and function – resurrected from the 1980s, with an historical focus to many of the chapters – but it takes the future firmly in its sights, and that is a future still beyond our grasp. In this sense, it fills two substantial gaps in the available scholarship on anarchism: first, it is scholarly work from an anarchist perspective three decades before any mooted 'anarchist turn' in the academy (Blumenfield, Bottici and Critchley 2013); second, like the vast majority of anarchist literature on the planet, it was not written in English, and this means that it has remained largely 'hidden' from an anglophone audience. The language barrier still haunts the movement. Even figures as famous as Bakunin, Proudhon and Malatesta have only very recently benefited from an attempt to fully publish their works in English, which should give you some idea of the paucity of translated work elsewhere.

At the tail end of the 1950s, Colin Ward (cited in Goodway 2006: 313) exclaimed that 'ideas and not armies change the face of the world', before lamenting that 'in the sphere of what we ambitiously call the social sciences, too few of the people with ideas couple them with anarchist attitudes'. Graeber (2004) expressed a similar sentiment half a century later. It is, as Ibáñez (2019) notes, no longer possible to bemoan the lack of 'anarchist academics', but the majority of those within the academy who identify as anarchists are scholars *of* anarchism; we still await a moment where anarchism becomes a common current in work focused outwards, away from itself. *Volontà* should be seen as an instructive forerunner in this regard even if this introduction is not. For whilst it made a concerted effort to link to 'the most interesting strands of the social sciences' (cited in Codello, Chapter 13), it remained thoroughly grounded in a militant, public-facing and culturally vibrant anarchism that did not and does not – and to our minds should not – fit comfortably into the confines of the bureaucratic, competitive, hierarchical, statist university system. The authors featured in this volume were not striving to be scholars *of* anarchism, but to live an anarchist life where thinking, writing and acting were all interconnected. Theirs was an anarchism of intellect and action, where the two terms are mutually constituted, not an *academic* anarchism in the institutionalised sense of the word. They were consistent militants, and the remarkable author biographies featured at the end of this volume give a sense of this.

As for ourselves, this book was more of a labour of love than an act of work. But, as always for scholars, the line between the two (if you are lucky) is sometimes hazy. We therefore sit in a position of institutional and salaried privilege, and have tried to approach this as custodians of a body of work whose political vitality is by no means beholden to us as editors, a role we have taken on through a mixture of interest and happenstance.

'A New Analysis for the Usual Strategy'

Having sketched out a sense of the origins of this work, we now offer a brief overview of the key ideas that its authors were focused on tackling. These ideas emerge from a particular milieu, a 'galaxy' composed of stars that shone across a myriad of interconnected groups, not least the CSL and the Milan-based anarchist magazine *A/Rivista Anarchica*, as well as the organising committee of Venice 1984, with plenty of overlap. Several of the key figures who would come to make up this galaxy co-authored a book published in 1973 by Pio Turroni's L'Antistato under the title *Anarchism '70: A New Analysis for the Usual Strategy* (on Pio Turroni see footnote p. 244). We quote here from Bertolo's (translated from Ambrosoli et al. 1973: 6) introduction to that book, for we feel it helps to convey the shared vision of those involved, the vision that became central to the work in this book.

> The very title of this book [A New Analysis for the Usual Strategy] captures quite well, in our opinion, the direction in which we must move: to graft onto the 'old' trunk of anarchism, cleaned of dead branches, the most fruitful shoots of modern economic and sociological thought; to analyse reality with new available forms of knowledge in order to employ the 'usual' method in the most profitable way, for the 'usual' purposes.

The 'usual' here [*di sempre*] is an anarchism that endures, an ever-lasting anarchism. Here is a joyful double-turn between an insistence on that quality of anarchism that makes it an 'always', a constant, whilst insisting on the need to forge it anew. All the contributions to the present volume were written in a similar mindset.

In his 1983 essay on 'Power, Authority, Domination' (Chapter 4), Bertolo asks why it is that anarchism, 'which can be considered the most radical critique of domination to date', is missing a mature and fully developed theory of power. In many ways all the chapters in this volume coalesce around that challenge, to question how we might see, imagine, live and think without domination in its various forms, whether in the imaginary, the state, patriarchy or the economic. Domination defines a relationship which is characterised by asymmetry between unequals: unequal in terms of power and so of freedom;

it defines a situation of superordination/subordination; it defines systems of permanent asymmetry between social groups. From an anarchist perspective, domination is thus a defining feature of both the state *and* capitalism, but it is not reducible to either (pre-dating, and most likely postdating, both). Bertolo attempts to disaggregate this 'jolly' word power into three separate concepts, 'power', 'domination' and 'authority', not aiming at an historical or etymological reconstruction of how the terms originated and evolved. The polyvalence of the terms remains. Instead, he uses 'power' to indicate the processes (neutral in themselves) through which society regulates itself with the production and enforcement of norms. This is 'necessary, not only to the existence of society, culture and of humanity itself, but also to the exercise of freedom as freedom to choose between determined possibilities' (Chapter 4, p. 73). By domination, Bertolo instead signifies hierarchical social relationships which are exemplified by relationships of command/obedience and which characterise systems 'in which the access to power is the monopoly of one part of society (individuals, groups, classes, castes . . .)'. Crucially, if we consider domination as a social characteristic that historically emerges rather than an intrinsic or natural factor of human evolution, we can conceive of a world in which new relations of power consistently aim at dismantling relations of domination and authority.

This distinction between domination and power is important. As Ibáñez (Chapter 3) points out, if we accept that power is inherent in all social relations, then clearly anarchism cannot be 'against power' *tout court*, for 'to speak of a society without political power is to speak of a society without social relations', and that is '*unthinkable*'. If, as he suggests, we need to think not only of the political power that anarchism posits itself against, but also what a 'libertarian power' might look like, then we must conceive of power that can overcome domination, hence the conceptual separation is crucial to animate the revolutionary spirit of anarchism. This is markedly distinct from a theory of generalised power, for when domination is not disaggregated from power more generally, 'rebellion becomes futile' (Colombo 2015: 145).

A radical account of power as domination (and its reproduction) could not ignore the problem of the imaginary. The imaginary occupies a central place in the intellectual journey of anarchism in the 1980s and 1990s, and this is reflected in the engagement of the *Volontà* group with the thought of Cornelius Castoriadis (*Volontà* 1/1984), René Lourau (*Volontà* 4/1980), and the important contributions of Eduardo Colombo on the topic (*Volontà* 4/1980, 2/1983, 3/1984). It is not by chance that Bertolo's investigation of power took place a few years after a thorough investigation of the 'subversive imaginary' (Chapter

9). This contribution was not included in the original manuscript, but it is a necessary piece of the puzzle. In 1998, Chapter 8 arrived to complement Chapter 9. Originally written for the conference 'Les Incendiaires de l'Imaginaire' organised in Grenoble by the Atelier de création libertaire, the two essays form a formidable intellectual diptych on the topic, and our feeling as editors was that they should really be read together.

Bertolo is preoccupied with two key concerns across both chapters. The first is the usual conceptual clarity and terminological rigour. The imaginary is often a misunderstood notion, as it is usually associated with the unreal, the false and the future conceived as something with no direct impact on the present. As Colombo (1987: 19)[8] points out elsewhere, the social imaginary should be considered 'a decentralization of modern thought that erases the essentialist dichotomy between the real and the imaginary and shifts their mutual frontiers within the semantic space of reality'. The imaginary is thus an inherently social institution with very real effects. Secondly, Bertolo argues that our social imaginary has been profoundly colonised by domination, in the sense that we often internalise a view of the world where domination is natural, and its absence unthinkable (Di Leo, in Chapter 12, aptly exposes those who jump from mundane asymmetrical relations, like that of teacher-student, to claim some innate truth at the societal level; these gymnastics of the mind are key to how we are taught to rationalise intolerable relations of domination). The key question then becomes: how and when was domination naturalised?

Lourau's (1978) analysis of the 'Unconscious State', regrettably never translated into English, provides the background against which Bertolo (Chapter 8, p. 149) sketches the possibility of subversion:

The 'mummy-daddy State',[9] as Lourau maintains, shapes our representations, rational and otherwise. It shapes the social imaginary, legitimising hierarchical institutions and herd-like authoritarian behaviour, drawing legitimacy from them in a self-feeding vicious circle: the circle of domination.

---

[8] This quote comes from the preface to an edited book featuring contributions from Cornelius Castoriadis, René Lourau, Alain Pessin and Pierre Ansart, further illustrating the flow of ideas. *The Upside-Down Imaginary*, sadly unavailable in English, was published by elèuthera, an anarchist publisher based at the CSL. Founded in 1986, it continues the legacy of *Volontà* by producing beautiful and affordable editions of essential anarchist texts, including the work of the late David Graeber in Italian.

[9] Lourau uses the refrain *'l'État papa-maman'* ('the mummy-daddy State') to synthesise in one powerful metaphor the paternalism of the state. Unfortunately, to date, Lourau's important book has not been translated into English.

The circle can only be broken through a *subversion* of the social imaginary, with an anti-hierarchical cultural process and a constant struggle against the State-unconscious.

This links closely to Colombo's argument (in Chapter 5) that we should see the state as a 'paradigm of power'. This is a fascinating development of Gustav Landauer's (2010: 214) insistence that 'the state is a social relationship', a statement that is often asked to carry a heavier theoretical load than it can bear without further elaboration. The state, in Colombo's eyes, is the political form that domination takes; its long historical emergence was enabled by the colonisation of the collective imaginary such that domination is both normalised in our minds and externalised to this supposedly 'autonomous' entity. There are echoes here of those protracted debates around state-theory that took place largely between Marxist intellectuals in the same period, but the focus is distinct. Instead of focusing on the state as a locus of power in a society governed chiefly by *capitalist* relations, in which (understandably) we might become preoccupied with questions of class power, or the autonomy of the political from capital, Colombo is concerned with domination more broadly. Through this lens, the state is 'a particular historical form of legitimization and organization of political power' (Bertolo 2013: 53) that institutes domination as the norm. Framing the state as a 'paradigm of power' prompts us to ask how this particular way of organising political power incorporates, extends, embellishes, enforces, reflects and upholds relations of domination in all realms of life. What makes this insight explicitly *anarchist* is its political implication, where 'smashing the state' becomes an ongoing struggle to propagate (both in thought and in action) social relations that are not built on domination.

In line with the aim of exploring new analyses for the 'usual purpose' (a society without domination), it is interesting to note how anthropological explorations of stateless societies are a constant point of reference. Bertolo, Lanza, Di Leo and Berti all invoke a spirit close to the work of the late David Graeber (2004): an openness to taking seriously those examples of social organisation that might be considered 'fringe' or 'pre-historic', 'peripheral' or 'archaic' to those who venerate modernity as a one-way journey to Progress. This is a recurrent motif of the book, one of the characteristics that make it stand out as anarchist in its method of reading history as much as in the histories that it chooses to read. One of the most notable influences here is certainly French anthropologist and ethnologist Pierre Clastres, whose work is central in Di Leo's 'The Source of the Nile: In Search of the Origins of Male Domination' (Chapter 10). Mirroring and deepening Bertolo's analysis of domination as asymmetry, Di Leo embarks on a metaphorical journey to the sources of the Nile to provide a sophisticated map of patriarchal domination. Di Leo draws from an impressive range of ground-breaking studies across disciplines (from anthropology to philosophy and political theory). She discusses at length two 'analytical simplifications' that were common currency within the mainstream feminist movement. The first is the *essentialisation* of the false dichotomy between a positive female element and a negative male element. This crystallisation is not only a caricatural abstraction but is also linked to 'a very specific historical and social category – the man and woman of the white middle class in Western countries' (Chapter 10, p. 181). The *situatedness* of patriarchal relations as understood by the feminist movement and sectors of feminist academia in the 1960s and 1970s may seem obvious today, but it was less so in 1983. The second is the *naturalisation* of power. The feminist movement fails to engage with an in-depth analysis of power itself. Di Leo points at the fact that 'male power and the structure of the sexual hierarchy have been analysed down to the deepest, darkest recesses, down to the slightest shades of meaning. But power without qualifications, power as an absolute social category has not been discussed. Virtually unchallenged, power appears to be more or less a "natural" fact of human society which is questioned only because of its degeneration into male power' (Chapter 10, p. 181). In pointing at essentialisation and naturalisation as two inherent fallacies of a certain understanding of patriarchy, the essay was ahead of its time and opens up an extremely fertile space to undertake a more radical critique of patriarchy *as* domination.

Anthropological and literary materials are also at the core of Lanza's two chapters (6 and 7), which should be read in sequence, for they are closely linked. He seeks to identify another logic for the economic where this latter is not governed by domination. If the economic lacks a foundation of its own, does not have structural autonomy, it is because it is a product of history. Its guiding rationality, understood as a science in its own right, is recognisable only in Western societies, as it is only there that we see the emergence of an anthropological type, *homo oeconomicus*. The lack of an autonomous statute of the economy demonstrates the historical possibility of another economic logic not subservient to domination.

In Chapter 7, the domination/economy dynamic becomes more forceful, for Lanza argues that the latter is born from the former, and *not* the other way around, with domination underpinning economics. What makes these interventions all the more fascinating – and this is another characteristic that these chapters all share – is that they are not merely restatements of 'classical' anarchist positions, for they bear heavily the imprint of a fusing between late-twentieth-century

philosophy (in Lanza's case, specifically that of Baudrillard) and anarchist thinking. Thus 'the power that the anarchist utopia seeks to annul ... is no longer
merely (but was it ever?) a structure weighing on society; it has become an
element of society' (Chapter 7, p. 227). This is the difficulty that so-called 'postanarchism' seeks to tackle.

The relation between freedom and equality, and how they represent the defining characteristics of anarchism, is also the concern at the centre of Chapter 11.
There, Nico Berti – who is both a militant and an important contemporary
historian of anarchism (see Berti 1998) – engages in a bold overview of the
anarchist ideal in its irreducible difference from the anarchist movement. Berti
seeks to revisit the fundamental question of what anarchism is and was, by differentiating it from both liberalism and socialism. The 'endpoint' of anarchism
is fundamentally but uncomfortably incompatible with both, as they 'place
freedom *in* history, as an effect of modernisation, whereas anarchism places it
against history, as a cause of modernisation' (Chapter 11, p. 227). Berti's analysis is refreshing in part because it refuses (like so many histories of anarchism)
to be triumphant in the shadow of failure, but rather centres historical defeat
as the defining characteristic of anarchism's double nature: its ethical tension
towards an uncompromised freedom. Such tension is ultimately what makes it
both a part of history (as an historical movement) and a force resisting history
(as an ideology). The cruel irony here, as he brilliantly points out, is that in
being crushed (most dramatically in Spain and Russia) the historical defeat
of anarchist movements came simultaneously with the theoretical 'victory' of
anarchism. 'Victory' is meant here in the sense of being bitterly validated. If
the premise of your radicalism is a rejection of the inherent authoritarianism
in state-centric forms of 'communism' and your movement is then wiped out
(by a combination of bloodshed and ideological conformity) by authoritarian
regimes that emerge under the flag of 'communism', you reach ideological perfection only in death. For Berti, as for anyone sympathetic to anarchist politics,
this is a tragedy in the fullest sense of the word. He is not fatalistic, however, but
seeks to impress upon us that this contradiction between the fate of the ideal
and the fate of the movement continues to this day. The birth of anarchism
within the institutionalised academy renews the importance of holding the
movement(s) and the ideal(s) together, not in uniformity, but at very least in
dialogue.

The New Anarchism?

At its beginning anarchism was accused of being pre-modern, only to be redis-covered as postmodern later.

Rossella Di Leo (Chapter 12, p. 000)

In the months after Venice 1984, the Canadian anarchist journal *Black Rose* dedicated an issue to reflections on the gathering from those who were there. Alongside the 'picturebook' *Another Venice* (distributed by five publishers in five languages simultaneously, which gives you some sense of the avowedly internationalist outlook of the meeting and its organisers), this represents – to the best of our knowledge – the only substantial English-language considera-tion of this unique event in the annals of twentieth-century anarchism. In it, D'Attilio (1985: 12) wonders aloud about the implications of this moment that Bertolo (in Chapter 2) called 'a fundamental "passage" in the life of the anarchist movement'.

Had the *nipotini di Bakunin* (the grandchildren of Bakunin, as many Italian newspapers described us) come up with a 'new' anarchism, emphasizing ecol-ogy, feminism, and pacifism instead of the 'old' anarchism, proletarian, militant, revolutionary? Had Bakunin been put away up in the attic? Is the anarchism of today no longer a political movement, but a cultural/ethical influence? Is there a break between the 'old' anarchism and the 'new' anarchism? Did any compelling reformation of anarchist ideas and strategies emerge from Venice?

The 'new' anarchism mentioned here is not an intellectual phenomenon – 'new' is not to be confused with 'post', which we will come to shortly – but rather a refocusing of anarchism beyond itself, into whatever libertarian struggles it might overlap with, however imperfectly. That meant, in concrete terms (in the mid-1980s), the new ecological movements, anti-nuclear struggles, the radical feminist and gay liberation movements, the anti-colonial movements, the anti-militarism movements; an anarchism that, increasingly, began to resemble a *principle*, or set of principles and practices, that could be applied across a broad spectrum of struggles, spaces, movements. As Colombo (Chapter 5) reminds us, 'anarchy is a trope, an organising principle', and, as we see time and time again, that principle can thrive even in moments and contexts where a self-identifying 'anarchist' movement does not. What Graeber (2002) would later call 'the new anarchists' were certainly there, at least in germinal form, in the squares of Venice. It may be tempting, therefore, to see the texts in this collection as the dying gasps of an 'old' anarchism or the early shoots of a 'new' anarchism, but we believe that it is more interesting if engaged with as a bridge between the two that negates the notion of any neat division along those lines, both historically (helping us to understand how anarchists in the mid-1980s were grappling with these challenges) and beyond that history (helping us to think critically about the future).

Katsiaficas' (2006) account of the now not so 'new' social movements of the early 2000s traces a line from '1968' (in its broadest sense, not simply the year) via *autonomy*, focused on Italy in the 1970s and Germany in the 1980s. This provides an interesting counterpoint to the role of anarchism. In his telling, the political seeds of the Battle of Seattle are much closer to a Marxism whose material base has fallen apart and whose intellectual heart has eaten itself. What we mean by this is that the dual shift towards a post-industrial society on the one hand and the extension of radical criticism on the other (against the state, but also against the unions, against the bureaucracy of the welfare system, against the sexism of wage labour, the drudgery of work itself, the organised institutions of the working class and so on; in other words, against 'the left' no less than society itself) created a trajectory in which movements *not* beholden to the anarchist ideal came increasingly to *resemble* anarchist principles but did not, in the process, necessarily become anarchist. Perhaps the lineage of ideas matters less than the form that reality begins to take, but it is important to acknowledge that anarchism can only be seen to animate the twenty-first-century spirit of revolt when it is conceptualised fluidly and openly or, to use Ibáñez's (2019) appealing phrase, as 'anarchism outside its own walls'. These are walls that the *Volontà* group (and that wider 'galaxy' to which Ibáñez belonged) were trying not so much to knock down as to make more porous, and it is this double-character (of having pride in anarchism, as Bertolo puts it, whilst renouncing part of its identity, as Berti would add) that characterises all the chapters in this volume: this reflects, in an uncanny and sometimes uncomfortable way, the character of contemporary anarchism itself, which dances between a nostalgia for the past and a reverence for its shredding.

There is, however, a silence in this volume that we feel compelled to address. The papers have nothing explicit to say about those currents of autonomist Marxism that so vividly rocked Italy – and especially its industrial cities, not least Milan – in the 1970s (see Mezzadra 2009). Those expecting a link to *Operaismo* in its various incarnations will search in vain. Whilst it is laudable (and, for us, fascinating, both intellectually and politically) to explore the overlaps between autonomism and anarchism in this context, such an endeavour falls behind the scope of this introduction. What matters to us here is to point at the fact that the histories of anarchism and *autonomia* are two distinct and often avowedly separate histories, and especially so in the narratives of the movements as reproduced by their militants. Accounts of those close to *autonomia* (see Balestrini and Moroni 1997; Virno and Hardt 1996) suppress anarchist voices and influences to the point of non-existence, mirroring the absence of *autonomia* from this anthology.

This separation is reflected by a surge of interest in the wider workerist 'moment' in Italy through the work of such luminaries as Antonio Negri and Mario Tronti. In the anglophone academic context, there has been noticeable interest around Italian workerism and so-called 'Italian critical thought' (see Gentili, Stimilli and Garelli 2018), including the publication of many key texts into English for the first time, some four decades after the act.[10] Such interest spans disciplines, from political science and philosophy to geography and literary studies. Political and intellectual blind spots persist, however; the role played by anarchism in this is often foreclosed by scholars. The perceptive reader might well pause here and notice a striking contradiction: did we not just say that the authors herein have no comment to make on the matter? How dare we, only a few lines later, bemoan the siphoning off of these histories when the histories themselves appear to take place in silos? For us, it is important to do a bit of both, namely, to respect those distinctions without reifying them again and again in the twenty-first century. By way of example, who remembers the figure of Primo Moroni and his bookshop in Milan (*Calusca*, 'back alley' in Milanese dialect), which acted as a catalyst for encounter, convergence and dialogue between different political tendencies, with a marked sympathy for the workerist current and various anarchist strands alongside Situationist and internationalist tendencies? The texts presented in this volume are *part of* the afterlives of that 'moment', even if they are apart from it. The political complexity of how ideologies evolve remains elusive if we stick to the canon of a self-identifying cohort (especially, in the Marxist case, when that cohort strives for a theoretical unity).

There is no doubt that in the heat of 1977, when the autonomist movement was at its strongest, its proponents were largely ignoring the anarchists, who remained politically on the margins. Moreover, the anarchists largely returned the indifference, accusing the autonomists of trying to hegemonise the movement while grafting anarchist concepts and strategies into a new Marxism

---

[10] See, for example, the recent English-language publication of Tronti's *Workers and Capital* (Verso, 2019), originally published in Italian in 1966, as well as a collection of his writings edited by Andrew Anastasi (*The Weapon of Organization: Mario Tronti's Political Revolution in Marxism*, Common Notions, 2020).

which, despite differing from the Gramscian vulgate of the PCI, was seen as constantly reproducing authoritarian relationships and militarism (see Mudu 2012). In essence, as suggested by Day (2005), *hegemony* became one of the defining distinctions between anarchism and autonomism in this era. For Day, autonomism still holds on to the need for a grand strategy. Its revolutionary vision is reliant on the realisation of a collective power that can be directed, somehow, to follow a plan; that seeks to become a counter-power disciplined and powerful enough to fight back at a scale that matches the interlocking forces of capitalism *tout court*. This is a significant fault line. It may look narrow, but it runs deep. This was a chasm often bridged through action but never through theory (as Day acknowledges, many autonomists and anarchists intermingled on the ground, especially through the social centres in the early 1980s; Mudu concurs, showing the fertile intersection through the practice of autogestion).[11] Here the line between friendship, comradeship and enemies becomes disquietingly fluid. Suffice to say, any account of those years – and more importantly the ideas that came out of them – that pays no attention at all to anarchist voices is an incomplete one, and an oddly incomplete one, given the fascination with a 'communism' that rejected the party and the state. If, as a good deal of anglophone scholars seem to rather suddenly believe, the 'post-political' leftism in late-twentieth-century Italy offers keys and insights into effective anticapitalism today, a roadmap charted during the birth-pangs of 'late capitalism' that might offer us a route out of it, then the voices of those included in this volume are surely an important part of that story. We do not wish to overemphasise this – there is no magical synergy herein, no secret bridge between these traditions – but we urge the reader not to forget this context.

There is another shift that we need to address. Intellectually, the 1980s were a transitional period in ways that clearly overstep the history of anarchism but impact upon it in no small way. This was the era in which 'poststructuralism' achieved dominance across the humanities and social sciences with remarkable speed, which presents something of a paradox: several intellectual themes that had long been key to anarchist thinking – 'poststructuralism may be seen as a broad critique of authority,' as Newman (2007: 158) puts it – became de rigueur

---

[11] Translating somewhat awkwardly as 'self-management', autogestion has specific connotations of workers' control, but its political vitality gets slightly lost in either English translation. If 'self-management' sounds oddly individualistic or business-like, 'workers' control' limits politics to the realm of work, whilst the term denotes a collective claim that is – or at least can be – far broader. For this reason, we retain the word *autogestion* throughout the book.

intellectually without much attention being paid to anarchism at all, except to occasionally dismiss it out of hand. As Shukaitis and Graeber (2007: 15) point out, the rise to dominance of this critique of dominance then created its own paradox, in which 'academics who see themselves as the most subversive of all structures of received authority have been spending most of their time establishing and preserving an authoritative canon'.

If poststructuralism seemed to intellectually mirror some of the concerns of anarchism (as a philosophy if not a political movement, and the distinction is important) whilst becoming intellectually dominant within the academy, it was arguably only a matter of time before a new cohort of scholars would attempt to filter anarchism itself through a poststructuralist lens (May 1994, 2009; Newman 2007, 2011, 2016). This project has not been without its critics, for in juxtaposing poststructuralism against so-called 'classical anarchism', this scholarship tends to ossify the latter, reducing it to a particular reading of a small number of texts (Kinna and Prichard 2009). To put it bluntly, we are not keen on the word 'postanarchism' for all the reasons that Kuhn (2009) outlines, which can be captured most succinctly by disquiet with the idea that anarchism is 'post' anything coherent or convincing. We rather maintain, with Berti, that anarchism is *in* history, yet *against* history. The dimension of resistance and the capability of *untimely* thinking, against the immediacy of the present, are inherent to anarchism, leaving room for a constant exercise of renewal. The constitutive openness of 'thinking as anarchists' does not point to a mere dismissal of that which comes under the label 'postanarchism'. On the contrary, it seems to make more sense to think openly and creatively about what the poststructuralist critique and anarchism can learn from one another, to what degree they are compatible (Ibáñez 2019; Kuhn 2009; Vodovnik 2013). The answer, somewhat glibly, is surely 'a bit', and all the chapters in this anthology are testament to that, but only up to a certain point. It is important to recall that 'poststructuralism' – as a packet, a brand, an identity, a recognisable conglomerate of thinkers – did not exist in the early 1980s, and we do not mean that as a slice of postmodern poetics. As Colombo (2015) reminds us, the 'canonical' texts of what was later assembled under the (sloppy, as many maintain) label of poststructuralism were not, when they were first published, considered as necessarily linked. This matters, because it changes how we read the texts herein. It is one thing for Lanza to productively cite Baudrillard (as he does in his contributions to this volume), but this does not make him a 'Baudrillarian' any more than it makes him a 'poststructuralist'; it makes him an anarchist who reads widely and thinks openly.

Conclusion

The poster for Venice 1984 (see Fig 1.1) was designed by Fabio Santin and Enrico Baj, whose links to anarchism were longstanding and went beyond aesthetic rebellion (see Heath 2004). The image of *Cagacazzo* is taken from Baj's installation *L'Apocalisse* [*The Apocalypse*], created in the years just prior to the gathering (see Eco 1979). In an interview for *A/Rivista Anarchica*, Baj declares that the inspiration for *The Apocalypse* came from Konrad Lorenz's book *Civilized Man's Eight Deadly Sins* (1974). Lorenz 'denounces man's destruction and indiscriminate exploitation of nature' (translated from Baj 1984). Baj was equally impressed by the Massachusetts Institute of Technology report on the energy crisis, for 'everyone seemed blinded by the myth of progress. This was my starting point. It is a work of fiction that wanted to represent a return to a "monstrous visionalism", it is a painting populated by monsters that we can identify with destruction, pollution, information technology, etc.' (ibid.).

A lot has changed since 1984, but we are still living in a world depleted by rampant ecological exploitation, gaping inequalities, patriarchy and ungraspable levels of surveillance, where states hold the power to murder us all, and bureaucracy balloons into an endlessly remembered and endlessly monetised network. This is brought into sharp relief by resurgent forms of xenophobic nationalism across the world, where the 'strong state' and the 'pure nation' go hand in hand with corruption, militarism and racism, a broadly conceived *dehumanisation* under which the vast majority of the world's humans are now governed. It is perhaps too easy to talk in sweeping terms of these horrors but, suffice to say, there is a *need* to learn how to 'think as anarchists' just as surely as there was forty years ago. We need this not only as a riposte to the axis of reactionary-conservative-fascist thinking that stamps itself on to the world with growing confidence, but as a reminder to those on 'the left' not to easily lapse into a nostalgia for the 'state-as-saviour' as we wait for the collapse of capitalism that is always just around the corner and forever out of reach. And we need intellectuals to think creatively with concepts such as power without deconstructing all ambition into an ephemeral niche of hyper-focused theorising, where all is only for the here and now, individualised as mirror to the 'abstract totalising' of an earlier era, where the telescope fails both ways around.

We are not under illusions about the contribution of this volume, which asks as many questions as it answers, remains grounded in a faded context, and will no doubt be derided by some for its academic density, but we are convinced that the issues it seeks to tackle are of profound importance. We are already witnessing how easily the cocktail of financial crisis and ecological collapse lends strength to a surge of walls and a psychological closing in of bitter rhetoric resplendent with familiar antisemitic conspiracies, anti-migrant hatred, militarised misogyny, and a *certainty* that haunts political discourse like a cluster-bomb both rigid and fluidly everywhere. We live in an era where 'chaos' intersects with authority in ways that are deeply disquieting, and in that juncture, 'anarchy' is hardly an appealing word, certainly a deeply misunderstood one. But we cannot seek solace in the shining armour of the police as a bastion against all these tensions unravelling. Instead, we need sustained thinking from an avowed leftist perspective that remembers how important freedom is to socialism and vice versa. We need, in other words, to spend a little bit more time *thinking as anarchists.*

The texts in this anthology suggest that this means, first and foremost, reconnecting with our future, to claim it. In this era of disasters and dystopias, where we are constantly engaged with the imagining of an ending that never comes – 'apocalypse forever!' – relearning how to connect the future with the present becomes truly revolutionary. We are asked to take our social imaginaries very seriously: they are real, they produce reality. The future cannot be severed from the present; the future is contained in the present, like the past. And not merely as a potential. The future incessantly acts on the present, through the effect of 'psychological feedback' (Bertolo, Chapter 9).

This tension, 'through which tomorrow is present already today' (ibid.), is the real meaning of utopia. This said, utopias can well move within the space of domination and, as Bertolo (ibid.) notes, it is 'terroristic' to use horrifying projections of the future to justify a 'least worse' present. This is all too familiar in the present moment. The monsters of Venice 1984 have mutated and are accompanied by new ones, but today it is arguably even more important to ask: what happens? What happens when 'someone begins to feel the need to open up some cracks in the wall and let in a decent image of the future' (ibid.)? The defining characteristic of *Thinking as Anarchists* is its consistent stance against domination. All of its interventions (on the domination inherent in the economic, in patriarchy, in the state and so on) are invitations to imagine a future where that domination is undone; to seek out an image of the future without domination.

This does not mean that we, or the authors in this volume, presume that a world without domination *tout court* is close at hand. It helps to recall Ward's (1961, cited in White 2007: 14) words on the possibility of freedom, for whilst 'the concept of a free society may be an abstraction . . . that of a free*er* society is not'. It is one of the longest-held stereotypes of anarchists that they demand all or nothing *now*, a kind of childish grasp for a utopia that arrives fully functioning in one fell swoop. Ibáñez (Chapter 3) reminds us that 'libertarians are not against power, but against a certain type of power'. He then poses the possibility of a 'libertarian reformism' that, like Colin Ward and his 'anarchist gradualism' (White 2007), reminds us that 'the revolution' will never come and go in a day or so, but relies on patient and ongoing work. This, for us, remains a particularly fertile and crucial observation, for it avoids the pitfalls of 'demanding the impossible' without giving up; it opens anarchism up to a whole host of 'meanwhile' radicalisms whilst *also* reminding us of the importance of connecting those moments to something that transcends the sum of its parts. It is not about finding comfort in a retreat to the small, a revolution of everyday life severed from the world in which it is lived, but rather urges us to consistently and patiently cultivate relations that are *not* patriarchal, that do *not* adhere to the hierarchical strictures of the state, that do *not* reward the fruits of exploitation with a hierarchical promotion; in other words, to cultivate relations that are – as far as possible – not based on domination. To put that more positively, and in words no doubt familiar to anarchists, it means imagining, devising, cultivating, propagating and enacting relations and institutions built on mutual aid and collective power.

Let us finish this introduction by returning to its beginning. This volume is not merely an act of translation in the linguistic sense of the word. We want it to be seen as part of a cultural and political effort to broaden the conception of anarchism – its history and its ideas – beyond the 'classic' texts that have long been available in English. The hegemony of English is not an issue specific to anarchism; it overshadows academic discourse itself. And as Müller (2021: 2) points out, linguistic privilege 'reduces the diversity of thought that we can learn of and from'. He is speaking to our own discipline (Geography), but this insight belongs to all of knowledge. Just as we can speak of 'worlding' Geography – which means decentring English as a language as much as 'Anglocentrism' as a worldview – we can imagine an anarchism that exists beyond and outside these boundaries. In fact, we do not need to *imagine* such an anarchism, for it already exists, and has done for a very long time – it is anarchism in all its multifaceted incarnations, but these are not incarnations that can be neatly cajoled into a linear history. Ask us what 'anarchism' is, and of course we start with the familiar names – Proudhon, Bakunin, Malatesta . . . (none of whom, of course, wrote in English) – but ask us to trace the life of the ideal or the principle, and that story becomes much harder, but oh so much more interesting to tell. It might seem a step too far to posture this volume as an act of *decolonisation*, in the vein of Ramnath's (2011) work on the Indian struggle for liberation, and we are well aware of what gets politically erased when that word is used too broadly. But it is clear to us that when we speak of 'Europe' as a homogeneous entity, we erase those parts of Europe that are still so often invisible to English-language accounts. 'Worlding' anarchism means blowing apart that notion of the homogeneous 'European' anarchist, which hides such richness of thought. *Thinking as Anarchists* is one woodpecker in the effort to chip away at the barricades of language. The driving force behind this is personal – every conversation we have had in the long process of pulling this together has been one of translation, of linguistic bartering and contextual mutual aid – but, as we hope we have shown, it also has nothing to do with us. An 'anarchism outside its own walls' (Ibáñez 2019) is only possible when its internal walls are porous enough to talk through.

Faremo del nostro peggio!

References

Ambrosoli, Roberto (2019), *Anarchik. Farò del mio peggio. Cronache anarchiche a fumetti*, Milan: Editrice A – Hazard Edizioni.

Ambrosoli, Roberto, Nico Berti, Amedeo Bertolo, Paolo Finzi and Luciano Lanza (1973), *Anarchismo '70: un'analisi nuova per la strategia di sempre*, Cesena: L'Antistato.

Amster, Randall, Abraham DeLeon, Luis A. Fernandez, Anthony J. Nocella II and Deric Shannon (2009), 'Introduction', in Randall Amster, Abraham DeLeon, Luis A. Fernandez, Anthony J. Nocella II and Deric Shannon (eds), *Contemporary Anarchist Studies: An Introductory Anthology of Anarchy in the Academy*, London: Routledge, pp. 1–8.

Anderson, Benedict (2007), *Under Three Flags: Anarchism and the Anti-Colonial Imagination*, London: Verso.

Another Venice (1986), *Another Venice: Images of an International Anarchist Meeting*, Montreal: Black Rose Books.

Ascherson, Neal, Michael Davie and Frances Cairncross (1969), '480 held in terrorist bomb hunt', *The Observer*, 14 December, pp. 1–2.

Baj, Enrico (1984), 'Intervista', *A/Rivista Anarchica* 14 (121); available at <http://www.arivista.org/index.php?nr=121&pag=121_07.html&key=Baj> (last accessed 17 May 2021).

Balestrini, Nanni, and Primo Moroni [1988] (1997), *L'Orda d'Oro*, Milan: Feltrinelli.

Balsamini, Luigi (2021), *A History of the Centre for Libertarian Studies – Giuseppe Pinelli Archive (1976–2009)*, Milan: Centro Studi Libertari; available at <https://centrostudilibertari.it/it/node/1032> (last accessed 17 May 2021).

Benello, C. George (1985), 'Incontroversion', *Black Rose* 11: 15–18.

Berti, Nico (1998), *Il pensiero anarchico dal Settecento al Novecento*, Bari: Piero Lacaita Editore.

Berti, Nico [1976] (2009), 'The New Masters', in Robert Graham (ed.), *Anarchism: A Documentary History of Libertarian Ideas*, vol. 2, Montreal: Black Rose Books, pp. 394–407.

Berti, Nico (2016), *Contro la storia. Cinquant'anni di anarchismo in Italia (1962–2012)*, Milan: Biblion Edizioni.

Bertolo, Amedeo [1999] (2013), 'Libertarian Democracy', in Robert Graham (ed.), *Anarchism: A Documentary History of Libertarian Ideas*, vol. 3, Montreal: Black Rose Books, pp. 53–60.

Blumenfield, Jacob, Chiara Bottici and Simon Critchley (eds) (2013), *The Anarchist Turn*, London: Pluto Press.

Bookchin, Murray (1985), 'Incontroversion', *Black Rose* 11: 21–3.

Centro Studi Libertari (1984), *Venezia 1984: Last Information Circular*, Milan: Centro Studi Libertari.

Christie, Stuart (1984), *Stefano Delle Chiaie: Portrait of a Black Terrorist*, London: Anarchy Magazine/Refract Publications.

Clark, John (1984), *The Anarchist Moment: Reflections on Culture, Nature and Power*, Montreal: Black Rose Books.

Colombo, Eduardo (ed.) (1987), *L'immaginario capovolto*, Milan: elèuthera.

Colombo, Eduardo (2015), 'Anarchism and the Question of Postmodernity', *Anarchist Developments in Cultural Studies* 1 & 2: 129–52.

D'Attilio, Robert (1985), 'Incontroduction', *Black Rose* 11: 4–12.

Day, Richard (2005), *Gramsci Is Dead: Anarchist Currents in the Newest Social Movements*, London: Pluto Press.

Di Paola, Pietro (2017), *The Knights Errant of Anarchy: London and the Italian Anarchist Diaspora*, Edinburgh: AK Press.

Ealham, Chris (2010), *Anarchism and the City: Revolution and Counter-Revolution in Barcelona, 1898–1937*, Edinburgh: AK Press.

Eco, Umberto (ed.) (1979), *Enrico Baj. Apocalisse*, Milan: Mazzotta.

Ferretti, Federico (2018), *Anarchy and Geography: Reclus and Kropotkin in the UK*, London: Routledge.

Gentili, Dario, Elettra Stimilli and Glenda Garelli (2018), *Italian Critical Thought: Genealogies and Categories*, London: Rowman & Littlefield International.

Ginsborg, Paul (1990), *A History of Contemporary Italy: Society and Politics 1943–1988*, London: Penguin.

Goodway, David (2006), *Anarchist Seeds beneath the Snow: Left-Libertarian Thought and British Writers from William Morris to Colin Ward*, Liverpool: Liverpool University Press.

Graeber, David (2002), 'The New Anarchists', *New Left Review* 13: 61–73.

Graeber, David (2004), *Fragments of an Anarchist Anthropology*, Paradigm 14, Chicago: Prickly Paradigm Press.

Gramsci, Antonio [1920] (1977), 'Address to the Anarchists', in *Antonio Gramsci: Selections from Political Writings 1910–1920*, ed. Quintin Hoare, New York: International Publishers, pp. 188–9.

Heath, Nick (2004), 'Baj, Enrico, 1924–2003', *Libcom*; available at <https://libcom.org/history/baj-enrico-1924-2003> (last accessed 17 May 2021).

Honeywell, Carissa (2011), *A British Anarchist Tradition: Herbert Read, Alex Comfort and Colin Ward*, New York: Continuum Books.

Ibáñez, Tomás (2019), *Anarchism Is Movement*, London: Freedom Press.

I Nuovi Padroni (1978), *Atti del Convegno Internazionale di Studi sui Nuovi Padroni*, Milan: Antistato.

Katsiaficas, Georgy (2006), *The Subversion of Politics: European Autonomous Social Movements and the Decolonization of Everyday Life*, Edinburgh: AK Press.

Kinna, Ruth (2016), *Kropotkin: Renewing an Anarchist Tradition*, Edinburgh: Edinburgh University Press.

Kinna, Ruth, and Alex Prichard (2009), 'Anarchism: Past, Present, and Utopia', in Randall Amster, Abraham DeLeon, Luis A. Fernandez, Anthony J. Nocella II and Deric Shannon (eds), *Contemporary Anarchist Studies: An Introductory Anthology of Anarchy in the Academy*, London: Routledge, pp. 270–9.

Kuhn, Gabriel (2009), 'Anarchism, Postmodernity, and Poststructuralism', in Randall Amster, Abraham DeLeon, Luis A. Fernandez, Anthony J. Nocella II and Deric Shannon (eds), *Contemporary Anarchist Studies: An Introductory Anthology of Anarchy in the Academy*, London: Routledge, pp. 18–25.

Landauer, Gustav [1910] (2010), 'Weak Statesmen, Weaker People!', in *Revolution and Other Writings: A Political Reader*, ed. Gabriel Kuhn, Oakland: PM Press, pp. 213–14.

Lanza, Luciano (2003), *Secrets and Bombs: Piazza Fontana 1969*, London: Christie Books.

Levy, Carl (1989), 'Italian Anarchism, 1870–1926', in David Goodway (ed.), *For Anarchism: History, Theory, and Practice*, London: Routledge, pp. 25–78.

Lourau, René (1978), *L'État-inconscient*, Paris: Éditions de Minuit.

Löwy, Michael (2013), *On Changing the World: Essays in Political Philosophy, from Karl Marx to Walter Benjamin*, Chicago: Haymarket Books.

May, Todd (1994), *The Political Philosophy of Poststructuralist Anarchism*, University Park: Pennsylvania State University Press.

May, Todd (2009), 'Anarchism from Foucault to Rancière', in Randall Amster,

Abraham DeLeon, Luis A. Fernandez, Anthony J. Nocella II and Deric Shannon (eds), *Contemporary Anarchist Studies: An Introductory Anthology of Anarchy in the Academy*, London: Routledge, pp. 11–17.

Mezzadra, Sandro (2009), 'Italy, Operaism, and Post-Operaism', in Immanuel Ness (ed.), *The International Encyclopaedia of Revolution and Protest*, doi:10.1002/9781405198073.wbierp0799.

Mudu, Pierpaolo (2012), 'At the Intersection of Anarchists and Autonomists: Autogestioni and Centri Sociali', *ACME: An International E-Journal for Critical Geographies* 11 (3): 413–38.

Müller, Martin (2021), 'Worlding Geography: From Linguistic Privilege to Decolonial Everywheres', in *Progress in Human Geography*, doi:10.1177/03 09132520979356.

Newman, Saul (2007), *From Bakunin to Lacan: Anti-Authoritarianism and the Dislocation of Power*, New York: Lexington Books.

Newman, Saul (2011), *The Politics of Postanarchism*, Edinburgh: Edinburgh University Press.

Newman, Saul (2016), *Postanarchism*, Cambridge: Polity Press.

Pernicone, Nunzio (2009), *Italian Anarchism, 1864–1892*, Edinburgh: AK Press.

Ramnath, Maia (2011), *Decolonizing Anarchism: An Antiauthoritarian History of India's Liberation Struggle*, Edinburgh: AK Press.

Pozzoni, Federico (2021) Art Against the Nation. The Relationship between the Anarchist Movement and Italian Nationalism in the Artwork I funerali dell'anarchico Pinelli by Enrico Baj (1972). *Anarchist Studies* 29(1): 79–87.

Senta, Antonio (2015), *Utopia e azione: Per una storia dell'anarchismo in Italia (1848–1984)*, Milan: elèuthera.

Shukaitis, Stevphen, and David Graeber (2007), 'Introduction', in Stevphen Shukaitis, David Graeber and Erika Biddle (eds), *Constituent Imagination: Militant Investigations, Collective Theorization*, Edinburgh: AK Press, pp. 11–34.

Toscano, Alberto (2019), 'The Ignoble Savage: Racism, Myth and the Anthropological Machine', *Theory & Event* 22 (4): 1,106–24.

Turcato, Davide (2015), *Making Sense of Anarchism: Errico Malatesta's Experiments with Revolution*, Edinburgh: AK Press.

Virno, Paolo, and Michael Hardt (eds) (1996), *Radical Thought in Italy: A Potential Politics*, Minneapolis: University of Minnesota Press.

Vodovnik, Žiga (2013), *A Living Spirit of Revolt: The Infrapolitics of Anarchism*, Oakland: PM Press.

Ward, Colin (1984), 'Colin Ward reports from Venice: Anarchy rules', *The Guardian*, 1 October, p. 15.

Ward, Colin (ed.) (1987), *A Decade of Anarchy: Selections from 'Anarchy', 1961–70*, London: Freedom Press.

White, Stuart (2007), 'Making Anarchism Respectable? The Social Philosophy of Colin Ward', *Journal of Political Ideologies* 12 (1): 11–28.

Wright, Steve (2002), *Storming Heaven: Class Composition and Struggle in Italian Autonomism*, London: Pluto Press.

2   The Venice Connection

Amedeo Bertolo (1984)

Originally published in *Volontà* 38 (5)

Venice and Surroundings

Venice: before, during, after. By 'Venice' I mean, predictably, the conference and, more generally, the international anarchist gathering[1] that is to take place in a month. And by 'before, during, after' (which is not paraphrasing the well-known formula of the Virgin Mary but rather Gauguin's 'Who are we? Where do we come from? Where are we going?') I would like to take the conference and the gathering as a particular sign, as the threshold between a before ('Where do we come from?') and an after ('Where are we going?'); as a particular point in the time-space continuum of anarchism from which we can look at ourselves and our surroundings and ask: 'Who are we?'

To assign such a meaning to Venice is, of course, quite arbitrary, just as is the appointing of a certain age, whether eighteen or twenty-one or any other, as the beginning of maturity. I am convinced that, in both personal and collective lifetimes, the 'moments', the individual events, are only conventional and symbolic signs of processes of mutation and transition. I have been talking about a 'sign' and nothing more and, to reduce yet further the emphasis which, on rereading the above, seems to me to be excessive, I would like to state at once that I do not intend to overrate the actual conference and gathering in Venice. I do not expect great things of that conference (or of the gathering) in itself. I do not intend to surreptitiously give it the importance of a 'Refoundation Congress' for anarchism. Most definitely not. And, if for no other reason, this

---

[1] Whilst 'gathering' was the English translation chosen during the event, some nuance is lost from the Italian word *incontro*. See Chapter 1 for further detail.

is because it will not be (and was never intended, nor planned, to be) a congress but rather a conference and an informal gathering. The former will produce ideas rather than resolutions and the latter will be a meeting place not for delegates but for the individual members of the international libertarian tribes who, like the gypsies at Saintes-Maries-de-la-Mer, will be representing no one but themselves.[2]

I know (or I believe that I know) that Venice will be, at its best, a 'big feast',[3] a great emotional and intellectual feast, and that it will not provide the solutions for any of the great theoretical or practical problems facing anarchism, that none of the lacerations, deeper or shallower, of the anarchist movement will be healed, that we will, all-together-but-apart, meet, talk, even come to blows, but also that we will – I hope – have a taste, however fleeting, of a libertarian community. Many will go home feeling that nothing special has taken place (and, in a certain sense, nothing important *could* happen in Venice), that they have taken part, or even just been present at, a rather chaotic collective *brainstorming* [in English in the original], within the framework of a festive, anarchist Tower of Babel . . .

And yet I still maintain that, symbolically, Venice (the gathering plus the work that has preceded it and the long, slow digestive process that will come afterwards) will represent a fundamental 'passage' in the life of the anarchist movement.

I must repeat that Venice is not that passage, but rather its sign. In fact, the anarchist movement, more or less throughout the world, has, for some years and quite independently of Venice, been coming to the realisation, in various ways and to various degrees, of its deep-seated crisis. It is, paradoxically, from that very quantitative and qualitative rebirth of the 1960s and 1970s which saved it from extinction that anarchism has drawn (or can draw) the elements which will allow it to see that what it believed to be merely a conjunctural crisis was instead a structural crisis, and so draw the energy, the will and the imagination necessary (even if not sufficient) to resolve it. Anarchism today is being (and is ever more aware of being) forced to a dramatic step from the old to the new, even if it is not yet sure just what is 'new' or 'old' within it.

[2] Saintes-Maries-de-la-Mer is a town in southern France, where thousands of Romani pilgrims gather every year to venerate their saint.

[3] Bertolo is hinting at the title of the 1973 French-Italian movie *La Grande Bouffe*, directed by Marco Ferreri. The film is a satirical critique of bourgeois excess, focusing on a group of friends who retreat to a villa in the countryside to eat themselves to death.

Now that 1968 (not, obviously, the year but the process of cultural change that began some years earlier, particularly in America, and which lasted until some years afterwards) has carried it above the quantitative and qualitative threshold of survival, anarchism must now pass that other quantitative and qualitative threshold that will transform it into a true agent of social transformation. And unless it can cross this second threshold it runs the risk of being, sooner or later, thrown back beyond the first one.

For some years now there has been a growing feeling (more or less conscious) that, in order to cross this second and critically important threshold, it is, above all, necessary to make, and to make as soon as possible, a qualitative leap. And this is what gives its symbolic value to a gathering such as Venice; a symbolic crucible for the different anarchist cultures, a symbolic ground for the blending of intellectual work and activist experience, of pragmatism and of deep-rooted traditions, of lucidity and passion, of good sense and utopia . . .

This is the real significance of Venice, or at least the significance that I and the many others who have worked for nearly two years to prepare this gathering hope that it will have. Over and above this general 'sign' there will be many others. Each of us will interpret it in his or her own way. I too, obviously, have my own opinion and those who read my last editorial in *Volontà* a year ago will have an idea what this is (Bertolo 1983).[4]

---

[4] Bertolo is referencing an editorial he was asked to write for *Volontà* in the summer of 1983 (issue no. 3) as a commentary on the Italian elections that took place in June that year. Bertolo begins (with evident disdain) by reflecting on Antonio Negri's attempt to avoid prison by standing as a political candidate for *Radicali* (a liberal-democratic party, perhaps best described in contemporary political parlance as aspiring 'centre-left'). Negri was duly elected and promptly escaped to France. Bertolo writes: 'What a satisfaction to see the disintegration of that area of super-revolutionaries that labelled themselves as "Autonomia Operaia". We listened to their Supreme Pontiff . . . declaring on television: "My comrades and I were not against entering the parliament" – they were always up for using libertarian spaces within institutions – they were even the only forces able to stop terrorism . . .' Rather than indulging in a predictable bashing of the election, Bertolo uses the remainder of the editorial to discuss the crisis of anarchism. He continues: 'So, let's spill the beans, let's speak the truth: The anarchist movement is in a crisis. A serious crisis, both qualitative and quantitative. The anarchist press keeps on losing readers. We no longer sell books, our groups are disintegrating, our encounters are less frequent and often merely formal, or based on personal friendships. The circles (those that are still running) are deserted of people and ideas. Both external activity and internal discussion are at an historical minimum. Comrades are escaping in big numbers, with various personal motivations . . . We are fragmenting, and our edifice is threatened by ruination. Some are happily moving, others are riven with guilt . . . If things continue this way we will be left with a simulacrum of a movement . . . I

The Pride in Being an Anarchist

In September 1972, at a conference organised to commemorate the centenary of what is (once again conventionally) considered as the birth date of the anarchist movement,[5] I concluded my address (Bertolo 1972) with a call for pride in being anarchist. Of those hundreds of people who applauded my address (but who really – and quite rightly – applauded their own sense of pride as anarchists) few are still here twelve years later. Many of the older ones have died, many of the younger ones have obviously taken their pride elsewhere – although I doubt that they now have the same reasons for pride. Few are left (although not so very few). And, nevertheless, I still feel the same pride in being anarchist, not (I hope) due to premature senility – 'you can't teach an old dog new tricks' – and not just (I hope) because I am, in this as in other things, rather out of date – coherence, it seems, is no longer a virtue – but because I can see no reason to modify my rational judgement of anarchism nor my emotional adherence to it. On the

was afraid of telling the truth, as I was afraid of worsening the situation. I was afraid of amplifying the depressive effects of the crisis, giving a voice to it . . . the crisis of the Italian anarchist movement (as the Spanish movement, or the French movement ten years ago) is not a mere conjunctural crisis, it is a structural one.' So for Bertolo, the new watchword, at least for himself if not for the movement, was to be 'let's save pessimism for better times', a reinvention of Gramsci's (1977) famous demand for 'pessimism of the intellect, optimism of the will' (first used by the Italian Marxist in a polemic against anarchism). As he puts it towards the end of the piece: 'I have engaged for years in anti-repressive campaigns, now I deem more urgent an anti-depressive campaign.' He concludes with an impassioned cry for a renewed anarchism: 'I am rationally convinced that anarchism has inexhaustible strength and richness that ideological revivalism (neo-Marxist, neo-liberal) highlight with the indecorous use of libertarian make-up on their new ideological looks. The counterculture of the 1960s, the feminist movement of the 1970s, the pacifist movement in the 1980s and the new ecological awareness, not to mention the socio-musical-folkloric phenomena, such as the Punk movement, have many fragments of anarchism within themselves. Many comrades are led to think that these can be substitutes for the anarchist movement. If this is not cultural necrophagy, it certainly means that anarchism is a sound and nutritious food.'

[5] Bertolo refers here to the centenary anniversary of the conference held in Rimini on 4–6 August 1872. During the Rimini conference the Bakuninists publicly announced that they had split from the International and formed a separate organisation. This declaration is traditionally regarded as the constitutive act of the socialist and anarchist movement in Italy (as a separate entity from Giuseppe Mazzini's movement), as well as the beginning of the fracture between Marxists and Bakuninists within the First International.

contrary, that pride, now filtered through the experiences and reflections of these dozen years, is more solid now than it was then, less fuelled by enthusiasm and perhaps because of this more solid.

This reference to what I said in 1972 is not merely a pretext for a somewhat narcissistic reaffirmation of faith. It is rather because it seems to me that the very pride in being anarchists, as I asserted it then and assert it again now – that is, not a self-satisfied pride but a proud assertion of identity – must now, more than ever, be systematically declared and cultivated. Just as it is not true that courage is something that one has or does not have – it can be mutually given – so it is with pride. We can and must 'give ourselves' a sense of pride in being anarchists. Only with a strong, widespread and proud sense of identity as anarchists will anarchism be able to go through that deep-reaching transformation that I believe (as many of us feel and believe) is urgently needed, without losing what makes it different and unique, without being assimilated or absorbed. Anarchism must change but must still remain a mutation, unshaken by the reigning cultures (Christian, Marxist, Liberal, Muslim . . .).

Our pride, which will serve us before, during and after Venice (that is, throughout the entire process of transition from the old to the new), is not presumption or arrogance. On the contrary, it allows that intellectual humility that is necessary if we are to remain open to doubt, to discussion, to verification, to curiosity about everything both inside and outside of ourselves. Because, contrary to what it seems, it is only those who are certain of their own identity who can allow themselves this humility. Those who do not have this sense of security waver before the opposite poles of a dogmatic closed-ness (a weak identity's armour against the 'other') and a continual Zelig-like mimesis of the other.

Our pride is fully justified, if not on the grounds of strict rationality, at least on those of reasonableness: even if, in our more than one hundred years of history, we have won neither battles nor hearts, our balance sheet is paradoxically less negative than those who have (as Berti explains in Chapter 11);[6] our pride is therefore a collective state of mind which is functional in the anarchist 'mutants' and their 'enlarged reproduction' and, in particular, in the ambivalence of the present crisis, of which Venice is to be the symbolic moment. Depression, self-

---

[6] Bertolo is referring to Berti's chapter in this volume, which we translated as 'Towards an historical and ideological appraisal of anarchism', and was originally published in the same issue of *Volontà* as this editorial. The Italian word used by Berti (*bilancio*) means 'balance sheet' and is commonly used metaphorically with the meaning of an 'appraisal'.

Figure 2.1 Bertolo had seen the slogan 'let's leave pessimism for better times' on an anarchist poster in Switzerland in 1982 (image courtesy of the Centre International de Recherches sur l'Anarchisme, CIRA, Lausanne). The slogan is sometimes (erroneously) credited to the Uruguayan radical Eduardo Galeano, who used it as a rallying cry at the 2001 Social Forum in Porto Alegre (having also seen it daubed on a wall).

pity and inferiority complexes can be fatal to anarchism in this historical phase ('let's leave pessimism for better times' redux; see Fig. 2.1).

Pride in one's own identity is, moreover, useful for the existence and collective action of every social group. Our thoughts go immediately to the pride in being black, in being a woman, in being gay . . . But we can also, more traditionally, think of the pride of the bourgeoisie (during the period of its rise) and of course the pride of the working class. In the past this latter was expressed in the *proud* passing on of a trade or at least of a social position from father to son. How many metalworkers' fathers today dream of a future for their sons as metalworkers and how many would rather they become doctors or at least civil servants?[7] The pride of the worker is on the road to extinction together with Cipputi and the traditional working class.[8] And speaking of workers . . .

[7] The Italian word *metalmeccanico* has particular connotations of the archetypal industrial worker. The British equivalent would probably be the coal miner, imagined as a signifier not only of a profession, but of a way of life and a particular class consciousness.

[8] Cipputi is an Italian comic strip character created by the comic artist and satirist Francesco Tullio Altan (1942). Cipputi has become an ironic term to define the leftist

The Worker and his Bicycle

In past generations of anarchists, blue-collar workers were an important element, and in certain times and places the great majority, whatever Marxist
historiography may maintain. And today, when we are far more likely to find a
teacher rather than a metalworker within the movement, there is still a ghost
among us: the Worker as a rhetorical figure, the Worker as a category in our
nostalgic libertarian imaginary, partly inherited from traditional anarchism and
partly adapted from the culture of the Marxist left,[9] owing to an ill-posed ideological continuity. When reading and listening to the words of many comrades
(including, to tell the truth, my own of some years ago) especially, although by
no means exclusively, within the realm of 'Latin'[10] anarchism, it would seem that
this Worker does indeed correspond to a working class (*the* class) which is to
have the task of changing the course of history and the face of the world.

To me it now seems that this very Worker, at this moment in time, is only
an obstacle in the way of our understanding reality (although not of our understanding our roots and our past, of which this figure explains a great deal)
and which inhibits our discussions, our actions. I am talking of that mythical
Worker, not of those flesh-and-blood workers, whether revolutionary or not,
libertarians or not. Libertarian syndicalism (and perhaps even revolutionary
syndicalism in certain social and political contexts) is quite realistic, even if
recent history – including that of the National Confederation of Labour (CNT)
in Spain – does not leave much room for optimism, but only if the theory and
practice of those models and myths which, to put it kindly, have not worked are
overhauled. This is, obviously, my own opinion and may not be shared by the
friends and comrades who will come to Venice. But it is certain that the idea of
the Great Proletarian Revolution is one of those that is tottering everywhere in
the international libertarian community (as well as in the far wider sea of the
various contemporary societies where libertarian currents are fermenting).

Some days ago, I read in a newspaper the results of a survey of 'the Milanese
on Two Wheels'. The social and occupational make-up of those Milanese whose
normal means of transport is the bicycle put office workers in first place (30.3%),

---

industrial worker (*metalmeccanico*) who has de facto capitulated to perpetual exploitation by his masters.

[9] Bertolo uses the Italian word *sinistrese* here, which is very difficult to neatly translate.
It has specific connotations of the jargon used by leftist militants in Italy, especially in
the 1970s.

[10] The word 'Latin' here is used to indicate a linguistic belonging, most of all, hence an
anarchism which is practised and thought in Romance languages.

followed by students (25.6%). Workers came second to last with only 2.5% and yet many will remember, as I do, the days not so long past when in Milan the bicycle was almost the symbolic workers' vehicle. You may say that the worker on his motorbike or in his car is no different from the worker on his bicycle (which is not altogether true) but this is not the point. For me, that statistical curiosity is symbolic of the deep-reaching cultural transformation of the working class in advanced industrial societies and, even more, as a transparent metaphor. The manufacturers of bicycles have, in the last thirty years, changed either their product or their clientele. We cannot continue producing bicycles in the old style and expect to sell them to the same clientele. To be sure, the metaphor proves nothing. And it is by no means sure that we are faced with the drastic choice between giving up 'producing' anarchist ideas or radically changing our clientele. It may well be that we can think and act (and live) as anarchists without renouncing any audience, directing our efforts towards all the various categories of the vast and differing peoples of the oppressed (as demonstrated by Bookchin). Nevertheless, I like the metaphor. I have a weakness for metaphor and I have a suspicion that I will resort to yet more before the end of this article.

Thinking as Anarchists

Thinking as anarchists today is just as important as acting as anarchists, in the realm where acting does not only mean activism, propaganda and struggle but the whole framework of life, that is of interaction with the human and natural environments (see Ambrosoli 1982). In fact, I feel that thinking is by far the most urgent need, given the dramatic delay that we have accumulated in the last half-century, of which the intellectual efforts of some individuals over the last ten or fifteen years, many of them excellent (and it is quite without false modesty that I include among these the work promoted and carried out by the Centro Studi Libertari), have only scratched the surface. We need thought in every direction and on every level. Thinking in order to act, naturally, but *thinking*, not just banal chewing of the cud or a cribbing of incongruous elements. And we need thinking *as anarchists*; an opening up, neither dogmatically nor uncritically, towards every aspect of contemporary culture which is or seems to be moving in a libertarian direction and the confrontation of every aspect of reality with that extraordinary interpretive criterion that is our radical critique of domination.

Thought for the day: 'the true realist is a man who knows both the world and his own dreams' (Le Guin 1980: 97)!

There is one task that seems to me to be particularly urgent if we are indeed to be able to 'think as anarchists'. This is the settling of accounts with our roots so as to gain for ourselves an identity devoid of nostalgia for the past, an identity reduced to the essential and, for this very reason, more suited to every time and place, to every situation, to every context. Our anarchist identity at present is a heavy load, a mish-mash of essential and non-essential elements that are universally valid and of those which are historically dated and/or specific to particular geopolitical realities. I have already used the examples of the Worker (with a capital W) and the Revolution (with a capital R), both mythologies of a certain reality or at least of a potentiality connected to a European social context which existed during the second half of the last century and the early decades of the present one (emblematically up to the Spanish Revolution) but there are innumerable other examples to be found.

Our luggage then is rich, but it is also cumbersome and contradictory if taken in a jumble. One need only think of the apparent irreconcilability in the anarchist tradition of individualism and communism, of class analysis and humanism, of violence and non-violence . . . Our luggage is cumbersome and apparently contradictory and so, every now and then, someone tries to lighten it and to make it unilaterally coherent by throwing out this piece or that, but in doing this we risk throwing away, each time, a bit of anarchism.

And yet the load must be lightened. We have a long journey ahead of us in unknown territory and we can only take the essentials; we may well enrich our load en route, depending on what we find in front of us in all the directions in which we set off. The problem is to decide what is essential because if we keep too much or too little we will not manage to go far. And I believe that our journey is to be a *very* long one. Abandoning the metaphor, the immensely delicate task which is facing us today in 'thinking as anarchists' is that of identifying the essence of anarchism, that which defines the anarchist identity over and above the concrete historical and geopolitical manifestations of anarchism to date. Our task is not to disincarnate anarchism, reducing it to a pure philosophic essence for contemplation, but to re-immerse it in the differing forms of reality which alone can give it the possibility of becoming a real expression and instrument and reference for all existing forms of theoretical negation of and practical resistance to domination in any social context.

So perhaps a different metaphor will serve us better than our load . . . Our task is to distil anarchism in all its manifestations, both past and present, because the essence of anarchism is to those manifestations as pure alcohol is to the innumerable alcoholic drinks which – infinite thanks be to human nature – have been invented at all (or almost all) latitudes and longitudes. And just as pure alcohol is undrinkable, so, probably, is 'pure' anarchism, and just as the various peoples have produced and still produce alcoholic beverages of differing concentrations and flavours to suit differing environmental and climatic circumstances, so has anarchism, in the past, given rise to differing forms of thought and action and so will it, in the future, be able to give rise to forms of thought and action which are immensely more diversified, and so more functional and more enjoyable. But whether it comes from grapes or from coconuts, from agave or from rye, from corn or from apples, whether it is diluted or concentrated, alcohol is the essential element of all alcoholic beverages. All the producers and consumers of wine, beer, vodka, cachaça, toddy, cider, whisky . . . have always known it intuitively – and today there is the scientific and technological evidence to prove it.

Now, to take the metaphor still a little further, whatever may be the tastes of those who set out on a long voyage towards unknown shores, it would be better for them to carry concentrated alcohol (like the barrel of rum on a pirate ship) than alcohol in a diluted form which is less functional even if the overall proportion of alcohol per volume is perhaps more agreeable. And it would be still better to take the knowledge necessary to produce alcohol in any new context. Anarchism is going to set out (it must set out and will perhaps do so whether we, the more or less legitimate heirs of the tradition, wish it or not) on a long voyage of thought and action in various directions. It would be better for anarchists to fill their flasks with a high-strength anarchism and their heads or notebooks with the knowledge essential for the fermentation and distillation of anarchism in any situation of domination and revolt.

State and Anarchy

Distilling anarchism does not, of course, mean reducing it to a simple formula. Anarchism is a philosophy of humanity and society (and is, or should be, as Bookchin rightly points out, of nature as well).[11] It is a view of the world which it would be ridiculous to try and reduce to one or even a few formal definitions. It is, nevertheless, possible and indeed necessary to identify the essential structures, to prune away the ambiguity and vagueness from its founding values and the key concepts.

For example: it is, I believe, quite evident that it is not enough to speak of the equality/freedom/diversity nexus to define our axiological foundations. We must clarify just what these three much-abused terms mean in the *specific*

---

[11] The enduring legacy of Murray Bookchin on the anarchist movement was to bring it into serious discussion with the modern ecological and environmental movements. See White (2008) for an accessible and critical overview of his work.

context of anarchism (see Berti, this volume). It is not enough to speak of direct action and direct democracy (even Gaddafi talks of direct democracy); it is not enough to say that anarchism is 'against' power and the State if we do not clarify what we mean by power and by the State. And, speaking of power, the Centro Studi Libertari has promoted original and in-depth studies which exemplify the type of work to be done. On the subject of the State, Colombo's chapter in this volume is, in my view, exceptionally important. His idea, stemming from an intuition on Bakunin and Landauer, is that the State is above all – essentially – a principle of organisation of social reality (today, in fact, it is *the* principle which explains and 'rationally' organises the society of domination in all its diverse concrete forms). In this way, the anarchists' seemingly ingenuous and outdated radical negation of the State regains a formidable scientific validity.

That same chapter puts forward the idea, potentially very fertile on an epistemological level, that anarchism is to be considered above all as an organisational *principle*, as the central element of a social imaginary – the anarchist one – which is completely alien to the dominant State imaginary. In this way 'State and Anarchy', the title of two plenary sessions at the Venice conference, can be seen, not as an anachronistic ideological-Manichean opposition, but as two different and incompatible ways of thinking and of organising reality.

This, and many other aspects (less general perhaps but no less important), will be discussed during the conference in Venice. I cannot list them all here – not only would I be repeating the programme, but I would also abuse the space allowed for an editorial. Before concluding, I will point out two methodological elements which, while implicit in the previous pages, may perhaps be missed or misunderstood.

First – the key to understanding 'Venice' which I have outlined is not only my personal approach but also, and in fact principally, the vision (debatable, certainly, but equally certainly worthy of serious consideration) around which the Centro Studi Libertari has worked since 1976, as reflected in *Volontà* since 1980. All the conferences, seminars, study groups and research programmes organised by the centre have sought to promote 'anarchist pride' (the pride in our cultural roots and in our history) and, *together*, the open-minded research into the new, a research open to the international libertarian (not only anarchist in the narrow sense) culture (see Chapter 13 in this volume).

Secondly, the task of 'refounding' anarchism is not the task of a handful of intellectuals but the collective task of the entire anarchist community, the task not of one conference (or of two or of three) but of a generation: ours. This is both fascinating and terrifying. On the theoretical level (not in terms of years) we are the fourth generation: the first laid the foundations, the second built on them, the third has lived off the income. We now have a choice: either to squander what is left or to rebuild the theoretical patrimony of anarchism.

To Venice, to Venice!

References

Ambrosoli, Roberto (1982), 'Volontà e natura umana', *Volontà* 4: 19–32.

Bertolo, Amedeo (1972), 'Anarchici e orgogliosi di esserlo', *A/Rivista Anarchica* 7.

Bertolo, Amedeo (1983), 'Lasciamo il pessimismo per tempi migliori', *Volontà* 3: 3–13.

Gramsci, Antonio [1920] (1977), 'Address to the Anarchists', in *Antonio Gramsci: Selections from Political Writings 1910–1920*, ed. Quentin Hoare, New York: International Publishers, pp. 188–9.

Le Guin, Ursula K. (1980), *The Word for World Is Forest*, St Albans: Granada Publishing Limited.

White, Damian F. (2008), *Bookchin: A Critical Appraisal*, London: Pluto Press.

The signage for Venice 1984 was created by the Venetian graphic designer Fabio Santin.

The exhibition space set up for Venice 1984 also featured a film festival titled 'Cinema & Anarchy'.

The choice of Venice as the venue for the meeting was mainly due to two factors: the first is that two anarchist groups with considerable logistical capabilities were active in the area (the Nestor Makhno group from Venice-Marghera and the Romeo Semenzato of Dolo); the second is that Venice, in addition to enjoying a worldwide reputation, is also an eminently pedestrian city that allows a 'street life' unimaginable in most cities. The narrow streets made transportation of all the necessary material complex and tiring. Over 100 people spent six days assembling and disassembling the materials.

The huge circus tent erected in Campo San Polo was used to host exhibitions, including one on the 'History and Geography of Anarchism', curated by the Centre International de Recherches sur l'Anarchisme (CIRA) in Lausanne, and 'Art and Anarchy', curated by Ark Studio in Milan.

Anarchik welcomes people to the canteen.

During the day, the spaces were packed.

Paolo Finzi (*A/Rivista Anarchica*), Rossella Di Leo and Elis Fraccaro (Nestor Makhno group of Venice-Marghera) in Campo Santa Margherita near the cash desk (at that time managed by Gemma Failla). The meeting was self-financed thanks to international donations and non-stop running of the kitchens.

Marianne Enckell (Switzerland), April Retter (New Zealand) and Rossella Di Leo (Italy) shortly before being interviewed by the BBC. In addition to the major Italian newspapers, the American NBC and the Danish Radio Christiania were also present.

In Campo Santa Margherita there were politically committed songwriters, punk groups (with related pogo) and traditional anarchist choirs.

Frontwoman of the all-women Swiss band 'Trotz Allem' performing at Venice 1984.

Ha Ki-Rak (1912–1997) was a university lecturer and one of the leading figures of Korean anarchism.

Dominique Girelli (1893–1991) hailed from Italy's Romagna region. After having actively participated in the Biennio Rosso (two years, 1919–20, of intense workers' and peasants' struggles), he sheltered in France, where he continued his militancy until the end of his days. Pictured here at Venice 1984, when he was ninety-one years old.

Silvia Ribeiro (Uruguay), Barbara Köster (West Germany) and Laura Prieto (Uruguay) at Venice 1984. In the background is Ruben Prieto from the Comunidad del Sur (Uruguay).

Part II: Power against Domination

3   Towards a Libertarian Political Power

Tomás Ibáñez (1983)

Originally published in *Volontà* 37 (3)

FOR DECADES, ANARCHISM has found itself in an undeniable phase of stagnation, both in theory and in practice.

At the level of theory, rare are the innovations that have occurred within a thought that can undoubtedly be qualified as radical, in the literal sense that it sticks to its roots,[1] as if they were made of glue, hampering its further developments and evolution.

For the most part, anarchism has remained anchored to concepts and propositions which have been developed in the eighteenth and nineteenth centuries.

At the level of practice, it can certainly be argued that anarchism has spread among large informal social movements, implicitly libertarian, leaving its mark on several social changes. Unfortunately, each libertarian transformation is matched by dozens of microevolutions drifting in an explicitly or implicitly totalitarian direction. Society seems to be moving more towards a reduction rather than an increase in fundamental freedoms and autonomies.

This double stagnation is obviously problematic insofar as it questions the very validity of libertarian positions. Can we try and outline the elements for a new beginning? I believe so.

Two coterminous concerns are at stake here. On the one hand, fundamental considerations point towards the elucidation of the social conditions for the production of emancipatory ideologies and social movements.* On the other

---

[1] The word 'radical' comes from the Latin *radix*, meaning 'root'.

* Why and how is libertarian thought produced? It would be interesting to consider anarchism as a social object obeying certain conditions of production (which conditions?). Such conditions ensure a set of social functions (which functions?) which

hand, the potential revitalisation of libertarian thought and action must necessarily undergo a powerful exorcism.

It is paramount to exorcise a whole set of taboos, whose ideologico-emotional charge blocks any possibility of reflection. Such exorcism is all the more necessary since what is at stake is the very essence [*noyau dur*] of anarchist thought.*

The concept of *power*, more precisely *political power*, is first in line to be desecrated if we want to unlock the conditions of possibility for a renewal of anarchism. Indeed, it has become customary to gauge its positioning vis-à-vis the issue of power and consider it as one of the main criteria to distinguish libertarian positions from non-libertarian ones.

In my view, the issue of power is the main *differentiator* between the degrees of libertarianism in socio-ideological thought, as well as between several socio-political attitudes, both individual and collective.

It is not acceptable to maintain that the only way to articulate the relationship between libertarian thought and the concept of power is in terms of negation, exclusion, rejection, opposition, i.e. of antinomy. It is true that there is a libertarian concept of power; it is false that it boils down to a negation of power. Until this is fully understood in libertarian thought, we will not be able to devise analyses and practices with some grip over social reality.

The Concept of Power

The polysemy of the term *power* and the breadth of its semantic spectrum often favour a dialogue of the deaf. During debates, we frequently observe the juxtaposition of speeches rather than their mutual articulation. This is because they deal with profoundly different objects, disguised under the use of a common designation, *power*. It is thereby useful to delimit the term *power* before stepping into its discussion. Noticeably, this does not imply that we can reach an *objective* and sanitised definition of the word *power*, since it is a politically charged term, analysed from a precise political standpoint, and could not be *neutrally* defined.

In one of its accepted meanings (probably the most general and diachronically the first), the term 'power' functions as an equivalent of the expression

---

in turn generate certain social and ideological effects (which effects?). The fact that Marxism has dealt with this question in a lamentable way does not diminish its importance. Perhaps this is where we can find the reason why anarchism is characterised by an absence of cumulative effects at the organisational, ideological and social level.

* It seems urgent to me to define what is the essence of libertarian thought and what are the *negotiable* elements which form its protective belt. The confusion of the two levels sometimes leads to unnecessarily sectarian attitudes.

'capacity to', that is to say, as a synonym of the set of effects that an agent, animated or not, may cause, whether directly or indirectly. It is interesting to observe that, since the outset, power is defined in relational terms, as for an element to produce or inhibit an effect, interaction must be established.

I imagine that no one, libertarian or not, would question this kind of power or consider it useful to challenge and destroy it. To be sure, there are no beings that are not endowed with power, as power is, in this sense, consubstantial with life.

In its second connotation, the word 'power' refers to a certain type of relationship between social agents, one which is usually characterised by the asymmetrical or unequal capacity of certain agents to affect the other pole of the relation. I don't deem it appropriate here to step into more refined levels of analysis and ask, for example, whether the production of these effects should be intentional or not, effective or not, desirable or not, and so on, in order to legitimately speak of a power relation (for a detailed analysis, see Ibáñez 1983).

The third meaning of the term 'power' refers to macrosocial structures and mechanisms of social regulation or social control. In this sense, we are talking about *apparatuses* or *dispositifs* of power, *centres* or *structures* of power, and so on.

I argue that it makes no sense to call for the *suppression of power* at any of its levels of expression, as what is true and obvious for the first level (power as capacity) is also true, although less apparent, for the other levels.

In other words, to speak of a society *without power* constitutes an aberration, whether viewed from the point of view of *power/ability* (for what would it mean to speak of a society that could do nothing?), or at the level of asymmetrical relationships (what would social interactions mean without asymmetrical effects?), or from the point of view of power as macrosocial regulatory mechanisms and structures (what would a system be – and society is obviously a system – if its elements were not *constrained* by the relations which define the system itself?). Power relations are consubstantial with the social fact itself, they are inherent to it, permeate it, they surround it and, at the same time, emanate from it. The social necessarily implies the existence of interactions between several elements: when these latter form a system (society), there are inevitably power effects of the system on its elements, just as there are power effects between elements of the system.

To speak of a society without political power is to speak of a society without social relations, without social regulations, without social decision-making processes; in short, it is to speak of an *unthinkable* because it reiterates a contradiction in terms.

The reason why I introduced the qualifier *political* to specify the term *power* is that, in its most general sense, it simply denotes the decision-making mechanisms and processes that allow a social formation to choose between various alternatives and the processes and mechanisms which ensure the effective implementation of the decisions taken. To be sure, there are a multiplicity of models of *political power*.

When libertarians declare to be *against power*, when they proclaim the need to *destroy power* and plan for a *society without power*, they cannot uphold an absurdity or something unthinkable.* Most likely, they simply commit a metonymic error by using the word 'power' to refer to a *specific type of power relationships*, namely, the type of power that we find in *relations of domination*, in *structures of domination*, in *domination dispositifs*, or in *apparatuses* of domination, and so on (be these relationships coercive, manipulative or of another type). Still, one should not consider as relations of domination all relations which constrain individual or group freedom.**

This is not only because it would equate relations of domination and relations of power (since all political or *societal* power is necessarily binding), but also because freedom and power are not in a simple relation of opposition. Indeed, it is true that power relations (inherent to the social, let us not forget) constrain the freedom of the individual, but it is equally true that they enable and can increase such freedom. This is how we should understand the beautiful formula 'A person's freedom ends where another man's freedom begins'. On the contrary, my freedom is enriched and expanded by another's freedom.

It is clear that the freedom of others constrains mine (I am not free in all that can encroach on their freedom), but it is simultaneously clear that my freedom needs the freedom of others in order to exist (in a world of automatons, my freedom would be considerably reduced). Power and freedom are therefore caught in an inextricably complex relationship of antagonism/possibility.

To return to the heart of the problem, we shall say that libertarians are, in fact, against social systems based on relations of domination (in the strict sense). 'Down with power!' should disappear from the libertarian lexicon in favour of 'Down with relations of domination!', even if this means having to define the conditions of possibility for a society of non-domination.

---

* However, we should consider whether the cry against power does not constitute, at the level of the social imaginary, a way of contesting, by displacement, the social bond itself, that is to say ultimately challenging ourselves as being inevitably instituted.

** No doubt a similar reflection should be devoted to the subject of freedom – one of the most difficult concepts – since it poses the problem of *self-referential systems*, which are closed on themselves.

Libertarians are not against power, but against a certain type of power. This implies that they are partisan of a certain variety of power, one we shall conveniently (and accurately) call *libertarian power* or, more precisely, *libertarian political power*. In other words, they are in favour of a libertarian mode of operation of the apparatuses of power, the dispositifs of power and power relations that characterise society.* To accept the principle of libertarian political power can have two types of effects.

The first effect is to force ourselves to think and analyse the concrete conditions underpinning the exercise of a libertarian political power in both societies with a *State* and *stateless* societies.

The easy solution is obviously to proclaim that power must be destroyed. This avoids the difficult task of having to define which are the conditions for the functioning of a libertarian power and which are the modes of conflict resolution in a non-authoritarian society.** Similarly, the focus on the State and the demand for its disappearance makes it possible to hide the fact that, even without a State, power relations and dispositifs remain within society. If we are convinced that with the disappearance of the State, power will also disappear, what is the point of worrying about this latter?

The second type of effect could allow for a dialogue between libertarians and their entourage, at last. Indeed, if people do not understand libertarian discourse, if they are insensitive to it, if they do not share its concerns, it is certainly not the fault of people themselves, but rather the fault of libertarians. Popular common sense is right when it remains impervious to libertarian arguments against power. Would it remain equally deaf to proposals which would not speak of suppressing power, but simply of transforming it?

I am aware that my analysis can evoke a *libertarian reformism*, and this impression will only grow when I say that, in order to establish a dialogue between libertarians and society, it is not enough to propose a change in power relations, but we must *give credibility* to the possibilities for change and plan their implementation, even if vaguely. The first condition to make change credible is for it to actually be possible. This sets the limits of an effective libertarian programme.

---

* Probably the functioning of a libertarian power should pass through the establishment of oscillatory mechanisms which avoid the crystallisation of a fixed directionality within power relations, and prevent effects of self-consolidation of power . . . But this is another issue altogether.

** I take this opportunity to emphasise the urgency of abandoning the deeply totalitarian idea of a *harmonious and conflict-free* society.

For a Minimax Libertarian Strategy*

As long as society is manageable,** even if only partially, it is obvious that a libertarian influence can only drive effective changes towards the *libertarianisation* of political power if a considerable part of the population favour it and act accordingly.

A reformist libertarian strategy necessarily presupposes the existence of a mass movement, insofar as it should bring together millions of people for a country like France and tens of millions for a country like the United States. Is it impossible? It certainly is, if we expect millions of *militants*; it is not if we refer to a movement of opinion which manifests itself more or less episodically or coherently, let us even say with scant coherence. Nevertheless, libertarians must help make this popular libertarian base possible by calling into question the usual maximalist strategy expressed in terms of *all or nothing*.

A vast libertarian movement of opinion or, if you prefer, a *libertarian gravity* in society can only be established through proposals which are both credible to the many and effective; that is, the proposed changes are likely to be achieved within a reasonable span of time and are sufficiently *motivating*.

Such proposals must conform to the necessarily hybrid character of movements which are neither entirely libertarian nor constantly libertarian. It is hence paramount to revise a whole set of *principles*, such as the systematic non-participation in any type of electoral process, the refusal of paid political shift-workers or the systematic rejection of alliances with non-libertarian sectors (note that these principles do not constitute the essence [*noyau dur*] of libertarian thought!).

This said, it would be completely untenable to count only on a *reformist* strategy, for several reasons. Firstly, it is simplistic to merely oppose reformism and radicalism. As discussed for the complex notion of *power/freedom*, many parts of the whole are inextricably entangled, the dichotomy is only superficial, or applies only to a certain level of reality, but not at all levels.

Reformism and radicalism feed on each other, oppose and complement each other simultaneously. On the other hand, reformism can produce perverse

---

* I do not use the term 'minimax' here in the technical sense that it takes in economics or in game theory [minimising the possible loss from a worst-case scenario]. I use it purely analogically.

** Whether society really is manageable is another question, but if it is absolutely not manageable then we can say goodbye to our militant speculations . . .

effects and lead to radical consequences, just as radicalism can lead to regressions or reform.

The second reason rests on the idea that radical action often increases its eventual effectiveness, or even acquires it, only insofar as there is a *movement* [*mouvance*] which fertilises the ground in advance.

The third maintains that radical positions and actions can constitute the social equivalent of random interactions and local fluctuations which allow physicochemical systems to *spontaneously* evolve towards specific and radically new orders (analogy with noise-induced order, order by fluctuations, complexity by noise, etc.). To be sure, society is sufficiently complex (in the technical sense of the term) and is situated *far enough from equilibrium* that it is strictly impossible to foresee the potential consequences of radical action, as exerted on a specific section of the social fabric (see, notably, May 1968). Only radical action seems capable of amplifying local social fluctuations to the point of causing *emergences* which are incompatible with the established social order. Nonetheless, it should be noted that radical action is a double-edged sword. Since society is an open, self-organising system, the disturbances (noise) introduced by radical action also improve the adaptability of the established system.

The fourth reason is that radicalism helps uphold concepts, propositions and questions that would otherwise be digested and transformed by dominant social models through the pre-digestion made by reformist movements.

The fifth reason pertains to historical experience. This shows how the coexistence of large *soft* sectors, *ideologically uncertain*, of *oscillating coherence* with radical, hard, uncompromising sectors has produced the most conducive situations to profound social change (see Spain 1936).

This said, the necessary dialectic between radicalism and reformism remains highly problematic.

Indeed, we must prevent reformism from breaking radical attempts by acting as a shock-absorbing mattress around it and thus erasing its effects. Likewise, we must prevent radical action from pulling the rug out from under reformers and making their task impossible. We must prevent reformist conceptual innovations from erasing the core [*noyau dur*] from which they originated and the background of radical criticism attached to ideological groups. Equally, we must prevent radical intransigence from clipping the wings of theoretical innovation.

Concluding, it is essential, and this is the most difficult of all, that radicals and reformists fully accept themselves as *antagonistic/complementary* elements and as being irreducibly *enemies/allies*.

I intentionally refrained from engaging with more markedly *dialectical* thought in order to express my deep conviction that insofar as we cannot grasp the irreducible complexity of realities, we will not be able to address them successfully.

Reference

Ibáñez, Tomás (1983), *Poder y Libertad*, Barcelona: Ed. Hora.

4   Power, Authority, Domination

Amedeo Bertolo (1983)

First published in *Volontà* 37 (2)

DURING MY RESEARCH on techno-bureaucracy, autogestion and utopia (Bertolo 1977, 1979, 1981), I found myself up against the problem of defining 'power'. On different occasions, I defined it more or less explicitly to suit the needs of my particular research, but these definitions were always partial and provisional, serving only to avoid possible misunderstandings while discussing other themes. The underlying question remained open, and even more so for me, it became ever more pressing as my thinking went both deeper and wider (or, at least, so I was convinced).

Indeed, the problem was and still is the need, if not to resolve, at least to focus clearly on an extremely complex concept which is central to anarchist thought, and not merely to agree on words. Paradoxically, anarchism, which can be considered the most radical critique of domination to date, both in theory and in practice, has not yet produced a theory of power that is more subtle and highly developed than the apologies of domination.

There has been no further reflection to do justice to the brilliant insights of the 'founding fathers' of anarchism. Those insights are still fertile – our anarchism, mine included, is built around them – but, more than a century later, they have remained little more than insights and run a serious risk of becoming mere stereotyped formulae, beliefs or taboos, thereby losing a large part of their value as a means to interpret and transform reality.

These insights become petrified and the relative vagueness of both concept and terminology, however inevitable and perhaps necessary this may have been initially, becomes an obstacle to further thought and action, originating both unjustifiable 'orthodoxies' and equally unjustifiable 'heresies', traditional immobilism and innovative absurdities, sterile discussions and social impotence.

Anarchists may find some solace in the fact that over the last century, mainstream science has thrown little light on that ensemble of 'things' (relations, behaviours, social structures . . .) that go under the name of power (or authority or domination). Power is undeniably central to anarchist critique but is equally crucial to any type of social and political thought.* Yet, the concept of power is, at once, one of the most controversial and one of the least debated concepts, and barely attracts academics and their proud analytic subtleties. When the analysis of power happens to be sophisticated, it is more in the rather negative sense of falsification than in the positive connotation of refinement.

Even a cursory reading of the literature on the subject will bring into evidence not only the considerable terminological confusion – a paradigmatic case is Weber's term *Herrschaft*, which is translated into Italian as both *potere* (power) and *autorità* (authority) – but also an equally considerable conceptual indeterminacy. As far as the interpretation and justification of the functions and genesis of power are concerned, academia seems unable to move beyond Hobbes and Locke, or even Plato and Aristotle.

This is, however, meagre consolation. Dominant science can afford the luxury of not being compelling at the logical level, since it is supported by the force of both circumstance and the unconscious imaginary, which both structures and is structured by it. Furthermore, a certain level of confusion is instrumental to it, as it hampers the identification of social domination in theory and its destruction in practice. Anarchist thought, on the other hand, *must* attain the highest level of clarity if it wishes, as indeed it does, to be a subversive social theory, that is, an instrument for understanding and *subverting* the existing reality.

This essay puts forward some definitions which could help improve the debate among anarchists, and facilitate dialogue between anarchists and non-anarchists, which otherwise risks remaining forever a dialogue of the deaf.

My definitional effort is not aimed at the *terms*, but rather at the *concepts* that are behind those terms, and the *contents* of these concepts. Just like the written (and vocal) sign 'house' may signal the concept of 'a man-made shelter', but its content may range from the hut to the skyscraper. In this essay, I will limit myself to the definition of wide categories of contents (and of concepts) instrumental to an initial, provisional answer to the following questions: what

---

* 'Power is the decisive formal category in both the analysis of the structures and the analysis of the processes in society' (Dahrendorf 1979: 155); 'The concept of power is perhaps the most fundamental in the whole of political science: the political process is the shaping, distribution, and exercise of power' (Lasswell and Kaplan 1950: 75); 'The study of power is the beginning of sociological wisdom' (Horowitz 1963: 11).

lies behind the common label of power? To what extent is it made of universal social functions or functions belonging to relations of domination?

It is customary, not only in academia, to begin a discussion on semantics with (1) an etymological approach and/or (2) an historical approach. In our case, neither would be particularly helpful. The etymology of the three terms that interest us stretches too far back into the past to be more than linguistic archaeology and, moreover, two of the three terms originally had meanings that were virtually indistinguishable.* As for their historical use, this reveals a level of polyvalence and interchangeability over time that makes any such analysis irrelevant to our purposes (see, for example, Eschenburg 1976).

To put it briefly, the origins and use of the keywords of our research, over time and in differing socio-economic contexts, only tell us that if we locate them in a spectrum of meanings stretching from a positive to a negative pole with respect to the (anarchist, but not exclusively) values of freedom and equality, the term 'authority' comes in a midway position of neutrality, the term 'domination' is generally placed towards the negative pole, and the term 'power' covers the entire spectrum, thanks to its particular double meaning of 'power to do' [*poter fare*] and of 'power to make someone else do' [*poter far fare*].

An analysis of the use of the three terms on the part of anarchists is of equally limited value (definitely more useful is an examination of the underlying concepts and contents): whether we consider the 'classic' writings or contemporary ones, whether in reflections or in propaganda, we usually find power/authority/domination used as synonyms (and thus with negative connotations).

It is true that we can probably identify some degree of distinction, more or less explicit, between power and authority, but this is not univocal. For Proudhon (2011), for example, power is a collective force, whereas authority is alienation, the monopolistic appropriation of this collective force (although he also uses the term 'political power' to define this expropriation of social potency). For Proudhon, therefore, authority could be seen as a negative term while power is, or could be termed, 'neutral'.[1] Bakunin (1970), on the other hand, recognised

---

* Power comes from Latin *potis* (lord, master), as does domination, from *dominus* (master, owner, head of the family). Authority instead comes from *auctor*, originally meaning 'he who nourishes or increases'.

[1] 'Neutrality' is here meant in the sense that Proudhon (2011: 654), like most revolutionary thinkers, was concerned with the question of how 'the collective force, an ontological, mechanical, industrial phenomenon, [can] become a political power'. In this sense, power is imagined as that which attains a fairer world as well as that which oppresses.

the existence of a 'neutral' authority,[2] and – moving from the classics to our contemporaries – Giovanni Baldelli (1971) gives a decidedly positive meaning to the word 'authority', which he generally uses in the sense of moral and intellectual influence.

Marginally more promising is analysis of the contemporary use of the three words, both in common and in scientific language. In everyday language the two adjectives 'authoritative' and 'authoritarian' illustrate the use, respectively positive and negative, of the noun 'authority' from which they come, a noun which can indicate a political role of power, a specific competency or moral excellence. Common language also applies the term 'power' to a whole range of situations, from the ability to be or do, to the structure of the social hierarchy. Only the word 'domination' is almost unequivocally used in the sense of power to impose (*de jure* or *de facto*) one's will on *others* by means of physical or psychological coercion.

Even with the social sciences, the term 'domination' (and the related verbs and adjectives) is less ambiguous compared to authority and power. Perhaps because of the negative affect surrounding it in its common usage, the term is only occasionally used, and usually with a negative value attached to it.* As far as definitions of power and authority are concerned, they can be found to suit all tastes. What, for some, is called authority is for others influence or prestige, or, conversely, some call authority what others call legitimate or formal power.**

---

[2] In one of his most famous passages, Bakunin (1970: 32–3) notes that 'In the matter of boots, I refer to the authority of the bootmaker; concerning houses, canals, or railroads, I consult that of the architect or engineer . . . I bow before the authority of special men [*sic*] because it is imposed upon me by my own reason.' If the summation that 'We accept all natural authorities and all influences of fact, but none of right' (1970: 35) may sound tautological, Bakunin's insistence on the importance of expertise remains an important bedrock of anarchist thought, for it helps to distinguish an anarchist society from a truly 'anarchic' lack of society.

* Domination is used with a 'neutral' meaning in at least three particularly relevant instances: Simmel (1978), for whom domination is a universal category of social interaction and power is one particular form of this; Dahrendorf (1959: 237), who proposes a definition of domination understood as 'the possession of authority, i.e., the right to issue authoritative commands'; and Lasswell and Kaplan (1950), for whom domination (in the Italian edition the term is 'dominio', but the word actually used by the authors is 'rule', not 'domination') is the model of effective power.

** Here are a few examples, in random order. *POWER*: 'Power is a) ability or natural faculty of action; b) legal or moral faculty, the right to do something; c) authority, especially in the concrete sense, as the constituted body exercising that given authority as government' (translated from Lalande 1971); 'Power is the participation in decision

In light of this, it seems necessary to try and define these terms by identifying the underlying concepts and contents, and circumventing lexical difficulties through an 'intuitive' use of certain terms (according to context), or by paraphrasing, whether elegantly or not. I will also resort to the frequent use of 'platitudes', that is, of concepts which are taken for granted by anarchists or which are widely known and accepted in the field of non-anarchist scientific and philosophical thought; from an unusual combination of various platitudes, we may discover something new.

Let us begin in an (apparently) roundabout way. Individual freedom, understood as the possibility of choice between alternative behaviours, is not, has never been and could never be unlimited. It operates in the presence of both natural and cultural limits and constraints. Any choice can only happen between *determined* possibilities. Even anarchists, those fanatics of freedom, concur with this (with the possible exception – more apparent than real – of some frantic individualists). Yet, this definition remains incomplete insofar as it paradoxically hints at a higher level of freedom through the attribution of *determining* restrictions to individual behaviour.

making' and 'A decision is a policy involving severe sanctions' (Lasswell and Kaplan 1950: 74–5); 'We can designate as power the ability of a social class to realise its specific objectives' (translated from Poulantzas 1972: 410). Power is 'the ability to make and carry out decisions even when others are opposed to them' (Wright Mills 1963: 18); power is 'a standing corporation which is obeyed from habit, has the means of physical compulsion, and is kept in being partly by view taken of its strength, partly by the faith that it rules as of right (in other words, its legitimacy), and partly by the hope of its beneficence' (De Jouvenel 1962: 25); by power we can understand 'all the means by which a man can bend the will of other men' (Mousnier 1973: 9); 'Power may be defined as the production of intended effects' (Russell 2004: 23); 'as the probability that certain specific commands (or all commands) will be obeyed by a given group of persons' (Weber 1978: 321) [Weber uses the German word *Herrschaft*, translated variably as 'power' and 'authority' in Italian or 'domination' and 'authority' in English]; power is communication regulated by a code (Luhmann 2012). *AUTHORITY*: Authority is 'any power exercised by one man or group of men over another man or group' (Abbagnano 1964); 'personal superiority or ascendancy . . . and the right to decide or command' (Lalande 1971); as Richard Sennett (1993: 10) puts it, 'a bond between people who are unequal', 'a way of defining and interpreting difference in strength' (118), or 'a search for stability and security in the strength of others' (178). 'The essence of authority . . . is to give a human being that security and that respect for his decisions that is logically given only to a super-individual and effectual axiom or to a deduction' (Simmel 1978: 41). 'Authority is thus the expected and legitimate possession of power' (Lasswell and Kaplan 1950: 133).

Let me clarify, I am not concerned, here, with the limits (whether external or internal) imposed by nature because they only *limit* the field of possibilities and do not *determine* behaviour. Hence, they are barely relevant to our discussion. Physiology and anatomy certainly limit the frequency and the modes of mating, but within those limits, the factors leading to specific models of erotic behaviour are exquisitely cultural. To put it with another example: in the game of chess, the chessboard can be seen to represent the natural limits (in fact the sixty-four squares are obviously an artificial limit, being part of the rules, but let us pretend that they are imposed by nature); the game rules represent the cultural limits (the bishop can only move diagonally, etc.); the moves of the players represent the freedom of choice within determined possibilities.

What I am interested in is precisely cultural determination. The two elements that, by mutual interaction, determine, to various degrees, animal behaviour, instinct and environment, are less important for those strange animals that are human beings. We are not governed by pure instincts (genetically determined behavioural reactions to given environmental stimuli) but, at best, by traces or residual instincts, with little or no social significance. Such are, for example, a newborn baby's instinct to suck or pseudo-instincts like the sexual 'instinct', which, in reality, is a need that can be satisfied in a variety of non-determined behavioural forms.

The environment for human beings is markedly more cultural than natural, not only because they have transformed and are transforming nature, but because their environment is made primarily of human relationships and their relationships with the world of 'things' are symbolically mediated.

During their long evolutionary process of hominisation, human beings have replaced instincts with cultural determinations, that is, with norms, rules, codes of communication and interaction. It is precisely in this substitution where lies human freedom at its highest level: *self-determination*.

To be sure, cultural determinations are not given (by God or nature), but self-given by humanity itself. Norms do not merely reflect natural necessities, they create arbitrary ones. That is to say that the creation of norms is necessary because it is 'written' in human nature (inhuman freedom's paradoxical self-determination) but the specific contents of these norms are not necessary. Human beings must create norms, but they can do so as they wish.

The production of norms is therefore the central, founding operation of human society and so of 'humanity' itself, as human beings can only exist as human as cultural products, that is to say, as social products.

The creation and re-creation of the social by inventing, passing down and modifying norms is, by definition, a collective function of the human species (that is, of its groups and subgroups). Just as, by definition, there is no individual code of communication, neither is there an individual norm of social interaction. Hence, while cultural determination represents the highest expression of human freedom, self-determination, it also originates a permanent asymmetry between the individual and the collectivity whereby the individual is determined by society much more than vice versa. Humanity collectively produces society, but it is individually shaped by it.

The creation of norms implies their application (a rule that is not applied is not a rule). However, the norm does not possess the same overriding force as the instinctual biochemical mechanisms, and the general consensus (which is infrequent, except perhaps in some highly homogeneous and static societies) cannot give the norm its compelling strength, the *sanction* that makes adherence to the norm, if not certain and universal, at least statistically probable. Every human group produces models of behaviour and related sanctions to which its members must conform; the severity of sanctions is proportional to the degree to which the norm is (considered as) fundamental for the group.

As Lasswell and Kaplan (1950: 74) point out, these sanctions are severe 'in terms of the values prevailing in the culture concerned. There is no doubt about the extremity of violence; yet disgrace – the drastic withdrawal of respect – may play a more important role in many situations.' Therefore, a sanction is severe to the extent to which the group's collective imaginary conceives it as such. Naturally, the same applies to the gravity of the infraction. The same behaviour may be judged very differently in different cultural contexts, and be consequently sanctioned in different ways. A loud belch may be considered a minor offence and so be greeted with only mild disapproval, or it may be considered a serious infraction and so give rise to a correspondingly severe sanction (for example, to expulsion from an exclusive club), or it may even be judged positively and receive a 'positive' sanction (laughter, satisfaction . . .). We must, in fact, remember that, beside negative sanctions, there are also positive sanctions (social recognition, esteem), which encourage approved behaviour. It is even possible, at least in theory, to conceive of a society in which individual behaviour is determined purely by means of positive sanctions (although in this case, the absence of positive sanctions could be considered a negative one).

The production and application of norms and sanctions, therefore, define the social regulatory function, which I propose to call *power*. Power is thus defined as a socially 'neutral' function which is necessary, not only to the existence of society, culture and of humanity itself, but also to the exercise of freedom as freedom to choose between determined possibilities, which we have discussed above. Indeed, the absence of cultural determination would lead to a meaningless vacuum, where choice is no longer possible, only pure chance. Freedom, as choice, can only be exercised in the presence of determinations, just as the friction of the air is necessary for the flight of birds.

Still, the fact that human behaviour can never be completely undetermined (nor, fortunately, completely determined*), and that its cultural determination is not only inevitable but, in its turn, an expression of freedom, does not imply that the ways and means of the social regulating function are neutral with respect to freedom itself.

It is paramount for freedom as choice that the mesh of determining factors be wide, elastic and modifiable, as the greater the range of possibilities left open by this 'mesh', the freer is the individual.

Equally paramount for freedom as self-determination is the level of participation in the regulatory process, as the freedom of individuals is greater, in this sense, when they have greater access to power. Equal access to power for all members of a society is, therefore, the first unavoidable condition for equal freedom for all: a condition necessary to *equal* freedom for all, but not sufficient to guarantee a high degree of freedom for each. Power can oppress all in the same degree and remain oppressive. There are examples of so-called 'primitive' societies where all have more or less equal access to power, but determined behaviours are so all-pervasive and/or traditionally immutable that they amount to a socially diffuse 'totalitarianism'.

A situation of 'equal power for all' is not only conceivable but has also been documented by anthropological research. It is, however, far from being the norm, either geographically or historically. It is far more common to find social systems in which the regulating function is exercised, not by the collectivity on itself, but rather by one part of the collectivity (generally, but not necessarily, a small minority) over another (generally the great majority); that is, systems in which the access to power is the monopoly of one part of society (individuals, groups, classes, castes . . .).

We are now stepping into another conceptual category which we could call *domination*. Domination defines the relationship between unequals – unequal in terms of power, and so of freedom; it defines the situation of superordination/subordination; it defines the systems of permanent asymmetry between social groups.

Domination typically manifests itself in relations of command/obedience whereby a command regulates the behaviour of the person who obeys. The command/obedience relation is not the regulating function in itself. One does not

---

* Crespi (1980) would say that humans 'oscillate' between the determined and the undetermined.

obey a norm (for example, that which forbids killing or requires us to drive on the right side of the road) but, rather, one abides by it. One obeys a command, that is, the form in which the norm is presented in a society of domination. The very fact that we conceive respect for the norm in terms of obedience stems from the expropriation of the regulating function by one part of society, which must *impose* it on the rest of society. The need to explicitly impose a norm is inversely proportional to participation in power, be it real or fictional. The social norm, in order to give regularity and predictability to cultural determination, must have an enforcing character. In other words, if important social behaviour must adhere to the norm for it to become a social norm, then it becomes *coercive* in situations of domination. This means that it is imposed along a hierarchical chain of subordination abiding to a general rule: command/obedience as a fundamental social relationship.

'From its beginnings', writes Clastres (1989: 16), 'our culture has conceived of political power in terms of hierarchised and authoritarian relationships of command and obedience. Every real or possible form of power is consequently reducible to this privileged relation which a priori expresses the essence of power.' But, 'if there is something completely alien to an Indian [Native American], it is the idea of giving an order or having to obey, except under very special circumstances' (ibid. 12). 'The model of coercive power is adopted, therefore, only in exceptional circumstances when the group faces an external threat . . . Normal civil power, based on the *consensus omnium* and not on constraint, is thus profoundly peaceful' (ibid. 30).

Evans-Pritchard also described a culture (the Nuer of Sudan) in which obedience is not conceived of, where command is an offence, and where no one obeys anyone else. It is not by chance that these are societies in which the regulating function is collective, where the word of the chief does not have the force of law, where the chief can be an 'arbiter' and express an 'authoritative' opinion (of this we shall see more when we consider authority and influence) but cannot act as judge or apply sanctions (Evans-Pritchard 1940). And even the Amba, whom Dahrendorf (1959) studies in his attempt to show the universality of the 'structures of authority' (by which he means, with an ease which goes ill with his usual accuracy, both what I defined as power and what I call domination), show, like the Nuer, the Tupinambà, the Guarani . . . the non-universality of domination. They demonstrate that the regulating function need not necessarily assume the coercive form of hierarchy and the relationship of command/obedience.*

---

* As Lasswell and Kaplan (1950: 223) write, 'As a rule approximates anarchy, it ceases to have the character of a rule at all. The scope of power shrinks to a minimum – in the

Domination, as we have said, is the privileged possession of power. The holders of domination reserve to themselves control of the process of producing the social, expropriating it from others. This phenomenon is similar to that of the privileged possession of the means of material production (to which it is often, although not necessarily, related) but even more concerning, as it pertains to human nature itself: domination is the denial of humanity for the expropriated, for those excluded from the dominant roles of the social structure.

Power, understood as the regulating function of society, is not the only form of cultural determination. There is a plethora of asymmetric relationships between individuals, in which certain behavioural choices can be totally or partially determined by the opinions or decisions of others, decisions to which is given a determining weight, so to say.

These relationships may be either personal or functional. By personal, I mean relationships whose subjects interact as persons; by functional, those whose subjects interact on the basis of roles which define social functions (the distinction, as usual, is partly arbitrary, insofar as all personal relationships are, to some degree, also interactions of roles and vice versa). In the case of personal relationships, we can define the asymmetry as *influence*, while for functional roles we call it *authority*.

In the first case, the asymmetry can be attributed to differences – moral, intellectual or of character – between individuals, resulting in one personality being somewhat 'stronger' than another, thus influencing rather than being influenced.*

In the second case, there is some sort of delegation of decision-making, due to the expectations attached to a role and justified (explicitly or implicitly) by 'competence'. The ambivalence of this term (which can mean ability or decisional capacity) conveys well the ambiguity between asymmetry of ability and decision-making capacity which characterises a full social division of labour into differing functions and roles.**

Now, neither influence nor authority, as defined above, necessarily implies a permanent social asymmetry. It is perfectly possible to imagine a social system

limiting case, no coercion is exercised. Social control remains, of course, in the various forms of influence; but the control is noncoercive.'

* This definition of influence is approximately the same as Sennett's (1993), although he extends it also to asymmetric interactions of role (including the roles of power and domination).

** This definition of authority is approximately the same as Sennett's (1993), although he applies it *only* to roles of power and domination.

in which a multiplicity of single asymmetrical relationships results in an overall equilibrium of influence and authority (or at least of this latter, which is conceptually closer to power and so to domination) for each subject. The asymmetrical parent/child relationship can be reformed over a lifetime in an 'egalitarian' cycle; the asymmetry of professional roles between individuals of differing professions can adjust itself through mutual services; coordination can be carried out in rotation . . . The authority attached to a role does not infringe the freedom of those who accept it voluntarily and critically; it can even be complementary to freedom by helping avoid its dispersion into a thousand insignificant rivulets: by simplifying a large number of individual choices, it allows us to 'focus' freedom on those choices that individuals hold truly important (individuals themselves, and not others on their behalf). Similarly, by choosing not to participate, or to do so only passively, in certain social decision-making processes (which is very different from being excluded from them) we are able to take full part in decision-making processes that matter to us.

Yet it remains true that societies organised around a hierarchical division of social activity necessarily feature a corresponding *hierarchy of authority and hence a permanent asymmetry* between the holders of different roles. It also remains true that some roles are 'authoritative' insofar as they are articulations of the social regulatory and so, within systems of domination, they are hierarchic articulations of domination itself and therefore are, by definition, permanently asymmetric. Thus differences of roles become social inequalities. In the same way, the existence of domination as a central category of the social imaginary determines permanent asymmetries of influence, since personal relationships are also perceived in terms of the hierarchy of domination. Thus individual differences also contribute to social inequality.

In abstract terms, the relationships which we have termed influence and authority can be 'neutral' categories, but in an existing social context of domination they take on a more or less pronounced value of domination and too often take the form of relationships of command/obedience.

To sum up, I have identified four conceptual categories which both common and scientific language put or can put under the same umbrella-term: *power*. I then proposed to limit this term to the first category: the social regulatory function, the sum of those processes through which a society regulates itself by producing and enforcing norms. If this function is carried out by only one part of society, that is, if one privileged (dominant) sector has a monopoly of power, it gives rise to a second category, to a set of hierarchical relationships of command/obedience, which I propose to call *domination*. Finally, I proposed the term *authority* for those asymmetries of roles which cause asymmetries of reciprocal determination, and *influence* for those asymmetries arising from personal characters.

I must reiterate that my main interest is not the terminology, the formal aspect of the definition, but its substance, the identification of concepts. The names that we give to colours are not important per se (even if agreeing on those names saves us time and spares us long periphrases). What really matters is that we agree on the existence of different colours, which correspond to different bands of frequencies of the visible range of light.

My contribution is (intended to be) a *first* distinction and identification of four groups of meanings, which can in turn serve for a general analysis of social phenomena. Further and different distinctions (corresponding to various forms and contents of power, domination and authority) will of course be necessary for deeper and/or more detailed analyses, yet I maintain that the four categories can serve well an initial anarchist approach to the problem.

Ultimately, what I deem *necessary* is the distinction between what I called power and domination. Anarchists have always perceived more or less clearly this fundamental qualitative difference (when, for example, they distinguish between society and the State); indeed, this is the essence of their thought. Yet, they have not always been able to draw the distinction explicitly in their analyses, by identifying two clear conceptual categories. Failing to identify them made anarchists fall prey to theoretical and practical aberrations, often in opposite directions (from the rejection in theory and practice of all norms and sanctions to the practice and semi-theory of domination, for instance during their participation in the Republican government during the Spanish Civil War).

Non-anarchist thinkers have generally been hardly capable of perceiving the difference between power and domination and have certainly not engaged with either the concepts or the terminology. As mentioned, this is hardly surprising, given their institutional role within a rationality belonging to an ideology of domination.

As mentioned, what I have proposed here – and what matters to me – is the identification of concepts, not terminology. Therefore, I would like future discussions – that I hope this article may trigger – to revolve around concepts rather than terms. I would like to see a critical analysis of the contents and concepts behind the proposed categories. For example: if a norm must be supported by strict sanctions is it 'simply' power or does it fall into the category of domination? Or, again, is it necessary, at this point in the debate, to distinguish between what I called influence and authority? Or would it be useful to distinguish between the asymmetries of actual ability and those of formal competence?

This said, it is worth spending a few more words on my terminology, as it is a delicate matter among anarchists. What I consider as neutral concepts under the labels of 'power' and 'authority' are not neutral for anarchists. Anarchists use the terms 'power', 'domination' and 'authority', particularly the first two, as synonyms, and with obvious negative connotations (they stand for the '-archy' which they reject and fight against). The question arises, why am I proposing an anarchist and neutral use of power and authority? In part, I am being provocative in order to point at the need to pay more attention to substance through a little semantic scandal. I try and highlight a conceptual innovation through a linguistic one. It strikes me as an absurdity that our own language, anarchist language, has three terms for one concept and none for the remaining two. But, above all, it is because I believe that both common and specialised language define as power and authority what in reality is power and authority *plus* domination. So if we subtract domination from power and authority, by making it a category of its own, even if in all existing societies (except the residual forms of primitive societies) it is in fact superimposed on the other two, we are left with those types of relationships which I call power and authority.

On the other hand, no anarchist would use the term 'powerlessness' (political, social, economic . . .) as a synonym for absence of domination, as the power whose absence is indicated by this word has the positive connotation of 'the power to do' [*poter fare*], to exercise one's own freedom.* And I am sure that the expression 'power of all'** does not sound heretical to most anarchists as it indicates the individual's capacity to decide and/or participate in the social decision-making processes.

Let us now leave definitional issues and move back to substance. How can the proposed concepts be useful to anarchist thought? They (or any other definitions which distinguish two or three or ten colours in that undifferentiated or ill-defined spectrum that we call power) allow us to better conceive the central *negation* of anarchist philosophy (that is, the anarchist interpretation of the world) and, consequently, its central *affirmation*, its founding value: freedom. Furthermore, this definition paves the way for a better formulation of a

---

* With regard to the relationship between will and freedom (which are, emblematically, defined in Russian with the single term *volija*) see Ambrosoli (1982).

** As, for example, in the following: 'The power of all . . . means that *each individual* must hold sufficient (real) power to influence and control political decisions concerning his life, to the degree that this is compatible with an equal power for every other individual in society, so that everyone has, in every moment, the maximum possibility that is compatible with the maximum possibility of every other person, to realise the best life he can' (translated from Pontara 1977: 61).

multitude of problems for anarchist social theory which studies both the 'laws' (uniformity, constantly recurring relationships, causal connections, necessary conditions) of domination and the 'laws' of freedom.

Let me provide a few examples – in the field of politics my definition allows us to think more clearly about the gap between norms and the law, and bring into evidence the substantial difference between the freedom of the liberals and anarchist freedom, to analyse the social, decision-making processes, to critically enrich the 'déjà vu' about assemblies, rotations, delegation, revocable mandates and so on. Perhaps, my definition of power, or any definition that distinguishes between its regulatory function and its monopoly by a privileged section of society, is the necessary starting point for an anarchist political science. After all, anarchists have always rejected politics, considering it the science and exercise of power, where this latter is identified with domination (and such superimposition is indeed the rule within existing societies).

Sociology can benefit from this definition to draw a neater, clearer distinction between diversity and inequality of roles and social categories; it could be useful to better identify institutions and mechanisms of domination, differentiating them from the structures of power; it could throw new light on the forms and contents of cooperation and conflict.

In economics, this definition will allow a more effective formulation of economic power (and domination), as a particular form of social power (and of domination). It allows us to distinguish between economic power and economic domination and between general economic 'laws', economic 'laws' which are common to all societies of domination, and those which are peculiar to specific societies of domination.

Psychology, in turn, will be able to distinguish between unavoidable and avoidable asymmetries between individuals, between differences attached to persons and roles (be they positive or neutral in terms of freedom) and inequalities which deny freedom. It [psychology] will also be able to better study both the 'libertarian personality' and the 'authoritarian personality'.* Perhaps it may

---

* Or, as De Jouvenel (1962: 340–1) puts it, the libertarian personality and the securitarian personality. '[T]here never was a time in any society whatsoever when some individuals did not feel themselves to be insufficiently protected, and others do not feel themselves to be insufficiently free. The former I will call "securitarians", and the latter "libertarians" . . . He who has grasped the conception of the libertarian and securitarian sentiments being measurable quantities of opposites can envisage any society whatsoever, at any given moment of its existence, as a multitude of specks, each corresponding to an individual which can be arranged in tiers by reference to their libertarian content. The most securitarian among them will, as I see it, be quite at the

even help us understand why, apart from a few exceptions, the anarchist message remains unappealing to the vast majority of people, why the Kropotkinian 'spirit of revolt' is usually less strong than social conformism.

Pedagogy could solve the contradiction between the authority of the adult and the freedom of the minor* and understand why permissiveness, as a form of tolerated anomy, is equally unsuitable for libertarian education, the process of building a libertarian personality, as is discipline imposed through coercion.

Finally (speaking among anarchists), we could spare ourselves many arguments and useless dialogues, turning them into a rational confrontation! We need only think of the recurrent debate on anarchist organisation in which, for a century now, the lack of understanding on a definitional level has played an equal part to disagreement on its substance.

Amongst the open questions that my proposal could help, if not solve, at least better formulate (in the paragraphs above I referred to examples within conventional social sciences) there is the question of the genesis of power. How, why and when are power, authority and domination born? If we are to strictly follow my definitions, in reality, the question arises only with respect to domination. The answer for authority and power is implicit in their respective definitions. If we accept the anthropological assumption that human beings are no longer subject to instinctual determination and that, vice versa, they are capable of producing a normative symbolic universe thanks to the particular evolution of their brains, it follows that the cultural regulatory function is both *possible* and *essential* for them.** In a similar vein, in my definition, authority follows as a corollary to the postulate that society structures itself in functional roles.

---

bottom, and the most libertarian right at the top.' And so, *voilà*, we have domination and the 'libertarians' become members of the dominant social groups. And thus an interesting idea turns into the same old story!

* We can consider, in this light, Bakunin's contribution (Dahrendorf 1979). For Bakunin (1869) the educative process is a progressive movement from 'authority' to 'freedom': the smaller the child the greater is their need for external determination; as they grow the asymmetry between them and the adult decreases and with maturity they become an adult in the full sense of the word and as such can and must reach the highest possible level of self-determination.

** 'The prime role of culture is to ensure the group's existence as a group, and consequently, in this domain as in all others, to replace chance by organization' (Lévi-Strauss 1971: 32). Culture provides a normative regulation for that which nature has 'forgotten' to regulate through biology: man's social behaviour. In this it seems that there is no clear-cut gap between man and other animals: 'It seems as if the great apes, having broken away from a specific pattern of behaviour, were unable to re-establish a norm on any new plane. The clear and precise instinctive behaviour of most mammals

Domination, on the other hand, has no necessary foundation in human nature and society. This is why its genesis becomes a problem for my definition. Let us start with some solutions put forward by non-anarchist thinkers. As mentioned, they failed to draw a clear distinction between power and domination. Even when they hint at a conceptual difference, they do not deem it necessary to demonstrate how we move from one to the other. They usually move from domination to power (my logical process is the opposite) and even those few who follow my logic do not challenge the process and consider the two as coeval, the necessity of one entails the other.

Let us now consider those explanations which during my research struck me as exemplary of the main arguments put forward to justify domination. Some proceed from domination to power and justify the former with bio-psychical arguments, that is, innate 'natural' psychological mechanisms: some personalities have a natural inclination for domination, others for subjugation.* After laying this first stone in their theoretical edifice, the apologists of power-domination hasten to vest it with more enthusing structural elements, and we are told that this 'natural' subdivision of humanity into two categories (tendential masters and tendential slaves) is beneficial to both parties and ultimately boils down to an admirable artifice of nature or providence to bestow on mankind its advantages.** Sennett's argument can also be seen to fall into this type

is lost to them, but the difference is purely negative and the field that nature has abandoned remains unoccupied' (ibid. 31).

* 'The majority of men[sic] are timid, modest, passive beings, who represent the plastic material of Power, being born to obey. The race of masters is a minority with a more intense vital force; they are the ambitious, the active, the imperious ones who need to affirm their superiority in thought and in action' (translated from Ferrero 1981: 39). This vulgar commonplace with its racist overtones follows, surprisingly enough, observations of a very different quality, such as the following: 'The beginnings of legitimacy are the justification of the right to command since, of all the inequalities between humans there is none that has such important consequences and so such a need for justification as the inequality deriving from power' (ibid. 27). And 'if, apart from some rare exceptions, all men have the same worth why should one have the right to command others and the others the duty of obeying?' (ibid. 28). Analogously, but more 'dialectically', Simmel (1978: 52) speaks of the 'will to dominate' and writes that 'the human being's feelings with respect to subordination are twofold. On the one hand he, in fact, wants to be dominated. Most men can not only not exist without a guide but also feel this: they seek a superior force which will free them from responsibility . . . Nevertheless they have a not lesser need to oppose this power of direction . . . Thus it could be said that obedience and opposition are the two aspects or elements of what is in fact coherent human behaviour.'

** 'This polarisation of man [sic] into masters and servants seems admirably suited to the of approach, although he formally starts from influence and then moves through authority to power and domination.*

The second type of argument is cultural, exemplified by Dahrendorf's (1959) thesis that no 'natural' explanation of power-domination is possible: power-domination is not the *effect* of a pre-existing inequality but, on the contrary, it is the *cause* of the first fundamental inequality between humans. However, as he does not distinguish between power and domination, he logically derives the necessity of domination from the necessity of power (which he terms authority), that is, from the regulatory function. For him, the regulatory function and the privileged possession of it are one and the same thing.

Another angle through which to look at and classify various approaches to the genesis of power-domination is whether they consider it coeval with humanity/society or postulate their appearance at a certain point in history. Remarkably (at least for theories which reduce power to domination), it is not power-domination but only domination that breaks into a social space which is either undefined or defined as the state of nature.**

Where does the problem of the genesis of domination fit within the logic of my definition? Since, within that logic, everything begins from the postulate

---

pre-arranged order in human nature' (translated from Ferrero 1981: 40); 'At its origins, power . . . is originally a form of defence against the two greatest terrors afflicting man: anarchy and war' (ibid. 39); '[Power] is a social necessity. By reason of the order which it imposes and the harmony which it creates, it enables men to attain a better life' (De Jouvenel 1962: 283).

* 'Authority is . . . a matter of defining and interpreting differences in strength. In one sense, the sentiment of authority is the recognition just that these differences exist. In another sense, a more complicated one, it is a matter of taking account of the needs and desires of the weak as well as the strong' (Sennett 1993: 126). Then 'the political synonym for strength [is] power' (ibid. 18). Finally, 'Power between two people is the will of one person prevailing over the will of the other' and 'The chain of command is the structure by which this imbalance of will can be extended to thousands or millions of people' (ibid. 170).

** One example: 'a natural society is a small thing. And for a small society to become a large one a new factor is necessary. For that there must be fusion, and this in the great majority of the cases comes, not from the instinct of association, but from that of domination. The large formation owes its existence to the instinct of *domination* [my italics] . . . Conquest and nothing but conquest gives birth to large formations. Sometimes the conquerors are a component society within a group, but usually a warrior band outside it' (De Jouvenel 1962: 99–100). And again: 'It follows that the state is in essence the result of the successes achieved by a band of brigands who superimpose themselves on small, distinct societies; [it] . . . behaves towards the vanquished and the subjected as Power in the pure state' (ibid. 100–1).

of human cultural plasticity, it excludes any hypotheses based on innate bio-psychological elements such as the 'will to dominate' or the 'instinct of domination' and so on (as a necessary counterpart to the propensity to obey, will to be ruled, etc.). If we are to take human cultural self-determination seriously then human behavioural models are not inscribed in nature, be they gregarious-authoritarian or of the anarchist type. My statement here does not intend to deny the possibility of a 'naturalistic' interpretation of anarchism, which used to be in fact quite common. Such an anarchism postulates human natural goodness as a natural self-regulative potential of society, which does not require normative determination. Still, even this anarchism cannot ascribe domination to nature and explains it in cultural terms, as arising from human invention.

If we follow a purely cultural interpretation of humanity, we should not be surprised to discover that in the context of domination, character traits are shaped by and for domination.

Nor should we be surprised by the absence of those traits in cultures characterised by the absence of domination – see the inconceivability of command and obedience, as Clastres (1989: 204–5) writes, the fact that 'no one in such a society feels the quaint desire to do more, own more, or appear to be more than his neighbour'. The cultural context gives meaning to the differences of character that are functional to it. In the context of domination, therefore, the individual character differences are forced into models leading to either pole of the command/obedience relationship.

But this still does not tell us when and how domination came into being. And I certainly cannot pretend to be able to answer this here. The problem is perhaps destined to remain open, as the present state of scientific knowledge does not allow us to empirically test our hypotheses, since they are empirically 'non-falsifiable'. We are therefore less likely to develop scientific theories about the origins of domination than 'myths' (apologetic or critical).

For now, I will limit myself to sketch an explanatory hypothesis from an anarchist and culturalist point of view. My hypothesis is that domination appeared at a certain point in the history of the human race as a 'cultural mutation'. We have recently begun to apply the principles of natural evolution (chance mutations and the positive selection of those characteristics best fitted to survival) to human cultural evolution (see Cavalli Sforza and Feldman 1981). Domination could be seen to be a mutation, that is to say, a cultural innovation which, in certain conditions, proved advantageous, in terms of survival, for those social groups who adopted it – for example, for greater military efficiency – and was subsequently imposed as a model either by conquest or by imitation for defensive purposes.

An alternative hypothesis, which I find reasonably convincing, maintains that the domination-mutation did not appear all of a sudden but rather elements of domination (that is to say, social relationships partly or temporarily modelled on the command/obedience relationship and the inequality of power that it entails) have always existed, or at least pre-date societies of domination, as for example in the man/woman, old/young, warrior/non-warrior, chief/tribe relationships. (In these relationships, domination could have existed as a cultural *imitation* of asymmetries seen in – or rather interpreted from – nature, that is, in 'social' animals hunted or reared or at least observed.* But this is yet another hypothesis.) These elements of domination would have been kept 'under control' in the earliest human societies and so could not become generalised as elements central to culture and society, until changed 'environmental' conditions, within or outside groups, made possible their transformation into dominant regulatory models. At this point the mutation spread by 'contagion' sparing only those groups which were made immune by their geographical and/ or cultural isolation.

The mutation hypothesis opens (or, better, rearticulates) a whole series of problems related to the project of abolishing domination, which is the central identifying feature of anarchism as the anarchist transformation is essentially a cultural mutation. Within that project, anarchists are mutants who tend to multiply and transmit their cultural anomaly (which is anomalous only vis-à-vis the normality of the dominant model) and, at the same time, create the 'environmental' conditions which will favour their mutation, that is, the generalisation of the mutant character. This could pave the way for novel interpretations of the relationship between existential, pedagogical or revolutionary anarchism. But we are now exceeding the scope of this text, which set out to offer some preliminary reflections on power, within the limits of a definitional proposal. Let us stop here. For now, at least.

References

Abbagnano, Nicola [1961] (1964), *Dizionario di filosofia*, Turin: UTET.
Ambrosoli, Roberto (1982), 'Volontà e natura umana', *Volontà* 36 (4).
Bakunin, Michael (1869), 'Equal Opportunity in Education', *L'Égalité*; retrieved

---

* This is one point of view from which we can consider Clastres's (1989: 44) observation that the politics of the primitive societies studied by him was organised around the understanding that coercive power in itself 'is no more than the furtive manifestation of nature in *its* power'.

from <https://theanarchistlibrary.org/library/michail-bakunin-equal-oppor tunity-in-education> (last accessed 20 May 2021).

Bakunin, Michael [1882] (1970), *God and the State*, New York: Dover Publications Inc.

Baldelli, Giovanni (1971), *Social Anarchism*, Harmondsworth: Penguin Books.

Bertolo, Amedeo (1977), 'Per una definizione dei nuovi padroni', in *I Nuovi Padroni*, Milan: Antistato.

Bertolo, Amedeo (1979), 'La gramigna sovversiva', *Interrogations* 17–18: 9–37.

Bertolo, Amedeo (1981), 'L'immaginario sovversivo', *A/Rivista Anarchica* 93.

Cavalli Sforza, Luigi, and Marcus W. Feldman (1981), *Cultural Transmission and Evolution: A Quantitative Approach*, Princeton: Princeton University Press.

Clastres, Pierre [1974] (1989), *Society against the State*, New York: Zone Books.

Crespi, Franco (1980), 'Mediazione, norma, potere', *Volontà* 34 (4).

Dahrendorf, Ralf [1957] (1959), *Class and Class Conflict in Industrial Society*, Stanford: Stanford University Press.

Dahrendorf, Ralf [1972] (1979), *La libertà che cambia*, Bari: Latzera.

De Jouvenel, Bertrand [1945] (1962), *On Power, its Nature and the History of its Growth*, Boston: Beacon Press.

Eschenburg, Theodore (1976), *Über Autorität*, Frankfurt: Suhrkamp.

Evans-Pritchard, Edward Evan (1940), *The Nuer: A Description of the Modes of Livelihood and Political Institutions of a Nilotic People*, Oxford: Oxford University Press.

Ferrero, Guglielmo [1970] (1981), *Potere*, Milan: Sugarco.

Horowitz, Irving Louis (1963), 'Introduction', in *Power, Politics and People: The Collected Essays of C. Wright Mills*, ed. Irving Louis Horowitz, New York: Oxford University Press, pp. 1–22.

Lalande, Pierre-André [1927] (1971), *Dizionario critico di filosofia*, Milan: ISEDI.

Lanza, Luciano (1981), 'Al di là dell'economia', *Volontà* 35 (3).

Lanza, Luciano (1982), 'L'economia dal dominio alla libertà', *Volontà* 36 (3).

Lasswell, Harold D., and Abraham Kaplan (1950), *Power and Society: A Framework for Political Inquiry*, New Haven: Yale University Press.

Lévi-Strauss, Claude [1949] (1971), *The Elementary Structures of Kinship*, Boston: Beacon Press.

Luhmann, Niklas [1968] (2012), *Trust and Power*, Cambridge: Polity Press.

Mousnier, Roland [1969] (1973), *Social Hierarchies, 1450 to the Present*, Berlin: Schocken Books.

Pontara, Giuliano (1977), 'Definizione di violenza e non-vioelnza conflitti sociali', in *Marxismo e non-violenza*, Genoa: Lanterna, pp. 59–80.

Poulantzas, Nicos (1972), 'Sul concetto di potere', in Franco Ferrarotti (ed.), *La sociologia del potere*, Bari: Laterza.

Proudhon, Pierre-Joseph [1858] (2011), 'Justice in the Revolution and the Church', in *Property Is Theft! A Pierre-Joseph Proudhon Reader*, ed. Iain McKay, Edinburgh: AK Press, pp. 619–84.

Russell, Bertrand [1938] (2004), *Power: A New Social Analysis*, London: Routledge.

Sennett, Richard [1980] (1993), *Authority*, London: Faber and Faber.

Simmel, Georg [1907] (1978), *Il dominio*, Rome: Bulzoni.

Weber, Max [1922] (1978), *Economy and Society: An Outline of Interpretive Sociology*, Berkeley: University of California Press.

Wright Mills, C. (1963), *Power, Politics and People*, New York: Oxford University Press.

5 The State as Paradigm of Power
Eduardo Colombo (1984)

First published in *Volontà* 38 (3)

> The promotion of anarchy is the ultimate – or perhaps the only – crime against the state.
>
> Georg Wilhelm Friedrich Hegel (1999: 21)

'TO MAKE ALL men equal – seditious dream . . ., impious, sacrilegious chimera . . .' (translated from Bossuet 1972: 97).[1] What is more apt than equality, that most absolute of prerequisites to human liberty, to threaten domination and privilege?

For Tocqueville (2004: 787–8), equality predisposes us to 'take a dim view of all authority'; it breeds unruliness and, he wrote, 'I admire equality when I see it deposit an obscure notion of, and instinctive penchant for, political independence in every man's heart and mind'.

The liberal credo may appear in 'neo-anarchist' clothing. It is bound, however, to come face to face sooner or later with its own allegiance to State control, proceeding as it does from the assumption of the fully autonomous individual as defined by Natural Law. The freedom of each individual human being does not come prior to society; nor is it an abstract whose expansion can be hindered by another freedom. Humans do not give up part of their freedom to build the political space of the *city*; they engage in no contract whatsoever; nor do they alienate anything of their own will.

---

[1] Jacques-Bénigne Bossuet (1627–1704) was a French bishop and theologian, who rose to fame not only for his proximity to the monarchy but for his defence of Catholic orthodoxy. He was a key proponent of the idea that monarchs derived their authority not from any earthly institution (even the Church), but from God directly. For one of the few introductions to his work in English, see Riley (1990).

Proudhon (1969: 118) is impatient with the swindle of the General Will and the Social Contract: 'Tyranny, claiming divine right, had become odious; he [Rousseau] reorganizes it and makes it respectable, by making it proceed from the people, so he says.'

When he came to define the positive principle of freedom, Bakunin (1980b: 237) founded it upon collective equality and solidarity since freedom – as well as oppression – is a product of the social activity of humanity. '[T]he isolated individual cannot possibly become conscious of his freedom. To be free means to be acknowledged and treated as such by all his fellowmen.' And, he adds (237–8):

> I am truly free only when all human beings, men and women, are equally free. The freedom of other men, far from negating or limiting my freedom, is, on the contrary, its necessary premise and confirmation . . . My personal freedom, confirmed by the liberty of all, extends to infinity.

Quoting these well-known words once again may seem banal to anarchists. Nonetheless, they sum up, in a way quite unparalleled, an articulation essential to anarchist theory: that of freedom and equality as the forces able to create the only political space in which the diversity of individuals and their varied means and talents find their possible complementarity. Or, to put it differently: *'we are convinced that liberty without socialism is privilege, injustice; and that socialism without liberty is slavery and brutality'* (Bakunin 1980a: 127).

When political power becomes autonomous and develops into a State, a wall soon to become unsurmountable is formed between freedom and equality. The State principle perpetuates social heteronomy, sanctions institutional hierarchy and perpetually reproduces domination. That is the reason why the critique of the liberal notion of the original covenant or so-called social contract – which is the legal basis of the State – has prevailed right from the very beginnings of anarchism, indeed from Godwin, through Proudhon, to Bakunin. 'The implications of the social contract are in fact fatal, because they culminate in the absolute domination of the State' (Bakunin 1973: 136).

From the liberal, individualistic point of view, characteristic of the ideological consolidation of the nation-State from the seventeenth century onwards, society is viewed as resulting from the relinquishment of the 'state of nature' and subsequent foundation of an autonomous 'body' politic. This is at once a hierarchical principle of institutional organisation: its logical consequence is that society dissolves into the State.

Anarchism conceives of the *political organ* [*l'instance politique*] as part and parcel of global society and posits the possibility, in organisational terms, of a complex, conflictual and incomplete structure, by no means transparent or definitive, yet based on overall reciprocity together with the autonomy of the acting subject as opposed to the fragmentation and distribution of Power.

Anarchy is a trope, an organising principle, a mode of representation of the political. The State is a different or antithetical principle. Fundamentally, the State is a paradigm in the hierarchical structuring of society; within the sphere of *political power* – i.e. domination – it is both necessary and irreducible. For this sphere is delineated out of the dispossession by a section of society of part of the overall ability any human group has to create relational modes, norms, customs, codes, institutions, in short of its symbol-instituting ability, which defines and constitutes the human level of social integration. Nor is such dispossession necessarily achieved by the use of force; it goes hand in hand with the basic premise of *political obligation*, that is, the duty to obey.

Closely intertwined within the contemporary notion of the Leviathan are in fact two different aspects of the State, which are too often fused or confused into one. One comes under the heading of what we called 'the State principle' that includes *domination* – whose core is command and obedience – as the inevitable form of the political. Here the hierarchical organisation of power is assumed, within the same discourse establishing the State as a principle or paradigm, to be necessary to the integration of complex societies. From the standpoint of contemporary political philosophy, with the only and notable exception of anarchism, the political organ [*l'instance politique*] at large is viewed as falling within the compass of this principle.

The other aspect for consideration is that of the composition and development of 'empirical' structures constituting a State in any given situation; that is to say, the institutions which make up national States, stretching as these do over a circumscribed territory, ruling over large or small populations and possessing a unique political organisation and a specific ideological system of legitimation within the larger generic model of the modern State. Making the right use at the right moment of these two semantic components, the ongoing social discourse conveniently constructs the State as a coherent, unified concept within the dominant political theory.

The Birth of the State

The following discussion will therefore bear, in a way that is bound to be both brief and cursory, on the general characteristics of the birth of the modern

State since, despite differences in the geographical, political and socio-economic nature of the various regimes, national States tally with the model which became prevalent in Europe between 1100 and 1600 (Strayer 2005).

As a rule, there is a general consensus that the historical origins of the State ought to be looked for in the particular kind of institutionalisation of political power which developed out of the conflict between Papacy and Empire within Western Christendom. In the mid-Middle Ages – from the tenth to the thirteenth century – political power appeared fragmented and scattered (Le Goff 1988). The feudal system looked like a random assortment of kingdoms, seigniories, church estates, imperial vicariates, free cities and principalities engaging in constant warfare to enforce or defend sovereignty over land, property and vassals. From the twelfth century onwards, the Papacy began to acknowledge sovereignty in temporal matters to princes breaking away from the Empire. Meanwhile, in France and Sicily, shrewd jurists were preparing the final formula: *Rex in regno suo est imperator*, thus paving the way for the nation-State to come (Guenée 1985).[2]

These considerations on the historical origins of the State allow us to concentrate on the word 'state' itself, which in Romance and Germanic languages is derived from the Latin *status*. The present meaning of the word is the result of the long period of gestation whereby the institutions and representations shaping the modern State gradually came into being (Colombo 1983). In the fourteenth and fifteenth centuries, the word *status* ('state')[3] took on its governmental sense to become synonymous with *potestas*,[4] *regimen*,[5] *gubernatio*.[6]

---

[2] This famous Latin phrase (meaning 'the king is ruler in his own kingdom') was one of the key points in the Peace of Westphalia (1648), a set of treaties that brought Europe's 'Thirty Years' War' to an end. The treaties supposedly enshrined a territorially bound, post-feudal, legally protected and non-clerical form of political power, but the shift to this idealised 'state' found neither its beginning nor its end therein. Regardless, the idea of sovereignty having such a neat beginning remains ideologically powerful (Miéville 2006).

[3] 'State' is here to be understood in its original sense, the Latin neutral word meaning condition or way of existence.

[4] *Potestas*, meaning power or faculty, was an important concept of Roman law. After the fall of the Western Roman Empire, Europe witnessed a fragmentation of power under the institutions of Christianity and Principalities. Political power in Europe was hence divided into two categories, religious government (*auctoritas*) and temporal power (*potestas*).

[5] The Latin word *regimen* means direction, government or rule, from the Latin verb *regere*, 'to rule, direct'.

[6] The Latin word *gubernatio* originates from *gubernum*, the ship's wheel. Hence *gubernatio* indicates nautical pilotage, direction, control and, by extension, government.

In the works of Machiavelli – who is generally recognised as having 'definitely fixed and popularized the modern meaning of the term' (Passerin d'Entrèves 1967: 30) – *stato* is used 'in connexion with what will, after him, be recognized as the basic and essential feature of the State, viz., that of being an organization endowed with the capacity of exerting and controlling the use of force over certain people and within a given territory' (Passerin d'Entrèves 1967: 32). Yet whenever such terms as *polis, res publica, civitas* and *regnum*, appearing in texts written prior to 1500, are translated as 'State', the past is invariably interpreted in the light of some of the mainstream ideas or prevalent views of contemporary political thought, namely the over-determination of the social due to the increasing autonomy of the political [*l'instance politique*] in its State form, and the often-implicit correlative inevitability of political power as domination.

The major political organisations of some historical import prior to the emergence of the State are generally divided into three types: the Greek city, the kingdom and the empire. Empires stretched over vast territories. Such was the case of the Roman Empire at the height of its expansion in the second century AD, or of the Qing Empire of the Ching Manchu dynasty which in the eighteenth century covered twelve million square kilometres (two million more than today's People's Republic of China). They were highly centralised and ruled over populations conquered by force of arms. Their frontiers stood firm against the barbarity and chaos foreign to the only 'world order' they knew. Yet, even if some of these empires, such as the Roman Empire, did develop a remarkable administrative apparatus, as well as a fully integrated judicial machinery, the whole system showed a low degree of cohesion, since it succeeded in integrating and involving in the political process only an extremely small section of the population, hence a total absence of any sense of allegiance or of belonging to the central imperial power.

Conversely, the characteristics of the Greek *polis* were: reduced territorial limits, smaller populations, and a high degree of internal cohesion and strong political involvement entailing a definite sense of community identity. Although its laws (*nomoi*) established the sovereignty of the assembly (one can trace as far back as the seventh century BC phrases such as 'the Polis decreed' or, later, 'it pleased the people . . .') as well as equality amongst its members, the *polis* came up against its own limitations and those they excluded: women, foreigners and slaves.

Yet if the Greek *polis* may rightly claim to have invented politics, it was still a far cry from the modern paradigm of the State. There is no autonomy of the political [*l'instance politique*] from religion. In its minimal definition the city was confined to one locus, near the *agora*, where the seat of government (*prytaneum*) used to be, 'that truly common home, religiously and politically speaking, the very heart of the City' (translated from Gernet 1982: 269). Nor was there any clear-cut division between the political system and 'the system of kinship'. Besides, political relationships were by no means universal, but rather involved a limited number of 'citizens' (Badie and Birnbaum 1983).

In the early Middle Ages, the kingdom was the most common form of political organisation in Europe. It was moreover the perfect antithesis of the modern State, as it was based not on an abstract principle or on more or less durable institutions, but rather on loyalty towards a handful of people. A kingdom would bring together populations accepting a certain person as their king or acknowledging the hereditary right of a certain family to reign; yet territorial limits, so vital to the nation-State, were a matter of indifference. Thus, within a few generations, the kingdom of the Visigoths moved from the Baltic to the Black Sea to the Bay of Biscay (Strayer 2005).

So, what were the first institutions, the very origins of the modern State? War and taxation invariably come to mind. History, however, is not as blunt. According to Strayer (2005), the first permanent institutions in Western Europe dealt with the internal affairs of the kingdom, especially justice and finance.

War was too expensive a business for these small political entities to be able to set up large armies and keep them over long periods. Not that military service for all – by levy or conscription – never occurred to kings. In England, in the name of the loyalty owed to him by each and every subject, the king proclaimed – the Statute of Winchester (1285) – that able-bodied men aged fifteen to sixty should report to the battlefield if need be, equipped according to their various means. And a few years later, Philip 'the Fair' of France enforced '*levée en masse*' or '*arrière-ban*' (Guenée 1985).[7] Thus, in the early fourteenth century, the concept of a national army begin to materialise both in England and in France. In practice, however, it proved a failure since populations feeling neither directly involved in nor sufficiently bound by loyalty to the kingdom shunned military service in massive numbers. Not to mention the traditional privilege of nobility vis-à-vis the use of arms, which is the opposite to the work of the commoner – a further layer of contradiction.

The taxation issue, on the other hand, developed on much firmer bases. In the Middle Ages the power of a prince was largely dependent on the size of his estates, but these were so fragmented and so far apart that tolls as well as other

---

[7] In mediaeval France, the *arrière-ban* ('retro-proclamation') was a proclamation of a king calling his vassals to arms.

feudal duties had to be shared with other members of the aristocracy, making it difficult to assess the revenue.

Thus the first full-time civil servants were the estate-managers whose function was to centralise and keep due record of all the sources of revenue from widely scattered territories (Strayer 2005). But what contributed most to the shaping of the nascent national State was the introduction of new forms of taxation. First to be introduced were indirect taxes, such as the 'salt tax' and customs duties. The latter, for instance, were adopted in 1274 by the small republic of Genoa, which collected two deniers per pound of merchandise imported or exported. In 1275 Edward I levied a customs duty on wool. And in 1277 Philip III of France banned the exportation of wool and other merchandise. 'What these three measures have in common', says Bernard Guenée (1985: 168), 'is that they were concomitant, differed in nature from the old circulation rights familiar to the feudal world and marked the first manifestation of the young States along their frontiers.'

However, the most fundamental changes were brought about by direct taxation, which not only encouraged the setting up of representational institutions but entailed the registration of the property of each inhabitant. It was not until the end of the fifteenth century that all Western States succeeded in imposing modern direct taxation on their various populations. But first two major obstacles had to be removed.

The first was popular opposition, for direct universal contribution required a certain degree of consent. This decisive step towards the establishment of the nation-State was achieved by the transfer of ancient loyalties from clan, city or province to the nation-State, which coincided with the recognition of a supreme and abstract authority endowed with the power to decide in the final analysis. It is in the light of this that the evolution of the 'Estates General' and parliament should be understood. In times of crisis, princes found themselves obliged to consult representative assemblies – or *parlamentum* – in order to obtain the funds they needed. By the middle of the fourteenth century, direct taxation could not be levied except in case of emergency and with the approval of the representative assembly of the country, be it parliament or Estates General.

The second major obstacle governments had to face was assessing personal capital or income or even taking stock of the number of households. First to appear, in Pisa (1162), was the *estima*, whereby direct taxation was no longer the same for every household but depended on an estimation kept in a register. Shortly afterwards, the *cadastre* followed in Italy and France and in 1300 the *percentage* was approved by the English Parliament. Widespread taxation led to more clearly outlined and centralised administrative techniques and to the creation of a body of specialised civil servants.

The administration of justice, which was also destined to play a part in the founding of the State initially, provided part of local revenue – most offences being liable to a fine. Besides, tax collection and the administration of justice were carried out by the same agents of the State. Sovereigns soon came to realise that justice could serve as a pretext for extending their power and strengthening their authority. The fact that major offences, such as murder, could only be judged in royal courthouses enabled them to have a say in provinces where they owned no land and had no right of local jurisdiction.

To conclude this cursory survey of the institutions which gave the modern nation-State its shape, it could be said that 'the two pillars of the mediaeval State were the Treasury and the High Court' (Strayer 2005: 33) and, further, that at this stage in the history of the Western world, bodies of specialised civil servants began to appear, ensuring regularity in administrative control, together with the 'chancery', a central, coordinating body.

Thus, by the end of the Middle Ages, all the components of the modern State can be said to have come to maturity. The first unmistakable sign was a certain permanence in political units, in both space and time. But what made its emergence possible was the establishment of impersonal and differentiated institutions. The decisive step was taken with the recognition, in Strayer's (2005: 9) words, of 'the need for a final authority' as opposed to a mere monopoly of power existing de facto.

This needs qualification, but first a word must be said about the failure of the nation-State to impose itself with any ease, owing to the resistance offered by hostile currents of thought, be they of a communalist or federalist nature. In his well-known pamphlet entitled 'The State: Its Historic Role', Peter Kropotkin (1970) traced the birth of the State to as late as the sixteenth century, thus taking into account the fact that the institutionalisation of the State form went hand in hand with the great peasant revolts and millenarianistic upheavals.

To quote Guenée (1985: 233): 'In the fourteenth and fifteenth centuries, the political life of Western states was the privilege of an elite and normally excluded the bulk of townsmen and country people.' The revolts of the peasantry and the paupers of the cities were long and violent. Rebellion broke out in Toulouse in 1322, then in Flanders one year later – where it was to last for five years; then in Cahors in 1336, culminating in the *jacquerie* in 1358 when 'over a hundred thousand villeins put the spade down to take up the pike. Cottages had been burning for too long – the time had come for the castles to burn too' (translated from Martin 1971: 12). Italy had already experienced uprisings both in Rome (1347) and in Siena (1355). And in England the insurrectionist movement shook the foundations of the social order in 1381 under the influence of Wyclif's demand for equality and common ownership of land, and thanks to John Ball's prophetic preaching: 'England cannot fare better nor ever will ere all property be held in common and there be no more villeins nor lords but we are all equal' (Cohn 1993: 199). In the course of the fifteenth and sixteenth centuries, with the secularisation of heresy, the rebellion became more widespread and 'political', as State and Church were encompassed in one unitary movement. The great Hussite rebellion that broke out in Bohemia in 1419 increased overnight the power of guildsmen who proceeded to lead the Prague movement along the revolutionary lines of its radical (Taborite) wing usually referred to as 'anarcho-communist'.[8] The Taborites recruited among unskilled workmen, paupers and outcasts in the cities, but what accounted for their remarkable ability to mobilise the masses was the fact that they penetrated deep into the country. The Taborite movement was practically wiped out at the battle of Lipan (1434) by the Bohemian Ultraquist army, which was made up of moderate Hussite elements. But rebellion was to rage again until 1535, with the breaking out of the Peasant War in Germany (1515), relayed by Thomas Müntzer and, later, by the Anabaptists. Many insurrections followed – up to the present day – yet, by the end of the sixteenth century, the nation-State was on its feet – ready to conquer the world.

---

[8] Suffering from starvation wages and high unemployment, Prague's urban population was, by the 1420s, restless and angry. The rural population, chafed by high feudal rents and a continued attack on their hereditary rights, were also under acute stress. The Taborite rebels held territory in Bohemia from 1419 to 1434, with a varied programme of demands that sought to tackle enduring issues of poverty and inequality as well as sources of hierarchy, corruption and idolatry in the Church. Norman Cohn's (1993) *The Pursuit of the Millennium*, which Colombo uses extensively, remains a fascinating overview of these eruptions of radical egalitarianism (see also Lea 1961). It is important to note that whilst the Taborites were anti-Church, and were considered extreme heretics by their enemies, they were not anti-religion, and in many ways their radicalism was born from a fusion of material need and theological critique. This is reflected in their name: their main point of defence was on a hill renamed to mirror 'Mount Tabor', said to be the point of the 'Second Coming' of Jesus Christ. There are, of course, different takes on the importance of the material versus the theological: whilst Federici (2004), following Engels, celebrates these radical Hussites as proto-communists, Fudge (2016) suggests that religion played the key role.

The Metaphysical Principle of the State

Four centuries later, in the Orwellian year of 1984, we are left wondering: how can a State possibly work? What is it that accounts for the coherence of this pattern, this structuring principle of society born right in the middle of the Middle Ages as the by-product of 'a sinister clerical conspiracy'? How did the three conspirators of Western Christendom, namely the priest, the general and the Roman judge, ever manage to take 'the decisive step' mentioned by Strayer? If these questions are to be answered, it should be understood that the institutionalisation of power into its *State form* is what entails, at the level of the *social imaginary*, a system of legitimisation which enables the same political power, i.e. *domination*, to be reproduced on the basis of an unconscious structure of participation.

The type of political power that appeared at the end of the Middle Ages succeeded in bringing together the primary sense of loyalty towards the immediate group and the notion of the 'absolute sovereignty' of an institutional complex both abstract and impersonal. The main characteristics of this institutional complex or body are that it constitutes itself as a unit – unifying the entire political sphere of society in the process, it conforms its action to the law and expresses itself through a system of prohibition and sanction.

Therefore, the modern State can be said to exist effectively when it has acquired the ability to make sure it is recognised, without resorting to force or threat. Once established, the concept of State is associated with the notion of an imperious power over and above individual will and implies *compulsory submission to the decisions of the political power*. This *duty to obey*, or *political obligation*, which inspired La Boétie* and astonished Hume,** is closely related to a theory of the legitimacy of power. The State is viewed not as an impassioned, whimsical tyrant but as an entity both abstract and 'rational' – of an instrumental kind of rationality dependent on the achievement of its ends – within the framework of the law. Yet, the law is made by men in order to produce social effects and as such is a product of political power. Mistaking legality for the State is a tautology inherent to power which legitimises everything it lays its hands on.

The incipient mediaeval State was nurtured on Roman law as interpreted and revised by the popes. In the early Middle Ages, there were two rival

---

* '[A] single tyrant who has no other power than the power they give him' (La Boétie 1975: 46).
** 'Nothing appears more surprising . . . than the easiness with which the many are governed by the few' (Hume 1963: 29).

conceptualisations of the 'legitimacy' of the origins of power. The first and oldest saw power as deriving from the will of the people, 'from below'. This was the case of the Germanic tribes who would choose their military chiefs or kings with the result that they retained a *'right to revolution'*.[9] The second maintained that all power came from God, or more prosaically from the Emperor, as in the caesaro-papistic doctrine of the Byzantine Empire – at any rate, 'from above', from the Supreme Being, the source of all earthly power. From the fourth century onwards, and by virtue of the decree of the Emperors Valentinian II, Gratian and Theodosius proclaiming Christianity the religion of the Empire, Papacy and the Church gradually came to assume responsibility for political affairs. The triumph of the Roman Church was to have two fundamental consequences. One was that for almost a thousand years the theory of power 'from below' did not find public expression. The second was that all political relations were dealt with in judicial terms. 'To the creators of Latin Christianity and Latin dogma the relations between God and man were legal relations, conceived in the framework of rights and duties, and moulded into a Roman jurisprudential scheme' (Ullmann 1975: 21).

Today we speak of 'political relations' as if the different categories familiar to us – social, political, economic, moral, religious and so on – were dissociable and autonomous. The Christian world, however, was a totalising entity and was far from imagining that religion and politics could be considered as distinct matters. In these early stages of Christianity, the insertion of human behaviour into the mould of the law was an important and insidious achievement for the Church of Rome.*

---

[9] The 'right to revolution' has a long and ambiguous history as a concept, at times implicit or explicit in the classic works of European political philosophy, not least in Locke's *Two Treatises of Government* in the late seventeenth century. It performs an interesting ideological role: whilst it can be dismissed as a classically liberal formula underpinning the legitimacy of state power (as choice, or 'contract'), it simultaneously threatens to undermine that power, invoking the idea of democracy in a more direct and (potentially violently) accountable form.

* We would like to draw attention to the fact that what relates, symbolically speaking, the manifest and latent strata of the prevailing *representation of power* is precisely the reference to the law. As Foucault admits, even if he refutes its consequences, this representation of power in judicial-cum-discursive terms 'prompts both the motives of repression and the theory of the constitutive law of desire'. He goes on to say: 'Moreover, one must not imagine that this representation is peculiar to those who are concerned with the problem of the relations of power with sex. In fact it is much more general; one frequently encounters it in political analyses of power, and it is deeply rooted in the history of the West' (Foucault 1978: 83; see also Colombo 1983).

According to Ullman (1975), Saint Jerome's translation of the Bible from the Hebrew and Greek into Latin was a decisive factor in this enterprise. The Vulgate emphasised the judicial aspects of the Old Testament and rendered all the political concepts in the characteristic style of Roman law. Thus did the Papacy, from the fifth century onwards, develop a political theory about the hegemony of the Church, and 'these ideas culminated – entirely in consonance with the theocratic standpoint – in the monarchic position of the pope' (Ullmann 1975: 22).

Since it is impossible, short of being incoherent, to trace in the history of the Western world the development of the ideas which, in the ever-changing social imaginary, gave shape to 'the metaphysical principle of the modern State',[10] we shall simply point out a few landmarks which can be regarded as essential. In the political theory of the mediaeval Papacy, three major antecedents can be isolated. First, one should bear in mind the fundamental distinction which Pope Leo I (440–461 AD), invoking Roman law, made between the monarchical function of the pontiff and his person, thus ensuring the abstract, institutional perpetuation of power together with all governmental decrees, laws and actions. Second, Pope Leo I also expressed the crucial tenet of the State when he formulated the *plenitudo potestatis*, which was taken up in the thirteenth century to give birth to the concept of *sovereignty*. Finally one should mention two related theoretical postulates. One was the invention of the *hierarchical theory* whereby the ramifications of power account for the dependence of each grade upon the one immediately above. Since power 'filters down', the subsequent duty to obey is confirmed at each level. The other is that those at the bottom of the ladder, that is, the majority of the people, should be treated like minors in need of protection and guidance.

With the rediscovery of the Justinian Code in the second half of the eleventh century, Roman law was again very much at the forefront of political thinking. But this time the papal theory suffered an important modification due to the increasing importance of corporations which demanded once more that the legitimation of power 'from below' be recognised and the community called upon to validate the laws. The 'fiction' of *representation* was born: the so-called embodiment of the collective will of deliberative assemblies or parliaments, either ecclesiastical or secular.

This was to lead, towards the end of the Middle Ages, to the key notion of an abstract normative power based on the law and applying conjointly to subjects and governments. Whether derived from the people or the Prince, the 'source' of

---

[10] Colombo is here referring to Hegel's *Philosophy of Right*.

power was now immaterial. A *summa potestas* or supreme power was beginning to emerge regardless of community or assembly or government or any other institution. The notion of a body politic endowed with absolute sovereignty was indeed the embryo of the State, and although the thirteenth century could not possibly have formulated it, the supreme power was gradually made to coincide with the boundaries of a kingdom or a territory. When the *respublica christiana* split up, each kingdom claimed for itself the whole of the Empire's *potestas* – and each king, the glory of the Emperor. Meanwhile the political, social and institutional structures making the new power possible began to appear – a long and by no means smooth process culminating in the Jacobin strain of the French Revolution.

The sixteenth century witnessed a turn towards the modern world and the State which represents it. In 1567 Jean Bodin in *The Six Books of the Republic* formulated the theory of sovereignty which must be absolute, indivisible and perpetual. The sovereignty of the republic is embodied in the person of the Prince, but if the Prince rules according to his whims the sovereign republic ceases to exist. Absolute sovereignty is not arbitrary. Bodin still smacks of old times. In fact, a few years earlier, Machiavelli had opened up the way for the making of the modern 'political object'. He described the struggle for the conquest and retention of power as dependent upon human action and the use of force or cunning.[11] The social sphere in which power was wielded was no longer protected either by the religious symbolism which had enveloped the reality of domination up to the eleventh century or by the abstract rationality of the State, which had not yet reached completion. For Machiavelli, what determined and legitimised the institutionalisation of power is the *logic of political action*, which alone justified command and obedience.

With the works of the Florentine Secretary the way was clear, and the Leviathan could now develop all its potentials. Nearly 140 years after *The Prince* (1513) was written, the nation-State had acquired its definitive modern form and Hobbes was able to write *De Cive* (1642) and *Leviathan* (1651). Whereas Machiavelli considered political actions from the point of view of the agent, whether he be prince or rebel, Hobbes inverted the perspective 'to speak not of the men, but, in the abstract, of the seat of power, (like to those simple and unpartial creatures in the Roman Capitol, that with their noise defended those within it, not because they were they, but there' (Passerin d'Entrèves 1967: 105).

---

[11] The Italian word *astuzia*, as Machiavelli used it, has no neat translation into English, where it is rendered variably as 'trickery', 'craftiness', 'shrewdness', 'astuteness', 'foxiness' and 'cunning'. The full meaning of the word is some combination of all six!

The logic of power was no longer the logic of the situation in which men found themselves but the logic of the political institution to which they submitted themselves.

By abolishing the 'state of nature', the Leviathan provided civil society with a legal basis. But the Leviathan was a 'mortal god', an artificial being created by men to evade the fear of violent death from the hands of other men. The body politic born out of the *contract* is 'more than consent or concord; it is real unity of them all, in one and the same person, made by covenant or every man with every man' (Hobbes 1967: 131). And the power resulting from it should be sufficient to protect them; and it is sufficient only insofar as 'he (Leviathan) hath the use of so much power and strength conferred on him that by terror thereof he is enabled to form the wills of them all, to peace at home and mutual aid against their enemies abroad' (Hobbes 1967: 132).[12] Any attempt to limit the absolute power of the Leviathan would be tantamount to destroying the legitimacy of the covenant which instituted it. According to Hobbesian theory, 'the body politic cannot exist independently of the sovereign who, as it gives it unity, gives it, so to speak, being' (translated from Manent 1977: 67). From the Hobbesian concept of a single contract founding at once sovereign power and civil society, as opposed to the older theory of the two contracts (*pactum societatis/pactum subjectionis*), it follows that the fundamental law of all States is *political obligation* or duty to obey.

Hobbes is the philosopher of political power; he gave the modern State, a State which is abstract, rational and 'atheist' – that is, without any transcendental legitimacy – its true imaginary dimension. 'The myth he [Hobbes] created was so forceful and challenging that it still haunts our minds and our hearts. If anything marks, once and for ever the birth of the modern State, it is the myth of Leviathan' (Passerin d'Entrèves 1967: 102–3). But it would be unfair to turn the seventeenth century into the preserve of Hobbes, and more so to overlook the fact that the thought structures institutionalised by sovereign power within the confines of Reason were already being undermined by the corrosive force of human liberty and social revolt.

Hobbes was writing at a time of civil war and revolution. The aristocracy in whose interest it was to defend the monarchy considered that Thomas Hobbes was no more than a Leveller, judging from the faith he had in equality of mankind (Hill 1975), so that countless 'vulgar profanes' had taken to dreaming of 'utopia and infinite liberty' (ibid. 34), making it possible for a radical like Winstanley to

---

[12] The gendered language here is difficult to avoid. Leviathan is invariably imagined not only as a 'body' representing the mass of the people, but as an explicitly male body, alluding to the 'deep structure' of masculinity in political theory (Di Stefano 1983).

write in 1650 that 'Law . . . is but the declarative will of conquerors, how they will have their subjects to be ruled' (ibid. 269).

It is not at all certain that Locke took his inspiration from the Digger Winstanley but, while in exile in Amsterdam, he reflected upon the right to revolution and proceeded to improve on the Leviathan. In 1690 the *Two Treatises on Government* were published and as it is by *consent* that individuals join the body politic, the right to revolution was overtly acknowledged. Consent, however, also implies an act of confidence, of *trust* [in English in the original] in the political institution, and, as subjects of a constituted body politic, individuals are bound by a civic duty to obey without exception. In Chapter VII, 'Of Political or Civil Society', Locke (1924: 159) wrote: 'There, and there only, is political society where *every* one of the members hath quitted this natural power, resigned it up into the hands of the community . . . And thus all private judgment of every particular member being excluded, the community comes to be umpire.'

David Hume stands out in the mid-eighteenth century as the critic of the concept of contract as a means of legitimising political power, denouncing firstly its historical invalidity and secondly the absurd logic that has the duty to submit derive from some original covenant – since we would be hard put to say just why we must keep our commitments.

According to Hume, the political duty to obey is determined by the very existence of the social order. If we look for historical evidence of the legitimacy of power, all we will find is usurpation and violence. And if we investigate further, we will see that possession and ownership turn out, at one stage or another, to be based on fraud and injustice. Which does not prevent him from reaching the conclusion that 'as obedience is our duty in the common course of things, it ought chiefly to be inculcated' (Hume 1963: 475).

In the meantime, Rousseau had conjured up the 'general Will', a daunting fiction which sanctions, as deriving from the social pact, 'the total alienation of each associate, together with all his rights, to the whole community' (Rousseau 1923: 15). For the original pact can be reduced to the following terms: 'Each of us places his person and strength in common under the supreme command of the General Will' (ibid.). And the consequence had always been present in the mythical structure of power: fate only echoes the oracle. Thus 'the social compact . . . tacitly includes the undertaking . . . that whoever refuses to obey the general will shall be compelled to do so by the whole body' (ibid. 18).

In a sense it could be said that with Rousseau the metaphysical notion of the modern State has come full circle, since he explicitly based the political duty to obey not on safety and social order but on individual freedom. 'Man was born free, and everywhere he is in chains,' the 'citizen of Geneva' exclaimed. And why is that so? Because of the social pact which, combining the law with force, imparts to the State sovereignty, supreme reason, *summa potestas*.

As a matter of fact, the process I have been dealing with, namely the birth of the State, reaches its climax eleven years after the death of Rousseau, with the French Revolution, when, under Jacobinic influence, the sovereignty of the people was transferred to the nation.

Yet the Great Revolution was not, at least not entirely, a bourgeois revolution. The radical pressure exerted by the *sans-culottes* set a precedent for an insurrectionary critique of power. In the words of the *enragé* Varlet: 'Why, the revolutionary government is a social monstrosity, a masterpiece indeed of pure Machiavellianism. To any being endowed with reason, government and revolution are simply incompatible' (translated from Harmel 1984: 85). Furthermore: 'The sovereign must constantly preside over the social body. He will not tolerate being represented.' Such, says Harmel, 'was the conclusion that the last of the *enragés* drew from the events of 1793. This conclusion was anarchist insofar as revolution must be carried out through direct action by the people, without the people entrusting their will to any authority whatsoever, no matter how popular, no matter how transitory it claims or promises to be' (ibid. 87).

By the end of the eighteenth century, the anarchist critique of the State was taking its first hesitant steps forward. William Godwin in *Political Justice* (1793) reproaches the social contract with enabling the autonomisation of the political and submitting individual reason to the reason of State. Later, Proudhon and then Bakunin were also to criticise the notion of contract and above all the Rousseauist formulation. Let us however return to the State.

The Structure of Domination

From our reading of the history of institutions and the political philosophy of the State, it is clear that the existing State, real or institutional, cannot be reduced to the various 'State apparatuses' it is made up of, namely government, civil service, the army, the police, the educational system and so on, any more than to institutional continuity in time.[13] The State demands that the socio-political

[13] It is likely here that Colombo is referencing Louis Althusser's (2006) famous piece on 'Ideology and Ideological State Apparatuses'. First published in 1970, it proposed an analysis of the state as a set of institutions and structures both repressive – e.g. police, army, law – and ideological – e.g. school, church, media. The phrase 'apparatus' carries with it an emphasis on use and function, and for Althusser, following Marx, the 'use' here was to impose and uphold class power. For Colombo, of course, this will not do, for it reduces (once again) the 'will to power' to the 'will to profit'.

sphere be organised according to its own model or paradigm, that is, the State paradigm. This in turn presupposes a predetermined ideology of power. In his analysis of the *Leviathan*, Manent (translated from 1977: 63–4) states that 'the Hobbesian definition is real, better still genetic or creative: the real at stake here is what is created by virtue or by means of the voluntary mental process of which the definition is a mere testimony'.

This accounts for the difficulty in finding a satisfactory definition of the State. While making allowance for this difficulty, Strayer remarks: 'A state exists chiefly in the hearts and minds of its people; if they do not believe it is there, no logical exercise will bring it to life' (Strayer 2005: 5). For belief is the fundamental argument which consecrates the credibility of the contract, the liturgy of the consensus, the legitimacy of the monopoly of coercion. 'I believe in the State because it doesn't make sense, because I just don't know – which is why the anarchist stand is not a matter of ignorance but misbelief,' says Louis Sala-Molins (translated from Sala-Molins 1982). And Georges Burdeau (translated from Burdeau 1970: 15) writes that 'the State is an idea . . . it exists only insofar as it is thought. There lies its essence . . . It is produced by human intelligence to account for and justify political power as a social entity.'[14]

Let us then concentrate on the heart of the matter: the State is a construction which explains and justifies the social fact of political power. This 'social fact' is neither neutral nor inert: it is in turn built upon by an attribution of signification, is dependent on the context which defines it, and is subject to the symbolical structure which includes it.

Society constitutes itself as such by instituting a wide range of meanings in a circular process whereby 'action' and 'discourse', action and symbol generate each other (Colombo 1983). In this respect, the organisation of social power into its State form defines the social sphere according to a *central imaginary signification* 'which reorganizes, redetermines, and reforms a host of previously available social significations, thereby altering them, conditioning the constitutions of other significations, entailing analogous lateral effects' (Castoriadis 2005: 363) upon the whole system.

Whatever the case may be, we must bear in mind that such key meanings – which organise the symbolic universe into a 'force field' dependent on these very significations, which in many cases remain virtual or latent (unconscious) – cannot be conceived of 'on the basis of their "relation" to "objects" as their referents. For it is in and through them that the objects and therefore the refer-

---

[14] Georges Burdeau (1905–1988) was a pre-eminent political scientist in France and a key figure behind the *Encyclopaedia Universalis*.

ential relation are made possible. The "object" [in the present case, the State] as referent is always co-constituted by the corresponding social imaginary signification' (Castoriadis 2005: 365).

In the long formative process of the State, the representations, images, ideas and values which make up *collective imaginary* as a representation of a supreme central power, distinct from civil society and endowed with 'the *monopoly of the legitimate use of physical force*' (Weber 2009: 78, emphasis in original) within a given population and within a limited territory, acquire or take on an intense emotional load which in the course of history binds each subject of the body politic to the 'Idea' constituting this body as commonwealth, *civitas*, republic, State.

The transition to the State form, a decisive step, is complete when the symbolic system of the legitimisation of State political power succeeds in capturing and draining most of the primitive loyalties which previously went to the *primary group*, that is, tribe, clan, 'family' or village. This is a fundamental process, for *primary loyalties* contain potentially what we have called the *structure of domination* (or second articulation of the symbolical) in the form of a largely unconscious system of integration into the socio-cultural world (Colombo 1983).

The structure of domination is dependent on the institutionalisation of political power as it is at once constitutive of and constituted by the said power. Political power here takes on the meaning of *domination* as defined by Bertolo (this volume, Chapter 4), that is, the appropriation and control by a minority of *the regulatory capacity of society*, in other words, of the 'sociality-producing process'.

Human societies, unlike other animal societies, are not regulated homeostatically but rather in a more specific, more complex, unstable fashion, namely through the creation of meaning, norms, codes and institutions, in short, of a symbolic system. Any symbolic (or semiotic) system requires a set of positive *rules*. Yet, if rules are necessary to the semiotic system, their relation to the *representation* which embodies them, or symbolic operator, is contingent. Selecting as symbolic operator the paternal metaphor – or, more precisely, the incest taboo central to it – our own socio-cultural order presents rules as Law so that the contingent relation becomes universal and essential to the whole system.

Sexuality and power are all the more closely linked as they relate lineage and exchange on the one hand, generations and sexes on the other, on the basis of a single taboo, that of incest. Thus, the symbolic order is conditioned by the primordial Law, which reproduces itself in the form of institutions and establishes the individual as a social subject. The law of the unconscious and the law of the State are mutually reconstituted. *Domination* is therefore normative insofar as it creates a hierarchy which sanctions and institutionalises the dispossession of the symbolico-instituting capacity of the social, at one extreme of the asymmetric relation thus established.

The modern State, or rather the notion or 'metaphysical principle' behind it, completes the autonomisation process of the political and permeates the whole of the social fabric with the semantic determination entailed by the structure of domination. Any social relation in a society of the State type is, in the final analysis, a command/obedience or dominator/dominated relation.

This led Landauer (2014: 214) to say that 'the state is a social relationship; a certain way of people relating to one another'. This totalising dimension of domination, which applies equally to the 'inner world' of the subject and to the mythical, institutional structure of the 'outer world' and is the basis of the reproduction of political power, has two major consequences. To put it briefly, the first is what Lourau (translated from 1978) has called 'the principle of generalised equivalence' whereby the entire institutionalisation of social action reproduces the State form. The second, closely related to the first, is 'voluntary servitude', that is, the acceptance of the duty to obey or political obligation which, surprisingly enough, is everywhere a fact.

Although it may be agreed that power is 'the name that one attributes to a complex strategical situation in a particular society' and that it is 'exercised from innumerable points, in the interplay of non-egalitarian and mobile relations' (Foucault 1978: 93–4), it should be remembered that these various networks of asymmetry and influence do not proceed from the base upwards to produce the State, but rather are set up by the State so that it can reproduce itself. Hierarchy institutionalises inequality. Where there is no hierarchy, there is no State.

To conclude, let us recall some of the concepts we have been using.

The *field of the political* can be defined as including all that has to do with the regulatory process of collective action in a global society. This regulatory process is a product of the symbolico-instituting capacity, which is characteristic of any social entity. This dimension is what Bertolo (this volume, Chapter 4) defined as *power*, and what we would rather describe as *capacity* or 'dimension of the political devoid of constituted or autonomous power'.

In the same spirit as Bertolo, Proudhon (2011: 92) said: 'in the natural order, power is born from society; it is the resultant of all the particular forces grouped for labour, defence and Justice.' Furthermore, 'according to the empirical concept prompted by the alienation of power, it is, on the contrary, society which is born of it' (ibid.). The alienation of power brings about *political power* or domination which, in fact, is the result of the appropriation by a minority or a specialised group of the symbolico-instituting capacity. The political organ [*l'instance politique*] becomes autonomous.

The State is a particular historical type of political power, as were 'the chieftaincy without power', the Greek city or the Roman Empire in other times.[15]

A society free from the State, free from political power or domination, is a new form to be conquered. It lies in the future.*

References

Althusser, Louis [1970] (2006), 'Ideology and Ideological State Apparatuses (notes towards an investigation)', in Aradhana Sharma and Akhil Gupta (eds), *The Anthropology of the State: A Reader*, Oxford: Blackwell Publishing, pp. 86–111.

Badie, Bertrand, and Pierre Birnbaum (1983), *The Sociology of the State*, Chicago: University of Chicago Press.

Bakunin, Michael (1973), 'State and Society', in *Michael Bakunin: Selected Writings*, ed. Arthur Lehning, London: Jonathan Cape, pp. 136–54.

Bakunin, Michael [1867] (1980a), 'Federalism, Socialism, Anti-Theologism', in *Bakunin on Anarchism*, ed. Sam Dolgoff, Montreal: Black Rose Books, pp. 102–47.

Bakunin, Michael [1871] (1980b), 'God and the State', in *Bakunin on Anarchism*, ed. Sam Dolgoff, Montreal: Black Rose Books, pp. 225–42.

Bossuet, Jacques-Bénigne [1689] (1972), *Oraisons funebres*, Paris: Tallandier.

Burdeau, Georges (1970), *L'État*, Paris: Seuil.

Castoriadis, Cornelius [1975] (2005), *The Imaginary Institution of Society*, Cambridge: Polity Press.

Clastres, Pierre [1974] (1989), *Society against the State: Essays in Political Anthropology*, New York: Zone Books.

Cohn, Norman (1993), *The Pursuit of the Millennium: Revolutionary Millenarians and Mystical Anarchists of the Middle Ages*, London: Pimlico.

Colombo, Eduardo (1983), 'Il potere e la sua riproduzione', *Volontà* 27 (2).

---

[15] The idea of a 'chieftaincy without power' is taken from the anthropological work of Pierre Clastres (1989). It implies a societal structure in which the 'power' of the nominal chieftain is a constantly renegotiated relationship, and in this sense devoid of 'power' as it would normally be understood.

* We have not been able in this brief study to deal with a number of points essential to the understanding of the State. More especially we have not concentrated on certain sociological aspects such as the class struggle, differentiation, bureaucratisation, social complexity, etc. – which does not mean we underrate their importance.

Di Stefano, Christine (1983), 'Masculinity as Ideology in Political Theory: Hobbesian Man Considered', *Women's Studies International Forum* 6 (6): 633–44.

Federici, Silvia (2004), *Caliban and the Witch: Women, the Body and Primitive Accumulation*, New York: Autonomedia.

Foucault, Michel (1978), *The History of Sexuality 1: The Will to Knowledge*, New York: Pantheon Books.

Fudge, Thomas A. (2016), 'Neither Mine nor Thine: Communist Experiments in Hussite Bohemia', *Canadian Journal of History* 33 (1): 25–47.

Gernet, Louis (1982), *Droits et institutions en Grèce antique*, Paris: Flammarion.

Guenée, Bernard (1985), *States and Rulers in Later Medieval Europe*, New York: Basil Blackwell.

Harmel, Claude (1984), *Histoire de l'anarchie*, Paris: Champ Libre.

Hegel, Georg Wilhelm Friedrich [1802] (1999), 'The German Constitution', in *Political Writings*, ed. Laurence Dickey and H. B. Nisbet, Cambridge: Cambridge University Press, pp. 6–101.

Hill, Christoper (1975), *The World Turned Upside Down: Radical Ideas during the English Revolution*, London: Penguin Books.

Hobbes, Thomas [1651] (1967), *Leviathan*, Oxford: Clarendon Press.

Hume, David [1758] (1963), *Essays Moral, Political and Literary*, Oxford: Oxford University Press.

Kropotkin, Peter [1896] (1970), 'The State: Its Historic Role', in *Selected Writings on Anarchism and Revolution*, ed. Martin Miller, Cambridge, MA: MIT Press, pp. 210–64.

La Boétie, Étienne de (1975), *The Politics of Obedience: The Discourse of Voluntary Servitude*, Montreal: Black Rose Books.

Landauer, Gustav [1910] (2014), 'Weak Statesmen, Weaker People!', in *Revolution and Other Writings: A Political Reader*, ed. Gabriel Kuhn and Richard J. F. Day, Oakland: PM Press, pp. 213–14.

Lea, Henry Charles (1961), *The Inquisition of the Middle Ages*, New York: Macmillan.

Le Goff, Jacques (1988), *Medieval Civilization*, Oxford: Blackwell Publishers Ltd.

Locke, John [1689] (1924), *Of Civil Government*, London: J. M. Dent & Sons.

Lourau, René (1978), *L'Etat inconscient*, Paris: Minuit.

Manent, Pierre (1977), *Naissance de la politique modern*, Paris: Payot.

Martin, Henri (1971), *La Jacquerie*, Paris: Maspero.

Miéville, China (2006), *Between Equal Rights: A Marxist Theory of International Law*, London: Pluto Press.

Passerin d'Entrèves, Alexander (1967), *The Notion of the State: An Introduction to Political Theory*, Oxford: Oxford University Press.

Prichard, Alex (2013), *Justice, Order, Anarchy: The International Political Theory of Pierre-Joseph Proudhon*, Abingdon: Routledge.

Proudhon, Pierre-Joseph [1851] (1969), *General Idea of the Revolution in the Nineteenth Century*, New York: Haskell House Publishers Ltd.

Proudhon, Pierre-Joseph [1858] (2011), 'Justice in the Revolution and the Church', in *Property Is Theft! A Pierre-Joseph Proudhon Reader*, ed. Iain McKay, Edinburgh: AK Press, pp. 619–84.

Riley, Patrick (1990), 'Introduction', in Jacques-Bénigne Bossuet, *Politics Drawn from Holy Scripture*, ed. Patrick Riley, Cambridge: Cambridge University Press, pp. xiii–lxviii.

Rousseau, Jean Jacques [1762] (1923), *The Social Contract & Discourses*, London: J. M. Dent & Sons.

Sala-Molins, Louis (1982), 'L'État', in *Le Monde*, Paris, 8 August.

Strayer, Joseph R. [1970] (2005), *On the Medieval Origins of the Modern State*, Princeton: Princeton University Press.

Tocqueville, Alexis de [1838] (2004), *Democracy in America*, New York: Library Classics of America.

Ullmann, Walter (1975), *Medieval Political Thought*, Harmondsworth: Peregrine Books.

Weber, Max [1918] (2009), *From Max Weber: Essays in Sociology*, Abingdon: Routledge.

6 Domination and the Economic[1]

Luciano Lanza (1984)

First published in *Volontà* 38 (1)

LET US BEGIN with the caveat made by Jean Baudrillard (1975: 21): 'In order to achieve a radical critique of political economy, it is not enough to unmask what is hidden behind the concept of consumption: the anthropology of needs and of use value. We must also unmask everything hidden behind the concepts of production, the mode of production, productive forces, relations of production.' Is the Parisian philosopher's suggestion enough to bring us to those roots which seem either so immediately available or, on the contrary, so distant and undecipherable as to frighten the researcher?

Understanding the nature of the economy from inside its categories and its logic, as Baudrillard's words would seem to suggest, can only produce satisfactory results if the very concept of economy is left unchallenged. That is to say, if the economy is considered to be just one of the possible ways to organise and determine social relationships. If we are to follow this, we must consider the economy within the wider context of the totality of social relationships. As humanity knows no other reality than domination, it is evident that the economy must be analysed together with this conditioning element. Domination is the central element of the social edifice, the producer of meaning, the inviolable taboo accompanying humanity throughout its history. It follows that we can

---

[1] The word *economia* in Italian has a broader semantic field which encompasses both of the words 'economics' and 'economy' in English. The word *economia* pertains to the organisation and the use of limited resources to satisfy individual or collective needs, and in this sense is closer to Greek roots of the word (*oikos* refers to the 'family', 'household' and the resources necessary to both). In this chapter, as well as in the next (Chapter 7), we translate the same word (*economia*) as 'economics', 'economy' and 'economic' according to the context.

assume with reasonable certainty that it imbues with meaning all aspects of society, including the economy. If this statement is correct, the economy can be considered to be one manifestation of domination, and therefore nothing more than the result of the institutionalisation of the reproduction of material means within the logic of domination.

The institutionalisation of the economy took place within a model of rationality guided by the founding principle 'the greatest possible return with the least possible effort'. This is of no little importance if we consider that economic theory, at the highest point of its 'economism', as personified by Lionel Robbins (1932), maintains that economic science would have no reason to exist without this basic element. The economy is one possible variable and, as such a product, a human creation without any real objective foundation.

Taking our cue from Cornelius Castoriadis (1987), we can think of the economy as a product of history that takes on a central significance in modern society and reorganises already-existing social meanings in a different way: the economy as an 'imaginary social meaning' (ibid. 211). Like all elements of society, the economy is not to be identified in the goods, the production, the relations of production, the means of production, but in the human symbolic and signifying structure. As Marshall Sahlins (1976) rightly shows, these two components mark the distinctive character of human beings, whose contact with the environment takes place according to a scheme of meanings of their own invention. From this descends a vision of the economy – which could well be extended to all the elements making up society – as an arbitrary phenomenon, decided by humanity, by its 'project-ability', by its possible modes of being.

The Birth of the Economy

Following this vision, we can consider the process of the institutionalisation of the economy to be a fairly recent phenomenon: at the turn of the seventeenth and eighteenth centuries, economics was founded as an autonomous science. The mercantilists and later the Physiocrats developed analyses and theories of certain aspects of human activity, identifying their particular characteristics and ways of functioning. It was at this point, particularly from Adam Smith (1991) onwards, that the materiality of economic relationships was codified in a theory that could not only explain but, above all, generate them. To be sure, in the seventeenth century there were merchants who were not so different from contemporary ones with a sense of profit and other characteristics that we ascribe to the economic sphere. What was still missing was an encompassing logic to interpret these 'signs' of political economy, to organise them into a system of their own. When such a system was explicitly formulated it entailed a deep-reaching qualitative transformation of the social imaginary.

Trade from one country to another, from one sea to the other, is lived and conceived differently by the merchants. Those very same actions, repeated (identically) for thousands of years, conquered a new symbolic space which became the building blocks of that edifice of meanings that we know as the self-regulating market. By stepping into the dimension of social signification, the self-regulating market and particularly its theory became elements of the central signifier: domination. The logic of domination, which is essentially the production of social meaning (of a particular meaning), also conquered that area of society that we normally define as the realm of material needs.

A true cultural revolution began, one which led humanity to think of itself and of society in economic terms. Such a transformation is hard to grasp today, as immersed as we are in a society governed by the economy, but, nonetheless, we can make sense of it by adopting an anthropological approach, through the analysis of archaic and primitive social structures. Up to that time there had been no autonomous economic logic, since economic relations were regulated by other institutions: religious, social, of kinship and so on. The investigations of Karl Polanyi (1957, 1977) and the substantivist school[2] help us make sense of the 'Great Transformation' (Polanyi 2001). Economic logic was born within the logic of domination and is thus regulated by it: since the only social signification was that of domination, the new institution followed the dynamics of the older ones. Before the 'Great Transformation' there was no intervention in the process of reproduction from within. 'The economy' was a marginal element in the social imaginary; those practices that we erroneously define as economic bear no, or very little, social signification.

Even in ancient feudal empires (Egyptian, Inca, Chinese, etc.) in which the imperial bureaucracy actively intervened in the production and distribution of goods, we cannot speak of economic logic in the modern sense but rather, more

---

[2] Lanza is referencing the formalist–substantivist debates originating in Polanyi's theory. Polanyi analyses the genesis of modern capital, which elevates profit and the market above society. He identifies other modalities, beyond market capitalism, through which the economy is constructed, and distinguishes between two meanings of the term 'economics'. The *formal* meaning, used by today's neoclassical economists, refers to economics as the logic of rational action and decision-making, as rational choice between the alternative uses of limited (scarce) means, as 'economising', 'maximising' or 'optimising'. The *substantive* meaning refers to the materiality of living and how humans make their livelihoods beyond a logic of maximisation and scarcity.

appropriately, of the preferential appropriation and hierarchical distribution of the means of livelihood. However, when domination gave birth to the economic logic it also initiated a process that transformed the logic of domination itself: economic rationality became the rationality of domination.

The birth of modern domination is organically linked to society. By invading the economic as well, domination absorbs the whole logic of society: no aspect of society falls outside its rules. Its logic permeates even more deeply the logic of society; its modes of reproduction are instilled into the modes of reproducing commodities. The interaction between domination and the economy, between the creator and its creature, is a process whereby the former finds itself conditioned and transformed by its product. Domination takes on a new form because, in regulating every aspect of life in society, it governs a space which is regulated by autonomous laws external to its functioning; this 'invention' can only be controlled if the economic laws are the same as those by which domination regulates society.

A citizen of Athens or a Guayaki hunter, a Chinese mandarin, an Egyptian pharaoh, an Indian brahmin or an Italian vassal could not even conceive that his life could be governed by the ultimate rule of profit and accumulation. Likewise, they could not conceive of limited resources in the face of unlimited needs. To come to such a conclusion, humanity must see itself as unable to be satisfied by the existing possibilities. Only then can economy in the full sense of the term come into being, and the economic logic and rationality become obvious and irrefutable necessities. Humanity has laid down certain premises which it considers as part of its very nature (limited resources and unlimited needs) and is left with no choice but to adopt the 'rational' rule: the maximum result with the minimum effort.

The Phases of an Encounter

The encounter between domination and the economy can be divided into two phases which are also two theoretically distinct aspects: the market economy and the planned economy.

The market economy (based on the self-regulating market) is the first form of this encounter. If we analyse the functioning of the self-regulating market against those of antiquity, we soon realise that their similarities are superficial. The markets of antiquity have widely differing rules and cannot be reduced to a single model as can those today. Furthermore, the markets of antiquity often lie outside the community, not only geographically but also, and above all, socially. Their transactions are regulated by criteria belonging to institutions outside the realm of the economic, and the same is true of the determination of prices. With the modern market the situation changes completely.

> A market economy is an economic system controlled, regulated and directed by market prices; order in the production and distribution of goods is entrusted to this self-regulating mechanism. An economy of this kind derives from the expectations that human beings behave in such a way as to achieve maximum money gains. (Polanyi 2001: 71)

In a few lines, Polanyi brings into sharp relief the qualitative and quantitative leap between the two types of markets. The modern market is not – many economists maintain – the legitimate offspring of that of antiquity. Between the two forms there is a break, a hiatus represented by a different conception of the world: liberalism. The modern concept of the market was born through the encounter with a liberal political regime that posed itself against absolute monarchism, and in so doing paved the way to the modern concept of freedom. This further complicates our analysis, as the two realities are coeval and contradictory. On the one hand, the self-regulating market is the first 'economic form' brought into existence by the encounter between domination and the economy; on the other, the birth of that very idea of freedom which in its most radical form is at the core of anarchist thought. Such a quandary is hard to overcome if not by appealing to simple causality, which is clearly an inadequate explanation. The difficulty is further increased by the fact that the economic form produced by liberalism, the self-regulating market, is theorised as a model of freedom and equality: many small sellers faced by many small buyers who can have no power over the determination of prices or over other operators. This theory can easily be rebutted as an abstraction, a fiction, an ideology created to justify a new form of exploitation. However valid this type of answer may be, it still partially evades the question. Proudhon's ideas of combining socialism and the market[3] cannot be liquidated by Marx's method of labelling him 'petty bourgeois'. Proudhon's analyses put forward a valid argument in favour of economic competition as the economic form on which to base the relations among free producers. The only objection that we can raise to the Besançon[4] thinker – and to most of his contemporaries – is that he could not move out of a symbolic universe in which the economic is supreme.

---

[3] Lanza is referring to Proudhon's idea of *mutualism*, the label often given to what was his attempt at describing an anti-authoritarian form of federalism (Prichard 2013).

[4] Proudhon was born in the French city of Besançon in 1809.

If, instead, we choose to follow the path indicated earlier, we must recognise that the self-regulating market is a product of the society of domination and is consequently untenable for the anarchist project. Still, as it was the first economic form to emerge from the contact with domination, it also helps us identify the shortcomings of such a blend (domination-economy). Indeed, the logic of domination pervades the logic of the reproduction of the means of livelihood, yet a division, a separation between the two elements, persists. Political domination and economic domination develop in parallel processes according to the same logic, but they operate in different fields. The political institutions are not superimposed on the economic ones; they occupy different social spaces. They could be seen, figuratively, as two rival brothers: biologically similar, but culturally enemies.

A greater degree of integration between domination and the economy characterises the planned economy. The underlying economic logic and rationality is still that of the market economy, but now the two terms are no longer separate at the level of the institutions. The economic is entirely within the structure of domination. Also, in the case of the planned economy, looking at its genesis proves instructive. Planning comes into being either as a capitalist instrument for regulation or as a socialist economic form. In the latter case, planning is seen as a means of bringing the economy back under human control, thus re-establishing an organic dimension for society which tends to abolish the separation between society and economy, which is seen as a product of capitalism. Hence planning too has an element of freedom and equality which must not be undervalued.

As with the market, planning – the reappropriation of the economic by society – develops in a context marked by the logic of domination. Economic rationality is thus not modified but adapted and directed towards aims which lie, in part, outside the logic of the market, although only in the sense that the political dimension has a primacy over the economic one. To continue with our earlier example: one of the two rival brothers has partly succeeded in subduing the other.

To date, the planned economy represents the most complete form of integration between domination and the economy. In light of this, we can argue that the potential disappearance of the economic would in no way mean the birth of a more just society, as many ingenuously believe, but rather the affirmation of totalitarianism in its purest form. Here we enter the realm of fiction, but not of the impossible: today the economic, as a product of domination, is one of the far from perfect sites of resistance to the evolution towards more sophisticated forms of domination. As a matter of fact, societies of domination – not only free societies – can also go beyond the economic (see Chapter 7).

Just as domination invades all aspects of life in society in a totalising way, as with perfect planning (which is, fortunately, still far off), economic logic could even disappear in the process of being remodelled by the logic of domination. Up to now, the encounter between domination and the economy materialised through two modes of allocation (exemplified by the market and planning) which existed prior to their encounter with and integration into the logic of domination. Both have, in fact, a social function which has been mystified and perverted by domination: exchange and choice, respectively. It is only through the encounter with domination that these two social functions become part of the economic logic and are transformed into 'economic forms' in the full meaning of the term. This also means that today we can think of both exchange and choice only within the single rationality which pervades our social imaginary – domination.

The Roots of the Economic

The analysis of the economy as a product of domination and the identification of its function in society raise questions about its very nature.

The definitions of the economists over these last centuries are of little use to us in drafting a reply, as they lie entirely within the economic logic: they define a product of domination without considering its producer. Even the Marxist critique of economics is of little help, as it criticises only one form of this manifestation of domination – capitalism – and, above all, falls into the error of maintaining that the planned economy is a path to the society without economics, the so-called second phase of communism. If there is a sense to my earlier objections to planning, it is clear that the Marxist contribution leaves me more or less indifferent. The path to be taken should lead us, as far as possible, beyond the current vision of the economy towards considering our capability to found (or to rediscover) the social nature of the economy at the level of the imaginary.

This very possibility sheds light on the dualistic aspects of the economy already identified by Carl Menger and Karl Polanyi. Menger writes (translated from Menger 1976: 162–3):

> I would call the two tendencies of economics which I have discussed in the previous section *elementary*; that is to say the technical tendency and that towards saving [or as Menger calls them elsewhere in the book, *economising*]. While in fact both almost always appear connected one with the other they nonetheless derive from *differing and independent causes*, and in some branches of economic activity they even appear separately . . . the technical

tendency of the economy does not therefore depend on that towards saving, nor is it *necessarily* tied to it . . . the two tendencies are therefore independent of each other – they are elementary tendencies – and their regular encounters in reality are owing to the fact that the causes determining them almost always coexist in the economy.

Polanyi (1957: 243) carries Menger's insight still further:

[T]he term economic is a compound of two meanings that have independent roots. We will call them the substantive and the formal meaning. The substantive meaning of economic derives from man's dependence for his living upon nature and his fellows. It refers to the interchange with his natural and social environment, in so far as this results in supplying him with the means of material want satisfaction. The formal meaning of economic derives from the logical character of the means-ends relationship, as apparent in such words as 'economical' or 'economizing.' It refers to a definite situation of choice, namely, that between the different uses of means induced by an insufficiency of those means. If we call the rules governing choice of means the logic of rational action, then we may denote this variant of logic, with an improvised term, as formal economics.

We can add another definition to those of Menger and Polanyi: the economy as an element of power relationships or the economy as an element of social relationships. In the first case it is one of the manifestations of power and takes on a certain structure to conform with the power that institutes it. In the second case, the economy can be seen as an instance of human relations that allows an increase in the possibilities and the attributes of the individual or of the group.

All these aspects of the dualism of the economy show us that humanity, even when immersed in the logic of domination, is still capable of conceiving of economic relationships which are not necessarily related to the central signifier of society. At the same time, they also show us how deeply rooted in our imaginary is the economy, to the point that we can only conceive of it in different forms, but not eliminate it entirely.

In this respect, the economy can be seen as a terrific analyser of domination. Our inability to nullify the economic points at our inability to nullify domination. The desire for rationality, for norms, for rules by which man tries to control and guide the reproduction of goods, is of the same stamp as the desire to attribute rationality, norms and rules to society as a whole. A legitimate desire, which is necessary for life in society, is transformed into instances of the reproduction of domination. The seemingly trivial economic necessity (how can we afford that commodity?) turns into the most complex and terrible necessity of domination.

Today, the decoding of domination must come about through the decoding of the economy. One becomes indispensable through the other, and vice versa. It is perhaps for this reason that the identification of the roots of that human creation that we call the economy seems impossible. Perhaps it is a rootless plant, or perhaps we must look for the roots in the simple gestures of the farmer sowing seed, of the woman weaving wool, in the adventurous voyage of the merchant, in the actions of the white-coated young scientist pressing the keys of the computer. The roots of the economy lie in everything and in nothing. Like domination, the economy is a construction of the imaginary and is both concrete and elusive at one and the same time.

Perhaps one way of escaping from this dead end could be to recognise that there is nothing to know over and above that which we can see. The economy would thus not present us with remote and unexplored zones, save perhaps for our minds, or, better, the collective mind. 'It can be said that if production reflects the general scheme of society it does so observing itself in a mirror . . . For us the production of goods is at the same time the privileged mode of symbolic production and transmission' (Sahlins 1976: 211).

References

Baudrillard, Jean (1975), *The Mirror of Production*, St. Louis: Telos Press.

Castoriadis, Cornelius [1975] (1987), *The Imaginary Institution of Society*, Cambridge: Polity Press.

Menger, Carl [1871] (1976), *Principi di economia politica*, Turin: UTET.

Polanyi, Karl (1957), *Trade and Market in the Early Empires*, Glencoe: The Free Press.

Polanyi, Karl (1977), *The Livelihood of Man*, New York: Academic Press.

Polanyi, Karl [1944] (2001), *The Great Transformation*, Boston: Beacon Press.

Prichard, Alex (2013), *Justice, Order and Anarchy: The International Political Theory of Pierre-Joseph Proudhon*, London: Routledge.

Robbins, Lionel (1932), *An Essay on the Nature and Significance of Economic Science*, London: Macmillan.

Sahlins, Marshall (1976), *Culture and Practical Reason*, Chicago: University of Chicago Press.

Smith, Adam [1776] (1991), *The Wealth of Nations*, New York: Everyman's Library.

Events were split between two Venetian squares, Campo Santa Margherita and Campo San Polo.

The more formal conference-style proceedings took place at the University of Venice School of Architecture (IUAV).

Nico Berti, Amedeo Bertolo, Colin Ward and Murray Bookchin during the session 'State and Anarchy' at Venice 1984.

Legendary embrace between Progreso Fernández (1897–1996), a *cenetista* who participated in the foundation of the Federación Anarquista Ibérica in 1927, and Murray Bookchin.

Marsha Hewitt (Canada), Rosanna Ambrogetti and Tiziana Ferrero Regis (Italy), Ariane Gransac (France) and Barbara Köster (West Germany) at the 'Feminism and Anarchism' session, Venice 1984.

John Clark (second left) at Venice 1984 alongside Jean-Jacques Gandini (France) on his right and Marianne Enckell, co-organiser of the *incontro* with the CIRA of Lausanne (Switzerland), Günther Hartmann and Wolfgang Haug (West Germany) on his left.

A spontaneous gathering at Venice 1984. Alongside the programmed events, conversations such as these were a common sight.

Paolo Finzi held an impromptu anarchy 'lecture' in Campo Santa Margherita before a female class who spontaneously asked for more information about the ongoing event.

Part III: The Imaginary Turned Upside Down

Anarchik upturning the hierarchy of the new masters, as published in *A/Rivista Anarchica* 22, June–July 1973.

7 Beyond the Economic: Preliminary Notes towards a Utopian Conception of Economics[1]

Luciano Lanza (1981)

First published in *Volontà* 35 (3)

PETER IBBETSON, A 1935 film much lauded by the surrealists, has its central character confined to his prison bed, dreaming of escape to meet the woman he loves. This same dream haunts the woman and the two dreams become one, lived by both as reality. They meet, run free, make love. The boundary between dream and reality is shattered by the force of their will despite the material impossibility: the reality of the dream.

Can utopia, humanity's great dream, be dreamed, desired, thought of as reality? Born out of the tension between its two constituent poles – rational planning and dreams – it points at the possibility of living the dream. The utopian dream, lived collectively rather than individually, could become the driving force for transformation as its social metamorphosis erodes the gap between dream and reality. Dream and reality are no longer at odds, since utopia no longer preludes disillusionment and awakening, but a transformation. In sketching out the ideal society, the social dream feeds on rational planning, which is born both as negation of its social context and as a liberation of unconscious desire. Thus, the utopian project is the force behind radical transformation, and yet it remains rooted in the reality it wishes to free itself from: even the 'boldest' utopia is never completely *other*.

The true utopian process must continue uninterrupted; once it reaches its 'objectives', they become the base for the next utopian project, in a continuum which is revitalised by continuing tension. We can think of the anarchist utopia as 'physiologically' dynamic; static objectives can only mean its death, since what we put forward today, however hard we may try, is inevitably tied to the present.

[1] See Chapter 6, footnote 1.

We must also recognise that the anarchist utopia, even when formulated in explicitly open terms – yet confined within a specific theoretical space – shows its relationship with ideology, revealing itself to be an ideological critique of the dominant ideology and of the ideologies of domination which seek to replace it.

Against these premises, can we formulate a utopian economics? What place does economics have in utopian projects? And, ultimately, is there a place for economics in the utopian vision?

Utopianists and Economics

Before we can answer these questions we must set our imagination sailing for the shores of Utopia, the land of the *Ajaoïens*, Terra Australis, enter the City of the Sun through the Gate of the Sunset, sail among the floating islands of Basiliade, enter the rooms of the Phalanstery, visit the one hundred provinces of Icarie, listen to the news of a wise old man from Nowhere or even board a space ship for the grey deserts of Anarres.[2] What will the inhabitants of these non-places have to say to us? Will they know how to resolve our dilemma? Will they be able to free our minds from the oppression of petty schemes?

'There being no property among them,' a citizen of Utopia (More 2016: 57) tells us before, forestalling a further question, adding that

> What is brought [to the market-place], and manufactured by the several families, is carried from thence to houses appointed for that purpose, in which all things of a sort are laid by themselves; and thither ever father goes, and takes whatsoever he or his family stand in need of, without either paying for it or leaving anything in exchange. There is no reason for giving a denial to any person, since there is such plenty of everything among them; and there is no danger of a man asking for more than he needs. (Ibid. 88)

This is the mythical 'taking from the heap'. And if we continue questioning our imaginary informant, we discover that ties between cities follow an analogous rule, together with a sort of 'family economy':

---

[2] Lanza alludes here to features in several utopias (in this order): Thomas More's *Utopia*; Bernard de Fontenelle's *Histoire des Ajaoïens*; Gabriel de Foigny's *Terra Australis*; Tommaso Campanella's *The City of the Sun*, Étienne-Gabriel Morelly's *Naufrage des isles flottantes, ou Basiliade du célèbre Pilpai*; Charles Fourier's *La Phalanstère*; Étienne Cabet's *Voyage to Icaria*, William Morris's *News from Nowhere*; and Ursula Le Guin's *The Dispossessed*.

In their great council at Amaurot, to which there are three sent from every town once a year, they examine what towns abound in provisions and what are under any scarcity, that so the one may be furnished from the other; and this is done freely, without any sort of exchange; for, according to their plenty or scarcity, they supply or are supplied from one another, so that indeed the whole island is, as it were, one family. (Ibid. 76)

A form of communism is also to be found in Campanella's *The City of the Sun*:

All things are in common; but there are officials who have control of the distribution not only of the necessities of life but also of learning and honours, and entertainments; but this control is such that no one can appropriate anything to himself. They say that property begins from having a house apart and one's own wife and children as these give rise to self-love; in order to hand on riches to one's son, people will begin to prey on the public sphere, if they are strong and without fear, or, if not, become avaricious, insidious and hypocritical. (Translated from Campanella 1977: 38–9)[3]

Bernard de Fontenelle (translated from 1979: 129), in his *History of the Ajaoïens*, tells us that 'in the island of Ajao the idea of "yours" and "mine" is unknown; but not everything is held completely in common. No one possesses land; it all belongs to the State, which is responsible for its cultivation and for the distribution of the fruits to all families.' All the products are collected and then redistributed among the various quarters by the members of the City Council (Minchiskoa-Adoë), and the local administrators (Minchiskoa) then distribute them among the various housing blocks, where the heads of the houses (Minchisti) distribute them among the individual families.

When someone needs a tunic, a cloak or a pair of trousers (which is the sum total of their clothing) he asks the Minchisti who immediately give him that which he requires. Other, less important things are acquired through bartering ... It also happens however that people seek the pleasure of forestalling the needs of others. So, for example, when those living in the same house but with different professions see that another lacks something they go to offer him what he needs without being asked; I must however add that the giver reserves the right to ask for the return of this favour when the occasion arises. (Ibid 130–2)

---

[3] Several English translations of Campanella's text are available; however, we chose to use our own translation from the original Italian.

All in all, the utopian writers have little to tell us about economic problems: they most often present us with situations of abundance and equal sharing. Gabriel de Foigny (1993: 40), creator of the first libertarian utopia, *The Southern Land, Known* (originally published in Switzerland under the title *La Terre Australe* in 1676), almost totally ignores the economic problem: 'To know one region is to know them all, and this arises from the natural inclination of the inhabitants to seek nothing more than their fellows so that even if one of them had something out of the ordinary, it would be impossible for him to use it.' Indeed, what matters to Foigny (ibid. 60–1) are the social structure and freedom:

> He implied that it is man's nature to be born free: that he cannot be subjugated without ceasing to be himself; that in subjection he sinks lower than the beast because beasts exist only to serve man, and captivity is as it were their natural state. A man cannot be born to serve another man . . . to subject a man to another man was to subject him to his own nature, to somehow make him a slave of himself, which could not be done without contradiction and extreme violence. He proved that the essence of man consists in his liberty, and to take this away from him, without destroying it entirely, was to make him live without his true essence . . .[4]

Foigny envisages a society without government in which all decisions are taken in local assemblies. 'If someone has found out something that displeases him or that he deems of public importance, he proposes it to the brothers, and they work out a more reasonable solution, having regard only for the national interest' (ibid. 87). There are certain analogies between Foigny's utopia and those of William Morris in 1890 and Ursula Le Guin in 1974, but whereas the latter two clearly showed their debt to anarchist theory, Foigny very much anticipated it.

Morris does not explicitly refer to anarchism in *News from Nowhere* (2003: 68), though he does write: 'in your sense of the word we have no government' and his economic vision clearly shows the influence of Kropotkin:

> The wares which we make are made because they are needed: men make for their neighbours' use as if they were making for themselves, not for a vague

---

[4] The 'he' Foigny refers to is an elderly 'Australian' (the 'Australia' of Foigny's imagination) who is explaining their customs. The gendered language should not be taken at face value here: one of the most remarkable aspects of the text, given that it was written in the mid-1670s, is that every 'Australian' is both male and female. 'My hermaphrodism would ensure my survival,' notes Foigny's (1993: 36) castaway-protagonist upon arrival.

market of which they know nothing, and over which they have no control: as there is no buying and selling, it would be mere insanity to make goods on the chance of their being wanted; for there is no longer anyone who can be *compelled* to buy them. So that whatever is made is good, and thoroughly fit for its purpose. Nothing *can* be made except for genuine use; therefore no inferior goods are made. Moreover, as aforesaid, we have now found out what we want, so we make no more than we want. (Ibid. 83)

The question that immediately springs to mind on reading Morris – how is it that no one produces more than is necessary? – is answered by Ursula Le Guin (1974) in *The Dispossessed* by means of a computer. Le Guin, a thoroughly modern utopian, eliminates the concept of economics: everyone takes part in the productive system according to their preference and with the mediation of a computer which distributes the tasks. Goods are distributed fairly according to need. Meals are served in communal refectories; people sleep in dormitories or in single rooms according to availability and preference. Everyone is free, there is no government, there is in fact explicit reference to anarchist ideas. As Le Guin describes it, the planet Anarres is an anarchist world, a modern world, not one looking backward to a mythical Golden Age, a vast and complex world in which productive activity is coordinated by science and held together by ethical tension.

To be sure, these are just a few examples out of the vast range of solutions put forward by various utopian thinkers. It would be impossible here to take even a cursory look at all that they have to offer with respect to the problem of 'economics'. What I would like to point out is that, while many (about two-thirds) of the best-known utopian writers argue for the abolition of private property, there are others in favour of it, or those who propose merely to limit it. Leaving aside strongly inegalitarian utopias such as Francesco Patrizi's *The Happy City* (1562), Samuel Gott's *The New Solima* (1648) or Fénelon's *Salento* (1699), even Joseph Fourier sketches out an economic system in which the factors of production receive differing degrees of recompense: 5/12 for labour, 4/12 for capital and 3/12 for talent or managerial ability.

Ernest Callenbach in *Ecotopia* (2004: 93) outlines a system of competitive enterprises in which all workers are partners: 'Ecotopian enterprises generally behave much like capitalist enterprises' but 'a man cannot just set up a business, offer wages to employees' and 'no Ecotopian can now inherit any property at all!' (ibid. 91).

At times, the economic problem is addressed with a significant degree of precision. In *La Basiliade*, Étienne-Gabriel Morelly (translated from 1753: 6–7) writes: 'Property, the mother of all the crimes that engulf the rest of the world, is unknown to them . . . It is in fact private property that creates the social and economic inequality from which classes are born, together with antagonism between the professions, distinctions and rank.'

Étienne Cabet in *The Voyage to Icaria* (1839) also argues for private property because everything remains planned by the State.[5] On this, he is partly antic-ipating Skinner in *Walden Two*[6] where property is held in common because everything is directed by a government of experts and by a system of psycholog-ical conditioning.

Despite this variety of examples, the lack of attention paid by utopian writers to economic problems, or the vagueness of their proposed solutions, is striking. Once the evil has been eliminated, life will organise itself joyously and without problems. Only thinkers like Kropotkin (2007) in *The Conquest of Bread* offer a more deep-reaching analysis, but it is evident that his image of a utopian society complements his analysis of the existing one.

The scant attention paid towards economics probably descends from the fact that it pertains to the realm of necessity, a sphere in sharp contrast with the utopian tension, which aims at realising the impossible. Another factor at play is a one-sided vision of the economy: the realm of oppression, greed and the 'corruption of human nature'.

In our view, the economy has a double nature and can be interpreted in two different ways: as an element of power relationships and as an element of social relationships.

[5] Cabet's utopia offers a vision that is 'symmetrical in design, obsessively clean, and highly ordered' (Parker, Fournier and Reedy 2007: 304). Whilst everything is collec-tively owned, censorship, sexism and control are uncomfortable parts of this commu-nistic vision. It is worth nothing that Cabet (1788–1856), as the founder of the Icarian movement, intended this to be a practical vision.

[6] Burrhus Skinner's (2005) *Walden Two*, first published in 1948, was notable not for its literary finesse, but for its vision of a society built through the psychological (re)condi-tioning of its members. The surface-level achievements of this rural American utopia are familiar from a slew of other utopian communes, but the distinction lies in the edu-cation system, where young children are 'kept in a completely controlled environment that is intended to weed out all behaviors considered unacceptable' (Kuhlman 2005: 9). Skinner frames this attempt at 'discarding outdated concepts of human nature' (ibid.) as a necessary step to utopia. This is in stark contrast to Huxley's (1932) *Brave New World*, where behavioural conditioning is distinctly *dys*topian, granting total control of human consciousness to a centralised authority.

The Two Faces of the Economic

In the first case [as an element of power relationships], the economy is one of the manifestations of power and is structured in conformity with the power that institutes it. As aptly pointed out by Clastres (1989: 198), the 'political relation of power precedes and founds the economic relation of exploitation'. Except for those rare cases of societies without power which Clastres studied, the 'constant' (or the 'independent variable') of society is power cum domination. This constant materialises in historical forms that are determined by contingent factors. The economic is one such factor, which merges forms pre-dating the 'new' power with those specific to it. A particular power *creates* the economic form that is most suited to asserting and reproducing itself, and from this arises a relationship of interdependence between power and the economy: given the former, the latter is necessary for its historical continuity. This interdependence develops to a point where it becomes impossible to separate the two elements and the operation would sound arbitrary, except perhaps in the situation of a 'rising power' where this interdependence is not yet well-established.

The economic relationship set up by power does not only move in the direction of power–society and vice versa but affects all social relationships in such a way that even relationships between 'subjects' undergo a process of generalised equivalence which compels them to conform to that model of a relationship, thus reproducing the relationships inscribed in the logic of domination. The economy of power is, therefore, the economy as we know it, but we can also consider it as the expression of one aspect of social relationships. In this latter sense, the economy represents a moment in human relationships which allows a broadening of individual possibilities, resources and obligations.

This relationship takes shape through exchange. Exchange is, in fact, a fundamental element of life in society. We exchange news, sensations, ideas; even love is an exchange, perhaps in its most complete form. Exchange is therefore a social act, even when goods are exchanged in that particular dimension defined as economic.

Moving from similar considerations, the economists, that is, a particular group of the ideologues of power, have founded their 'science' – political economy – but there is no reason why economics cannot be thought out and developed in a completely different way. Exchange may well follow different logics: 'The aim of exchange was to create a sense of friendship between the two people concerned and if this did not occur it did not achieve its end' (Radcliffe-Brown 1948: 84). And further: 'A great proportion of primitive exchange, much more than our own traffic, has as its decisive function this latter, instrumental one: the material flow underwrites or initiates social relations' (Sahlins 1972: 186). Karl Polanyi (1944: 46) declares: 'The outstanding discovery of recent historical and anthropological research is that man's [sic] economy, as a rule, is submerged in his social relationships.'

Exchange therefore receives its character from the given social structure: when power is not a constituent element, exchange is reciprocal and egalitarian; but as soon as society is reshaped by political power, the nature of exchange is turned upside down. Following Clastres (1989), we can say that power represents a breaking point for exchange, since the primitive human no longer produces for themselves, even when the law of exchange intervenes to mediate the direct relationship between a human and their product. Power infringes the egalitarian rules of exchange by replacing them with the fear of debt:

> It is there . . . that the difference between the Amazonian Savage and the Indian of the Inca Empire is to be placed. All things considered, the first produces in order to live, whereas the second works in addition so that others can live, those who do not work, the masters who tell him: you must pay what you owe us, you must perpetually repay your debt to us. (Ibid. 198)

Debt, as an instrument of dependence, is nullified in the reciprocity of exchange, a reciprocity that is also altered by the gift. The gift produces a particular form of indebtedness; it creates a state of dependence whereby 'the beneficiary of this generosity has been put under obligation: he is "one down"; so the donor has every right to expect equal good treatment the next time around' (Sahlins 1972: 303). For primitive peoples, the gift was reversible; giving, as a unilateral act, could only be resolved in the counter-gift.[7] Without this, the recipient would remain in a state of dependence on the giver. As Jean Baudrillard (1993: 48) rightly notes,

> The gift, under the sign of gift-exchange, has been made into the distinguishing mark of primitive 'economies', and at the same time into the alternative principle to the law of value and political economy. There is no worse mystification. The gift is our myth, the idealist myth correlative to our materialist myth, and we bury the primitives under both myths at the same time. The primitive symbolic process knows nothing of the gratuity of the gift, it knows only the

[7] Lanza is referencing Marcel Mauss's famous work on the gift as a medium of exchange, *The Gift: Forms and Functions of Exchange in Archaic Societies*, originally published in 1925.

challenge and the reversibility of exchanges. When this reversibility is broken, precisely by the unilateral possibility of giving (which pre-supposes the possibility of stockpiling value and transferring it in one direction only), then the properly symbolic relationship is dead and power makes an appearance.

Indeed, one of the key characteristics of modern power is to provide services when they have not been requested.

> What is new in the bureaucratic mode of production and domination is, if one dared to call it such, its 'altruism' . . . The bureaucracy not only offers its services to the collectivity but it also serves it really and effectively . . . [I]t works, it makes sacrifices, it administers, it directs and orients, it plans, it 'serves' (and in doing so alienates) . . . human beings, taking away their powers of decision, their initiative, their responsibility for their actions, communication . . . in other words it deprives them of their specifically human activity. (Translated from Lapassade 1974: 125)

At this point we may well ask whether the tribal chieftain described by Clastres – who does not hold power, works more than the others, and continues to give – does not already have the attributes of domination and whether it is not only the particular social structure that inhibits the realisation of this potential. Are the chieftain's gifts not merely a 'primitive form' of the non-requested services of the bureaucratic society? This digression leads me to the conclusion that unilateral services are a phase in the constitution of domination, as they shatter the egalitarian economic relationship. From this arises the re-evaluation of exchange as an instrument to maintain the equilibrium of society. Its non-reciprocity produces an unequal relationship which is a possible prelude to relationships of domination.

Another question follows: is 'value' a structural element of the reversibility of exchange? Unless we take the value of the exchange into consideration, we cannot understand why the 'savage' wishes to return the gift with a counter-gift. If the exchange takes place in a situation of reciprocity and equality it means that the values of the goods exchanged are considered to be equal; otherwise, the exchange would be unequal and would give rise to expectations of compensation to make the exchange equal or else to reverse the direction of the inequality, thus giving rise to further expectations. The existence of a category of 'value' even in societies without political power is anything but irrelevant. It is value that provides the foundation for that economy which I earlier defined as an element in a power relationship. 'The theory of value, on the other hand, is not a part of economic science but, rather, it is the *principle*[8] from which the entire science starts' (translated from Napoleoni 1976: 7). Nor does Joan Robinson's (1966: 29) amused irony reassure us:

> One of the great metaphysical ideas in economics is expressed by the word 'value'. What is value and where does it come from? It does not mean usefulness—the good that goods do us . . . It does not mean market prices, which vary from time to time under the influence of casual accidents, nor is it just an historical average of actual prices. Indeed it is not simply a price; it is something which will explain how prices came to be what they are. What is it? Where shall we find it? Like all metaphysical concepts, when you try to pin it down it turns out to be just a word.

At first glance, value, in its economic sense, would seem to be an integral part, indeed a structuring principle, of the 'economics of Power', thus invalidating its potential use for our utopian project. Can we imagine a social relationship devoid of value (in its wider sense and not in its strictly economic one)? To take an obvious example: one individual communicates an idea to another; this latter examines it and classifies it according to their cultural parameters, that is, as interesting or stimulating or of little to no interest, in which case they forget it. This process contains an element of value as the individual gives a certain value to the received idea. The culture of this hypothetical individual is hence structured on a scale of values which allow them to carry out this classification. Without such a structure, all the elements surrounding us would be amorphous: a beautiful landscape would be equal to a stinking alley; Mozart's D Minor piano concerto would be no different, except perhaps quantitatively, to a song by Orietta Berti.[9] One of the pre-eminent functions of a culture consists in assigning greater or lesser importance to a fact or event, a physical element, a cultural product and so on. We can say, therefore, that value, and the 'value judgement', is a category created by culture. To be sure, it is one of the constitutive elements of culture, an element that cannot be suppressed without depriving humanity of its capacity for evaluation and choice.

A similar process occurs with respect to goods: we attach greater importance to one good rather than another and when forced to choose, we choose what interests us more. Faced with the choice between a bottle of 1961 Gattinara

---

[8] *Principio* in Italian means both beginning and principle.
[9] Orietta Berti is an Italian light-music singer who was particularly popular in the 1960s–1970s.

wine (a particularly good vintage) and thirty litres of Coca-Cola, I would have no hesitation in choosing the former, even if quantitatively inferior. This does not preclude the possibility that some of my friends may prefer thirty litres of the horrendous American drink. Our choices between goods are also based on values and it could not be otherwise without risking the most deadening uniformity.

The idea of value is thus inherent to our culture and, in my view, is anything but a negative element. Up to now we have used value as synonymous with 'judgement of worth', but our problem becomes more complex when we include such a 'judgement of worth' or 'value' into the social relationship that we termed 'exchange'. In this phase the exchange, in order to be 'equal', tends to be based on an equality of values exchanged; that is to say, that the two subjects in the *exchange* define a 'quantification of the value' of the *objects of the exchange*. This quantification is not objective in itself but becomes so in the context of the social relationship. The resultant 'exchange value' arises from 'particular considerations' of the two subjects and is obviously arbitrary. However, this arbitrariness is freely sought, and allows the concrete realisation of the exchange. These 'particular considerations' are obviously the values attributed by the two subjects according to a preferential positioning of the goods in question, based on their current needs.

If we transfer this *simple* relationship into a more *complex* dimension such as a society, we witness the generalised objectification of exchange values, determined by a need to be able to predict the value-cost of a certain good. An entire mystifying ideology has been built up around this process, with 'bourgeois' and 'Marxist' economists mirroring each other. Both, in their respective roles, see exchange values as the good or the evil of society. Jean Baudrillard, in his *apparent* overcoming of the logic of value, is a perfect example: 'The phantasm of value is also the phantasm of order and the law' (Baudrillard 1981: 209):

> So the issue is clearly not 'mystified consciousness', nor whatever illusion the aforementioned revolutionaries had about the liberatory suspension of exchange value. They failed to see that there is no contradiction between exchange value and the satisfaction of desire – on the contrary. To be sure, such a contradiction would make the thought of revolution much simpler to grasp, but it is only possible from the perspective of an axiological idealism, and the idealization of use value in particular. In effect, this position is betrayed by its own, powerful sublimation, which leads its adherents to underestimate the radicality of its transgression. Having approached the problem so gingerly, they have, in effect, proposed a reformist strategy that contests value at only a relatively superficial level. (Ibid. 210)

These types of arguments are common within neo-Marxism, and are based on Marx's own error confusing an effect with its cause. In my view, the law of value is not the 'perverting' element of society, but it is rather the context in which this 'law' develops that determines more or less desirable situations.

If the logic of society is defined by a relationship of domination, the law of value operates according to the logic of domination, thus becoming the vehicle for social relationships which reproduce in the economic sphere the very logic of domination already established in the social sphere.

By force of equivalence, what conditions the whole of society and reproduces all social relationships according to its own logic is, by its very existence, power. René Lourau (translated from 1978: 82) writes:

> The principle of equivalence extended to all social forms means that the State, which is both the power of legitimation of the institution and the result of all institutional legitimacy, is what drives all social life, every innovation, every movement and often even revolutionary action, for new social forces to generate forms equivalent to those in existence, in a framework of changing equilibriums, regressive or progressive, but always defined by the sacred existence of a State as the metaphysical guarantee of the 'social'.

A great deal – probably all – therefore depends on the type of social relationships, whether they belong to relationships of domination or whether they develop in an environment in which freedom is taken as a fundamental premise. In this latter case we can very well imagine a 'neutral function' for the law of value: it can be considered as nothing more than a communication technique. Perhaps we may even conceive of the law of value with a positive function. To be sure, its suppression can happen only in a society completely reconciled with itself, in a transparent[10] society, in that second phase of communism in which, according to Marx (1978), values do not exist because they are unnecessary since 'in "socialized" man, the human species and the individual represent a realised unity. Every individual represents the species and the species is represented in every individual. The needs of "socialized" human beings determine production – and this means that the human species itself makes the decisions' (Heller 1978: 125). To me at least, this type of society seems anything but attrac-

---

10 The notion of a *transparent* society has specific ambivalences that are difficult to translate into English, for in this context it carries subtle totalitarian undertones, alluding to a 'surveillance society' where everything can be seen, recalling the Panopticon made famous by Foucault.

tive. If this is utopia, it is a totalitarian one, it is the dream of the 'total planner', a society where diversity gives way to mass equality, where individuals have lost their individual characteristics and each 'can be seen' in every other.

If, instead, the law of value operates according to the new logic of free social relationships, it will allow an increase in diversity without limiting equality. Furthermore, if the category of value should indeed disappear, how would the conditions by which 'the needs of "socialized" human beings determine production' (Heller 1978: 125) operate *in practice*? Needs manifest themselves according to a scale of values determined by the particular nature of the subject, but if this attribution of values did not take place, needs would be undifferentiated and left to chance. At this point, however, a question arises: if needs contain the category of *value*, we should be able to put a *value* on needs – but what is meant by evaluation of our needs?

In a complex society like the one we live in, the need for a certain good rarely arises autonomously in the subject, but rather descends from the knowledge that a specific good exists. Need arises from an exchange of knowledge and is satisfied almost exclusively through exchange. In modern times, the system of needs, as many have already pointed out, is a compound response to the system of production whereby the technocrats (those who guide our lives) can declare that 'they cannot trust what society designates as its needs; they "know" that society cannot know its own needs since they are not variable independent of the new technologies' (Lyotard 1984: 63). While overrating the role of planners, the technocratic vision also highlights an important aspect of needs: they rely on a system of relationships. The complexity of relationships feeds the complexity of needs; within this scenario, it is not viable to attempt to identify the 'natural needs' of humanity and differentiate them from those arising out of the society of domination.

What are natural needs? Even if we could define them, it would result in a list of simple needs pertaining to the 'minimum subsistence level' – therefore a tiny fraction of our needs – and we would have to argue that this minimum for subsistence, the realm of primary needs, varies greatly, more than we were expecting it to. Let us take the example of the so-called primitive people: they are indigent only when assessed through our cultural parameters, yet they may consider their needs satisfied with what we consider of insufficient quantity and quality. This is another culture with different 'primary needs': it seems that the minimum subsistence figure is determined by culture. Needs (a wide-reaching category which is in no way limited to goods) are anything but secondary in human culture and its production. When prehistoric humans began to 'produce' culture they parted from their 'state of nature', and their needs were no longer determined purely by physiological needs but also (and more and more so) by culture. Needs lost their 'naturalness' through the symbolic mediation of the imaginary which imbues them with new meanings.

Humans – the only *cultural animals* – are therefore shaped by the gap between nature and culture. These two elements, combining in what we could call a chemical reaction, brought into being a new element, to the point that they can no longer be analysed separately. The element we see and perceive – what matters to social analysis – is just humanity's cultural variations. The analysis of needs is in fact an analysis of the culture of needs. Still, historicising needs cannot explain their genesis, and is ultimately more description than interpretation.

Historicising exposes the persistence of both power and its culture – the duo nature/culture is rather a trio: nature/culture/power. It describes needs under conditions of domination. Today, we can only vaguely hint at needs under conditions of freedom, and to do so we extrapolate from a contradictory and complex context those needs that, according to our ideological choice, we deem to be symptoms of needs under conditions of freedom.

This, to me, is what hampers (the production of) a 'theory of needs'. Provided that such an undertaking is possible and useful, it restates something as obvious as it is little-known: we can freely articulate and express our needs only with the abolition of power.

Power and Society

Power, sadly, cannot be severed from society; it takes form inside society, situating itself around and within its strategically important functions. Power thus becomes indispensable, which makes the idea of eradicating it sound impossible even to those anarchists who more or less consciously buy the liberal-democratic theorem that the sum total of power in society is the same and then resolve it by dividing power equally among all members of society. On the other hand, the structure of modern society would seem to refute the theoretical invariance of the sum total of power. Shrewd ideologues of power such as Niklas Luhmann (2012) point at an increase in the quantity of power as social systems become more and more complex. Decision-makers meet this increased complexity with a greater quantity of decisions, so the total of socially active power circulating within society grows.

Luhmann (ibid. 193) discerns another 'preoccupying' aspect of power: 'The causality of power lies in neutralizing the will, but not necessarily in breaking the will of the inferior.' This brings him to deride the idea of an egalitarian division of power: 'Thus "emancipation" becomes management's last trick, denying the difference between superior and subordinate and thus taking away the subordinate's power basis. Under the pretense of equalizing power, this simply reorganizes the power which the subordinates on the whole already possess' (ibid. 212).

The power that the anarchist utopia seeks to eradicate, the power which we find ourselves up against, has changed considerably. It is no longer merely (but was it ever?) a structure weighing on civil society; it has become *an element of society*; it no longer has 'a heart to strike at' but many smaller hearts spread throughout the body social. Our analysis of power has stopped short at a vision of power which is now virtually obsolete; we must update our vision in order to strike it a truly mortal blow without wounding society as well. This is a truly difficult task: how to strike at something we do not yet know?

The analysis of the new masters – the techno-bureaucracy – was an important step in this direction, but not quite enough. Having identified the enemy and understood its general functions, we must now understand the social-psychological dynamics driving the new masters and the 'curvature' [*courbure*], as René Lourau would say, that they give to society. If power in its institutionalised form (the State) is our unconscious – 'The mummy-daddy State gives a form to our mental images, the more as well as the least rational' (translated from Lourau 1978: 20) – where can we strike at it?

Put in these terms, our problem is left with no foreseeable solutions, together with the related issue of conceiving of an economy that is not determined by power relations. Power provides us with the only 'possible' representation of the economy, and we all fall prey to its manipulation: we keep on dreaming the dream of power (we keep on dreaming what power wants us to dream). Perhaps in the depths of our dreams, there might be a corner not yet explored, weighed up, manipulated and distorted by power. It is not just a dream, it is reality; a reality that we do not often see because we see with the eyes of power. A reality that thousands of years of domination, empire, or more or less enlightened tyranny did not manage to silence. The deadlock of power, the crack that has yet to be closed, is complexity, the multiformity, the variety of social contexts. Notwithstanding the sad dreams of total planners, we are not mere grey, 'homogenised' objects; subjectivity is still alive even if scorned, afflicted, despised and humiliated.

The Economy of Freedom

The complexity of the social environment – which power seeks to weed out and reduce to a system regulated by its symbolic code – remains and reproduces itself. This is the basic fact from which the utopian project can gain new life. In our case, it is apparent how the economic system of power selects those aspects which it considers relevant and extracts them from the complexity of the environment. As it attempts to reduce its own complexity, the economic system develops a particular logic – defined as 'economic law'. Thus, we have a code of 'normal' economic behaviours, that is, in harmony with the system, but our knowledge of *normality* also points at 'deviant', 'transgressive' behaviours, which widen the range of possible alternative actions within the economic system. If it wishes to survive, its institutions must contemplate the widest possible range of deviance.

If this is indeed the logic of the system, we have a preliminary heuristic answer, as imperfect as it is: strengthening the capacity of deviance as a means to resist the reductionism of the power system.

'Beyond the economic' we find the non-place of the economy as opposed to the 'economic system' – understood as the process of reducing complexity. We oppose it through a multiformity that cannot be silenced: anarchy.

The economy is a 'cultural' product of humanity and *can* be conceived of in multiple ways since the economic laws operate according to the logic of social relationships. If, today, these take on an objectified form, this is because power objectifies our social relationships. Nonetheless, we can undertake a cultural operation which consists in identifying those economic relationships which do not contradict, or better are functional and complementary to, the desired social relationships. The logical process of constructing an *economy of freedom* would lie in an operation conceived of and decided on by the *social actors*. This operation consists in asserting those economic relationships which function and reproduce themselves according to a 'conventional' scheme which makes behaviour predictable.

A pact, understood as agreement between parties to carry out certain reciprocal acts, could, in my opinion, represent the moment of mediation and coordination between actors in society.

The utopian project, in its search for open forms, finds its positive affirmation in conventionality since, in realising itself in an order of stability/instability that is open to continual modifications, it finds its foundations in the expression of will, in the voluntary or decisional choice. This system would be 'open' because key to pacts is their relativity, a dimension that allows for and invites the emergence of other rules of agreement. Its very 'conscious arbitrariness' prevents it from becoming absolute since there are no external foundations for the decision-takers. Moreover, a pact, in the full sense of the word, is only possible between free and equal partners. If this is not the case, the pact is only a camouflaged imposition. Not even the pact instituting inequality or the loss of freedom of one party can be considered a true pact since the adherence to that pact modifies its nature by depriving it of a fundamental element – its revocability.

The term 'pact' could be replaced by 'contract' if the relationship at stake pertains to purely economic aspects; that is, if it has a more limited scope, without altering its essence. Such essence does not seek external legitimacy, even if everyone seeks a source of legitimacy for their actions, declarations and ideas. The source of legitimacy has changed over time, but perhaps we should ask ourselves if the postulation of legitimacy ultimately belongs to an authoritarian discourse because the search for an *absolute* principle is always a pyramidal structure of thought – which is inadmissible in an anarchist context. If we recognise that a horizontal socio-economic axis forms around the *extreme* and *radical* forms of the concepts of freedom and equality, we can assign self-foundation and self-legitimisation to these concepts. Freedom is self-legitimising because if we observe all the constitutive acts of society today (and for the last few centuries) we can see that their common foundation is freedom. This freedom may be mystified, adulterated, it may be an unfreedom masquerading as freedom, but it is, nevertheless, always declared. So, if the society of domination must always shield itself behind proclamations of freedom in order to have a shadow of legitimacy, this means that freedom is a fundamental element of our social being; that freedom is a value that no one, not even the worst dictator, can deny or estrange from men. This consideration may be seen as, and possibly is, arbitrary but it is in the recognition of arbitrariness that the anarchist utopia openly confesses its doubts – that is, its antidogmatic essence – and imagines pacts as the dubitative form of a project of transformation.

References

Baudrillard, Jean (1981), *For a Critique of the Political Economy of the Sign*, St. Louis: Telos Press.

Baudrillard, Jean (1993), *Symbolic Exchange and Death*, London: Sage Publications Ltd.

Callenbach, Ernest [1975] (2004), *Ecotopia*, Berkeley: Banyan Tree Books.

Campanella, Tommaso [1602] (1977), *La citta del sole*, Milan: Feltrinelli.

Clastres, Pierre [1974] (1989), *Society against the State: Essays in Political Anthropology*, New York: Zone Books.

Foigny, Gabriel de [1676] (1993), *The Southern Land, Known*, Syracuse: Syracuse University Press.

Fontenelle, Bernard de [1768] (1979), *La storia degli Agiaoiani*, Naples: Guida Editori.

Heller, Ágnes (1978), *The Theory of Need in Marx*, London: Allison & Busby.

Huxley, Aldous (1932), *Brave New World*, London: Chatto & Windus.

Kropotkin, Peter (2007), *The Conquest of Bread*, Edinburgh: AK Press.

Kuhlman, Hilke (2005), *Living Walden Two: B. F. Skinner's Behaviourist Utopia and Experimental Communities*, Chicago: University of Illinois Press.

Lapassade, Georges (1974), *L'analisi istituzionale*, Milan: Isedi.

Le Guin, Ursula (1974), *The Dispossessed*, London: Granada Publishing Ltd.

Lourau, René (1978), *L'État-inconscient*, Paris: Éditions de Minuit.

Luhmann, Niklas (2012), *Trust and Power*, Cambridge: Polity Press.

Lyotard, Jean-François [1979] (1984), *The Postmodern Condition: A Report on Knowledge*, Manchester: Manchester University Press.

Marx, Karl [1875] (1978), 'Critique of the Gotha Programme', in *The Marx-Engels Reader*, ed. Robert C. Tucker, New York: W. W. Norton & Company Inc.

More, Thomas [1516] (2016), *Utopia*, London: Verso.

Morelly, Étienne-Gabriel (1753), *Le naufrage des îles flottantes ou la Basiliade du célèbre Pilpai* (2 vols); available at <https://gallica.bnf.fr/ark:/12148/bpt6 k84452x.image> (last accessed 1 June 2021).

Morris, William [1890] (2003), *News from Nowhere*, Oxford: Oxford University Press.

Napoleoni, Claudio (1976), *Valore*, Milan: Isedi.

Parker, Martin, Valerie Fournier and Patrick Reedy (2007), *The Dictionary of Alternatives: Utopianism and Organization*, London: Zed Books.

Polanyi, Karl (1944), *The Great Transformation*, New York: Farrar & Rinehart, Inc.

Radcliffe-Brown, Alfred Reginald (1948), *The Andaman Islanders: A Study in Social Anthropology*, Glencoe: The Free Press.

Robinson, Joan (1966), *Economic Philosophy*, Harmondsworth: Penguin Books.

Sahlins, Marshall (1972), *Stone Age Economics*, Chicago: Aldine Atherton, Inc.

Skinner, B. F. (2005), *Walden Two*, Indianapolis: Hackett Publishing Company, Inc.

8　The Utopian Function and the Anarchist Imaginary
Amedeo Bertolo (1998)

Originally published in Les Incendiaires de l'Imaginaire
(Atelier de création libertaire, 2000).

> It isn't the material conditions that count, but what one thinks about them.
>
> Tibor Fischer, *Under the Frog*

A DEEP TRANSFORMATION of basic social structures – a 'revolution', whatever one might mean by that – also requires a deep transformation of psychological structures, and both of these transformations can only take place under the pressure of an extremely strong emotional charge, a strong and passionate will for transformation that spreads out across leading social agents ('vanguards' in the military-Marxist lexicon, 'active minorities' in that of the libertarian movement of 1968) but also through more sizeable popular milieu (the exploited, the dominated, the humiliated . . .). This implies that there has to be a sufficient spread of an imaginary that is not only lucidly rational but also emotionally rich, an imaginary that sets the soul alight (not one that only tepidly warms our nostalgic memories and alleviates our frustrations), an imaginary that can become *incendiary*. In my opinion, the *utopian* dimension is essential for the subversive function of the imaginary. I will therefore talk about utopia and I will, quite predictably, be speaking 'in anarchist mode'.*

Before beginning any critical reflection on utopia, it is important to provide some semantic definitions of the relevant terms, concepts and contents. Indeed, as with many other terms (e.g. 'socialism', 'freedom', 'autogestion', 'democracy'), 'utopia' is a container-word in which one can put many things – and indeed, many have done so; some of them had a certain coherence, others were quite

---

* I have written to a greater length on utopia in my essay 'The Subversive Imaginary' (see Chapter 9).

contradictory. These disagreements are due not only to different attitudes in relation to the existing social order, that is, the ideological assumptions of those who have expressed or express a certain opinion, but also to the multiplicity of meanings that can be attributed to the word 'utopia'.

Taking my cue from Bloch (2000) and Mannheim (1979), I will identify, schematically, five basic meanings of utopia, the 'non-place':

1. *Impossible social set-up*: that which is not, has never been, and will never be;
2. *Image of the future*: that which is not, but will be or could be;
3. *Tension of change*: the tension between that which exists and how we would like things to be;
4. *Model for a different society*: whether desired or feared (in this latter case one speaks more precisely of a *dys*topia);
5. *Project for a different society*.

In relation to the first meaning, one has to bear in mind a further important distinction: between that which is unobtainable in an absolute sense and that which is so only in a relative sense. This distinction between relative and absolute impossibility obviously cannot be left to the ideologues of the status quo who always confuse these two kinds of impossibility, transforming behaviour that has been *culturally* mediated by specific social contexts into 'natural laws'. All of human history shows that what is *relatively* impossible can become possible, in fact real – and this holds true not only for our dreams but, alas, also for our nightmares.

As far as the second definition is concerned, it is clear that human activity is impossible without an image of the future. It is fairly easy to see how, precisely within the utopian dimension, the future, as a radically different image from the present, can determine individual and collective actions, impacting on the present in terms of expectations and plans, in brief, a *tension* towards the new. Or merely as daydream, as escapism. But, in this case too, does utopia lose all meaning if matters are as the poet W. H. Auden (Auden and Garrett 1935) would have them: 'Man needs escape as he needs food and deep sleep'? Either way, the future – by which I mean an image of the future – is *never* without meaning, because the future lies within the present – just like the past, as an *image* of the past – and determines it. It is quite clear that dominant ideologies have always written and rewritten both the past and the future in terms of their *function* in the present.

We might say that utopia, on the contrary, tends to rewrite the present as a function of the future, of *its* future. There is no objective future, just as there is no objective past: there are only *representations* of the past and of the future that express different ideological relations to the present.

The expectation of a better social set-up in the future, however, is not enough to define the specific character of the utopian tension (save, perhaps, for its millenarian version). The dimension of hope must be accompanied by that of will, that is, the dimension of creative intelligence, the intelligence of planning. Thus we find the concept of utopia as a model, as an intellectual experiment, and utopia as a project.

In my view, the different meanings of utopia considered above – except for utopia as an absolute impossibility – can be considered as aspects of a single *utopian function*. A function characterised by a strong emotional and intellectual tension, directed towards the transformation of social structures. A function that is in itself *dynamic*, with a power of disrupting even if it descends from a static model. A function which belongs to anyone – individual, social group or movement – who cultivates the *hope* and *will* for a radical transformation of society.

At this point, the positive and necessary link between anarchism and utopia implicitly emerges. Anarchism expresses the hope and will for a social transformation so radical, so in contradiction to the existing order, for a future so different from the present, to make a strong utopian tension *possible*. But this strong utopian tension is in turn *necessary* in order to direct the social order and individual behaviour towards a form of change so exceptional as to entail a real qualitative leap, a real *cultural mutation*. Utopian tension is necessary in order to make possible the seemingly impossible, to allow the future and the non-place to live in the *here and now*.

'Be realistic, demand the impossible': the ostensibly 'absurd' slogan of May '68 captures well the utopian tension underpinning the uprising (now celebrating its thirtieth anniversary) as well as every social movement. And that other slogan – 'it is forbidden to forbid!' – brings out another important libertarian element of the utopian tension.

The utopian function is central to anarchism. Conversely, it is only in its anarchist version that utopia acquires its fullest, most extreme and coherent sense. It is only in the anarchist version that utopia is not doomed to contradict itself sooner or later, but can instead be imagined as a *permanent* function.

Why? Because the specific character of anarchism – and therefore also of the anarchist utopia – lies in its axiological basis that posits *freedom* as the 'central' value, a freedom driven to extreme consequences and inextricably connected to *equality*, *solidarity* and *diversity*, which are both its social premises and consequences. Precisely from this fundamental and indispensable choice of freedom derives the guarantee that the anarchist utopia can never turn into an ideology in Mannheim's sense of the term, that is, a justification of the existing state of things. Anarchism's utopian tension cannot be exhausted because the dimension of freedom is itself inexhaustible. The anarchist utopia cannot lead from one closed system to another, let alone to a totalitarian system, as instead happens with utopias that move within the imaginary space of domination.

There is therefore no *single* anarchist system that might represent humanity's point of arrival, whether near or far. The anarchist utopia contains a *space of freedom* to be explored, a space in which to experiment with infinite and chiefly anarchist social forms, a space of freedom in which to weave diversity and equality in infinite forms.

Ultimately, as anarchism – in coherence with its choice of freedom – does not believe in history's necessary and progressive unfolding but rather sees social change as a voluntary action, it attributes a positive value to utopia, even as a model. And to utopia as a project. In this context, models are used as intellectual experiments, as a means to acquire critical knowledge of what exists . . . and of what does not exist and challenges the existing. Here the project is neither a global, final plan, nor an *abuse of power at the expense of the future or of the masses*, nor a totalitarian dream of social engineers and *enlightened princes*. On the contrary, it exists as collective, open, dynamic, experimental creativity, in which theory and practice continuously realise each other.

The utopian function, therefore, is the anarchist utopia to the highest degree, and expresses itself as the subversive function of the social imaginary.

We can thus claim the positive sense of *both* utopia *and* imaginary, two terms which are normally coupled with a negative and derisory connotation. Indeed, in ordinary language and to common sense, utopia means illusion, just as imaginary means unreal. The 'imaginary invalid'[1] is a false invalid, someone who believes themselves to be sick without being so. Clearer than this . . . and yet, no. Psychosomatic medicine has already warned us, showing that the distinction/opposition between the real and the imaginary is all but clear-cut. Above all, what is at stake here is not the human body and its *physical* organs, but that of society and its *cultural* 'organs'.

Today, only a naive and crudely materialist social science can conceive of a clear distinction/opposition between the real and the imaginary. Society is not made up of things but of relations. The very possibility of building a social order is founded on a unity of representations, values, norms, models of behaviour

---

[1] This 'imaginary invalid' is the hypochondriac *par excellence*, from Molière's play of the same name.

. . . in a word, the imaginary. Social order is above all a symbolic order. In this respect, the imaginary is far from being unreal; it is one and the same with social reality.

Even the economy itself, often considered to be the *material* basis of society, is not composed of things, but of relations between people, and between people and things. Economic relations are based on the imaginary no less than political relations . . . or erotic ones. The economic 'structure' is no more 'material' in a strict sense than the juridical 'superstructure'.

The social world exists *because* we represent it and *how* we represent it. Obviously, this does not mean that everything that is imaginary is real. Yet one can, I believe, claim that in the social arena, all that is real is imaginary.

Erich Maria Remarque (2013: 15) said that 'Man lives seventy-five per cent by his imagination and only twenty-five per cent by fact'. Robert Musil wrote that 'the essential happens in the imaginary, the irrelevant in reality'.[2] These are two literary and slightly paradoxical ways of saying the same thing.

To say that everything that is real is imaginary does not mean to say, with Hegel, that all that is real is rational. Quite the contrary. As Eduardo Colombo (translated from 1984: 94) wrote,

> the rules, traditions, myths and great structures of meaning which make up the symbolic universe, which organize the imaginary representation of the world, do not appear all at the same time in the consciousness of men and women who live them, but on the contrary are for the most part unconscious.

The apparent rationality of the social imaginary today rests upon an abundance of material that is not only unconscious but even irrational. Such is the 'unconscious State' described by René Lourau (1978) that holds up the ostensible rationality of the current social order!

The 'mummy-daddy State', as Lourau maintains, shapes our representations, rational and otherwise. It shapes the social imaginary, legitimising hierarchical institutions and herd-like authoritarian behaviour, drawing legitimacy from them in a self-feeding vicious circle: the circle of domination. The circle can only

---

[2] In the most widely available English translation of *The Man without Qualities* (Musil 1997: 69), this line is rendered somewhat clunkily as 'the more important things take place today in the abstract, and the more trivial ones in real life'. The original German reads 'Im Abstrakten ereignet sich heute das Wesentlicher, und das Belanglosere in Wirklichken', which can be rendered as 'The essential today lies in the abstract, the irrelevant in the real'.

be broken through a *subversion* of the social imaginary, with an anti-hierarchical cultural process and a constant struggle against the State-unconscious.

The spirit of revolt does not arise by itself from the material conditions, not even from the most horrific ones, and much less from the relative welfare of the Western world. Indeed, it arises from conditions that are experienced as intolerable, but only when they are *lived* as such. The intolerable is not an objective category. It is a subjective one. A miserable wage, a hovel of a home . . . these are not intolerable per se. Hundreds of millions, even billions, of men and women have tolerated and still tolerate them. What divides the tolerable from the intolerable are expectations, values, fears, hopes – that is, the imaginary representation that an individual or a social group have of themselves and of the world.

The extraordinary meekness with which millions of Jews allowed themselves to be led to the slaughterhouses of the concentration camps, and the millions of Russians to the gulags, the incredible acceptance over centuries of the caste system by the inferior castes – or still more, the enthusiasm by which millions of men have massacred each other in so many wars, and the unbelievable millennia of woman's subordination to man . . . all of this can only be explained by a determining force of the imaginary. If a Jew imagines himself to be a victim then he allows himself to be victimised, if a woman imagines herself to be inferior to man then she will find it normal to be dominated, if a slave imagines himself to be a slave then he will feel the need for a master. If a worker believes himself to be a wage-earner he will only ever aspire to 'reasonable' improvements in the conditions of his wage and not to the 'unreasonable' freedom and responsibility of autogestion.

The roots of domination do not lie in *nature* but in culture, not in '*things*' but in the imaginary. Individual and collective rebellion against domination is thus possible only if *one conceives it as possible*, if one conceives to be possible all that the unconscious State and State rationality tell us is impossible, only if the non-place of the libertarian and egalitarian utopia denies the place of hierarchical ideology.

This means *creating* new images of humanity and of society, and spreading the idea that imagination is an *activity* and not the *consumption* of images, that it must fall to each and everybody. As Walter Bagehot (cited in Russell, 2004: 190) writes in *The English Constitution*: 'It is often said that men are ruled by their imaginations; but it would be truer to say that they are governed by the weakness of their imaginations.'

References

Auden, W. H., and John Garrett (1935), *The Poet's Tongue: An Anthology*, London: Bell & Sons.

Bloch, Ernst [1919] (2000), *The Spirit of Utopia*, Stanford: Stanford University Press.

Colombo, Eduardo (1984), 'Dell'obbedienza. Il potere e la sua riproduzione', *Volontà* 2.

Lourau, René (1978), *L'État-inconscient*, Paris: Éditions de Minuit.

Mannheim, Karl [1936] (1979), *Ideology and Utopia*, London: Routledge.

Musil, Robert [1930] (1997), *The Man without Qualities*, London: Picador.

Remarque, Erich Maria [1957] (2013), *The Black Obelisk: A Novel*, New York: Random House.

Russell, Bertrand [1938] (2004), *Power: A New Social Analysis*, London: Routledge.

9 The Subversive Imaginary

Amedeo Bertolo (1981)

Originally published in *A/Rivista Anarchica* 93 (4)

A map of the world that does not include Utopia is not worth even glancing at, for it leaves out the one country at which Humanity is always landing. And when Humanity lands there, it looks out, and, seeing a better country, sets sail. Progress is the realization of Utopias.

Oscar Wilde (1891)

UTOPIA HAS SEEN alternate periods of both fortune and decay, in which either its supporters or its critics have prevailed. Both groups are a constant presence: there are always those who use the term with a certain negative connotation and those who, on the contrary, imbue it with a positive value. Marx and Engels' well-known critique (which nevertheless was much less destructive than the attitude of their followers and of so-called 'vulgar Marxism') was followed by a prolonged period of decay. Subsequently, there has been a certain recovery of fortune, including with Marxists such as Bloch and Rühle, culminating in the 1960s, when utopia's positive connotation prevailed. In the meantime, however, a new critical tendency developed, this time under the label of 'liberal democracy' (i.e. Popper, Dahrendorf) rather than 'scientific-socialist', so that in the sociological and political literature of the last ten to twenty years (as has been the case with intellectual attitudes and social behaviour more generally) we find a plethora of arguments both for and against utopia, for all seasons: revolutionary, reformist, conservative, reactionary.

What emerges clearly from literature on the topic is that disagreements over utopia arise from (a) the many meanings attributed to the term, and/ or (b) the ideological bases of those who express such judgements. Among anarchists too there has been over the past century – and there still is – a wide range of attitudes, even while in general there has never been either absolute refusal or uncritical praise. In the anarchist's case, the positive or negative use of the terms 'utopian', 'utopic' and so on seems to derive in part from external cultural influences, to which anarchist culture responds each time – perhaps mechanically – through imitation and reaction, but above all due to the first of the two reasons given above, that is, the semantic ambiguity of the terms in question. Any discussion of the anarchist utopia – and of utopia more generally – must therefore begin with an analysis of the meanings that stand behind words.

The argument of this chapter is that utopia usually represents an ineradicable and positive dimension of humanity – the dimension of hope, of innovative will, of creativity – and that anarchists in particular must explore and expand this dimension – critically but without obsession. If Mumford (1971: 307) can write that 'our most important task at the present moment is to build castles in the air' (and he was no daydreamer, but rather a concrete reformist); if Riesman (1947: 173) can write that 'a revival of the tradition of utopian thinking seems to me one of the important intellectual tasks of today'; if Marcuse (1970: 63) can say that 'we must face the possibility that the path to socialism may proceed from science to utopia and not from utopia to science' as Engels argued, then anarchist culture, which expresses the hope and desire for the most radical social change in history, has even more reason to reappropriate all of the positive depths of utopia and underscore the 'utopian courage' of its tradition.

According to Bloch (1980), utopia serves three basic functions. The first is to show others that reality is not exhausted in the here and now, the second is as a working tool that allows one to systematically explore all concrete possibilities, and the third is to make us aware of the imperfections in this world, to not escape into a golden past or an illusory future, but to transform the world according to what is proposed by utopia itself. An anonymous editor in a popular interior design magazine defines utopia as follows: '[it] is the aspiration to a life that is different from what is offered by the society in which we live, it is the projection of society as we want it. Utopia, therefore, is no dream, nor a chimera, nor an escape from reality: rather, it is intellectual tension, thinking.'[1]

In these sentences, whether as affirmation or negation, we find all the relevant meanings that are attributed to the term 'utopia':

1. That which is completely unrealisable: a free play of fantasy, a schizoid escape into an illusory world;

[1] Translated from *Caleidoscopio*, XIV, n. 23, March 1978, 2.

2. An image of the future; a free play of fantasy, a schizoid escape into an illusory world;
3. Critical consciousness of existing reality and a 'tension' towards social change;
4. A mental model of a different society; and a 'tension' towards social change;
5. A plan for a different society.

What is left outside is utopia as a literary genre, which does not interest us here. Whether expressed as an essay or in song, through daydreaming or blueprinting, as travel tales or science fiction, utopia, as social function, falls always in the spectrum spanning from escapism to planning.

The first meaning of utopia, as something beautiful but impossible, the ideal but unrealisable society (and therefore a useless dream at best and damaging at worst, because it can lead to inaction or, on the contrary, to forms of irrational social action), is without a doubt the most widespread version, above all in everyday language. Still, there is no need to be intimidated by the ostensible authority of the 'good common sense' (often descending from the dominant ideology), nor by its seemingly unquestionable negative connotation.

Once again, conceptual clarity is necessary: what do we mean by 'impossible' and, more specifically, by stating that a certain hope or a project of social transformation is unattainable? Is it impossible in absolute terms, or with respect to a specific context? Is it impossible because it stands in contradiction to scientific, biological, physical, chemical laws and so on – that is, laws that are rationally determined – or is it unfeasible due to specific present conditions which are quite arbitrarily (and often in bad faith) sold as eternal and universal laws?

Mannheim (1979: 177) has very clearly described the error (or trick) of 'ignoring or confusing the distinction between what is unfeasible in absolute terms, or in relative ones', between what he calls absolute and relative utopias.

> This reluctance to transcend the status quo tends towards the view of regarding something that is unrealizable merely in the given order as completely unrealizable in any order, so that by obscuring these distinctions one can suppress the validity of the claims of the relative utopia. By calling everything utopian that goes beyond the present existing order, one sets at rest the anxiety that might arise from the relative utopias that are realizable in another order. (Ibid. 177)

He further notes that whenever an idea is called utopian, it is always from the perspective of a bygone era.

In turn, the utopias of emerging classes or even more modest projects of reform like the abolition of slavery, universal suffrage, improvements in living conditions of wage workers and so on have been held to be categorically unattainable by the ideologues of the ruling class. Until less than half a century ago, the abolition of private property was considered an absolute utopia, even though it is now an indisputable reality for more than a third of humanity. For while it is true that the techno-bureaucratic 'communism' which has replaced capitalism in these areas is clearly horrendous, the horrors of the master-State (entirely foreseen by anti-authoritarian socialists) do not impact on the basic argument: the realisability of that which was once held to be unrealisable, of that which we used to call an absolute utopia, whilst it was in fact a relative one.

To be sure, the utopia that interests us and to which we attach a distinctly positive value cannot be the 'absolute' utopia. Still, we cannot delegate the definition of what is absolutely impossible to *common sense* [in English in the original], nor to ideology (in Mannheim's sense), nor to the science of those who attempt to show how human behaviour is naturally determined and thus, for the most part, immutable. We are reasonably confident (though not dogmatically) that human social behaviour is essentially cultural – that is, learnt – and cannot be reduced to instinctive behaviour. Human specificity lies precisely within cultural mediation, which represents the qualitative leap between humans and the other animals, and in which lies the roots of human freedom.

On a closer look, within 'human nature', one can barely identify (and, to tell the truth, still not truly prove) vague traces of instinct, that is, of *genetically determined* behaviour, while those aspects which are commonly called instinctive are in fact mere impulses or physiological 'needs', whose behavioural expression is entirely *culturally determined*. In other words, we know that the human activities corresponding to elementary biological functions – feeding, mating and so on – are in their specific mode of explication determined by the symbolic world, reason, religion, customs, laws, ideologies . . . and by utopias. And we know that there is a cultural evolution, one which is not necessarily linear and progressive, that proceeds both through quantitative accumulation and through qualitative leaps. This is true for science as much as for ethics, for institutions as well as sexual relations . . .

We do not buy *tabula rasa* theories imagining a clean slate on which anything can be written with casual indifference. Still, we maintain an irreducible core within 'human nature', a core within which it is impossible – at least in the current state of knowledge – to discriminate what is nature and what is culture. Where the apologists of inequality see the ineradicable roots of aggressive and hierarchical behaviours, we prefer to see the unquenchable search for freedom and thus of equality, which is the necessary social dimension of freedom.

All the same, as we do not aim at demonstrating the natural necessity of our utopias (because we would then be very poor and contradictory utopians, and we would be committing the same error as the anti-utopians), we can admit, without risking our own logical coherence, that within 'human nature' there are potentialities for inequality, domination, exploitation and so on. We do know that non-aggressive anthropological types existed and exist (see, for example, the volume edited by Montagu (1981)); we do know that a non-hierarchical anthropological type is possible, if only because it existed in such a robust way that resisted millennia of cultural oppressions (see Clastres 1989 and also Evans-Pritchard's beautiful definition of the properly anarchic character of the Nuer).[*,2] Hence, even if it were to be convincingly demonstrated (which it has not been) that reciprocal aggression, hierarchy and other similar forms of behaviour so dear to the 'scientific' ideology of the status quo are 'inscribed' into human nature, we know that opposing forms of behaviour are equally inscribed therein, and that aggressive, hierarchical 'tendencies' can be eliminated through cultural mechanisms that rather than emphasising and empowering them (or, perhaps, generating them) are modelled on opposite 'tendencies' of solidarity, equality, emancipation . . . Such possibility exists, and that is what matters.

From one extreme to another: from the first definition which – with the due caveats – can be almost universally accepted as negative, we move to the second

---

* 'The Nuer is a product of hard and egalitarian upbringing . . . no man recognizes a superior . . . There is no master and no servant in their society, but only equals . . . Among themselves even the suspicion of an order riles a man and he either does not carry it out or he carries it out in a casual and dilatory manner that is more insulting than a refusal . . . In his daily relations with his fellows a man shows respect to his elders . . . so long as they do not infringe on his independence, but he will not submit to any authority which clashes with his own interests and he does not consider himself bound to obey any one' (Evans-Pritchard 1940: 181–2).

2 In Italian, Evans-Pritchard's book was published in 1975 under the title *I Nuer: un'anarchia ordinata* ['The Nuer: an ordered anarchy'] whereas in English it was published under the less provocative title *The Nuer: A Description of the Modes of Livelihood and Political Institutions of a Nilotic People*. Noticing this, we asked Rossella Di Leo if she would have been aware of the book had its Italian title been closer to its English one. No, she replied – one of many reminders during the editing of this project that translation matters! The Italian title was chosen by the translator of the book, noted anthropologist and Africanist Bernardo Bernardi (1916–2007), and the phrase 'an ordered anarchy' is used by Evans-Pritchard himself in the book, even if it does not appear in the original title.

meaning (utopia as an image of the future) which, to a certain extent, can be universally regarded as positive. Dahrendorf (translated from 1971: 199) himself, who represents one of the subtlest – but nevertheless no less convinced – enemies of utopia, feels himself compelled to add that 'there is a broader concept of utopia that includes any image of the future'. He does not refer to the second meaning of utopia here, because 'without an image of utopia, we cannot live, let alone structure our lives. Desires, dreams and hopes, plans and goals, are the moving forces of our activity' (ibid.). This view of utopia was probably on the mind of another great anti-utopian, Benedetto Croce (1913), when, seemingly contradicting the many instances in which he rejected the utopian dimension, he admitted that 'the utopia of today becomes the reality of the morrow', almost paraphrasing Oscar Wilde ('progress is the realization of Utopias') and Karl Mannheim ('it is entirely likely that the utopia of today becomes the world of tomorrow').

The point is that the future is contained in the present, like the past. And not merely as a potential, according to which 'a weighing of each of the factors existing in the present, and an insight into the tendencies latent in these forces, can be obtained only if the present is understood in the light of its concrete fulfilment in the future' (Mannheim 1979: 221). In my view, this is a mechanical and limited account of the relation between present and future, which does not take into account the effect of the psychological *feedback* [in English in the original] through which the future influences the present.

I feel much closer to Bookchin (1971: 274) when he writes that 'an outlook that ceases to look for what is new and potential in the name of "realism" has already lost contact with the present, for the present is always conditioned by the future'. It is inconceivable that people can exist purely in the here and now, other than as a cork that passively floats on an eternal present. If people act more or less *voluntarily*, if they choose more or less *freely*, it is thanks to their past and future, or rather their *image* of the past and their *image* of the future. Furthermore, even their representation of the past (which is not exclusively made up of personal experiences but participates in the social imaginary) is influenced by their predictions and expectations, that is, by their image of the future, because individual (and collective) memory is not a warehouse, but rather it is a vital function, continually re-elaborating the past, evaluating and reorganising the data that constitute it.

If it is the case that we concretely live only here and now, as cultural animals, it is equally true that in the here and now we also live symbolically elsewhere, yesterday and tomorrow. To use a spatial metaphor, we might say that in human time each moment is always 'three-dimensional', that is, it encompasses present, past and future.

Ideologues of the status quo (whether priests or scientists) have always known how important the future is for the present and have been charged with constructing an image of the future essentially akin to the present, by removing from the future – and therefore from the present – any expectations at odds with the existing social order, moving them into a mythic time or replacing them with small expectations of small changes. On the contrary, social groups opposed to the ruling class (whether in competing struggles *for* power or antagonistic struggles *against* power) have always used the future for utopian ends, that is, subversive of the existing order.

Yet today, when liberal utopia has disclosed itself for what it truly is or at least has become – bourgeois ideology – and Marxist utopia has been unveiled for what it was or at least has become – techno-bureaucratic ideology – nothing can justify the squalid *repechage* of a bourgeois 'utopia'; today, when not even that quantitative surrogate for utopia represented by progress as economic development seems to guarantee any kind of acceptable future, what happens? It happens that one can read the following in a mainstream Italian newspaper:

We are afraid of the future, we cannot even imagine it any more. Those who lived centuries ago . . . thought of the future more or less as the present. In a more recent era, with the development of science and technology, we have seen the spreading of the idea of progress: the future will be better than the present . . . Today, we are not in the condition to imagine how the world will be in a hundred years' time. If we extrapolate from the present like our ancestors, we would have to imagine a human anthill, in which everything is rationed, a city of hundred of millions, in which we do not know if anarchy or totalitarianism will reign . . . In any case, we cannot imagine something happy, not even something better. This means we have lost the future. But does a society that cannot see its future in a hundred years' time have any future in thirty, twenty, ten years' time? Does not the disappearance of the distant future also pathologically affect the near future? (Translated from Alberoni 1980)

In the same newspaper Alberto Cavallari (1980) sings the praises of a new utopia, a 'real-utopia' in which 'politics can rest on ethics'. Because 'this mad planet . . . is spiralling into the void of an unbounded spiritual crisis'. And 'the crisis is the lack of a future'.

Man has to enact a 'cultural mutation', he has to courageously take on global strategies and policies . . . Man has only another twenty years to make a 'rev-

olution' otherwise the 2000s will see the beginning of the catastrophe . . . We
are seeing the crisis of all ideologies, fragmented, 'realist' politics are creating
the catastrophe, all while the final scourge of the millennium is believing that
there isn't even any space left for utopias.

It feels like rereading René Dumont (1974: 6), when he writes that 'the Realists,
or at any rate the best of them, point out that "their" world is heading ineluc-
tably for catastrophe. They therefore hand over to the Utopians, who are called
. . . to look for ways to lay the foundations of various types of society'! What
happens? What happens is that the complete closure of the future is dangerous
for social stability as much as its total opening up; what happens is that someone begins to feel the need to open up some cracks in the wall and let in a decent
image of the future, to avoid the defenders of the status quo from having only a
'terroristic' use of the future (a horrifying projection that justifies a 'least worse'
present).

Or perhaps we might reawaken within the collective imaginary a truly utopian
version of the future, a truly revolutionary use – without any inverted commas.

There are thus three images of the future: one is the ideological reading of the
future as a copy of the present – whether a faithful copy or a slightly retouched
one, it serves a conservative purpose; then there is the image of the future
that projects some 'degenerative' tendencies of the present into an imagined
and worse future, which can serve either an ideological goal of preserving the
status quo ('terroristic' or correctional) or a utopian goal (or rather dystopian,
a negative utopia that criticises the present by amplifying its defects, like those
of Zamyatin, Huxley, Orwell); finally, there is the truly utopian reading, which
leads us directly to the third definition of utopia, well identified by Mannheim
in his classic distinction between ideology and utopia, and in his equally classic
definition of the utopian mentality.

[There are] two main categories of ideas which transcend the present reality:
ideologies and utopias . . . Utopias transcend the social context because they
orient conduct towards elements which are not present at all in the given
social context. (Translated from Mannheim 1978: 216)

For Mannheim, existing reality gives rise to utopias which, in turn, break down
its boundaries, leaving reality free to develop towards a new order – towards
the next 'topia', as Landauer (2010: 113) would say – while the transcendence of
ideology has a conservative, mystifying function. Furthermore, for Mannheim
(1979: 173),

> A state of mind is utopian when it is incongruous with the state of reality within which it occurs . . . Only those orientations transcending reality will be referred to by us as utopian which, when they pass over into conduct, tend to shatter, either partially or wholly, the order of things prevailing at the time.

Understood as creative tension, the utopian function can only be characterised with a positive value by anyone sharing a radical refusal of the existing social order. Any project of social transformation that does not limit itself to the mere renovation of an old building (i.e. that does not limit itself to clever conservation) but rather aims at a broader restructuring – and this encompasses wide-ranging reformist projects, as well as revolutionary ones – has to participate in the utopian mentality, in the conscious contradiction between aspiration and reality.

Those who oppose a reformist realism to a revolutionary utopianism have not understood that without a certain dose of the utopian spirit, no true reform is possible (just as without a certain dose of realism, no revolution is possible). Either that, or they want to try and disguise a realpolitik pure and simple under the adjective 'reformist'. They belong to the lot of those ideologues who attempt to exorcise utopia through platitudes such as 'better an egg today than a hen tomorrow'.

Instead the spirit of utopia – the tension through which tomorrow is present already today – tells us that *the egg of today can be made from the hen of tomorrow*, that without one we do not have the other.

Silone (1971: 26),[3] a Christian without a church and a socialist without a party (as he defined himself), wrote that: 'If Utopia is not used up in either religion or politics, this is because it responds to a need that is profoundly rooted within mankind. The history of Utopia therefore is the history of an ever-disappointed, but tenacious hope.' The utopian tension is indeed made of hope, but not only this. Hope for a different social order is not enough to define the specific character of the utopian tension (other than perhaps in its fideistic

---

[3] Ignazio Silone (born Secondino Tranquilli, 1900–1978) was a political leader, novelist and short-story writer. He was one of the founding members of the Italian Communist Party (PCI) in 1921. He quickly rose to prominence in the party, including a stint as a PCI delegate, along with Palmiro Togliatti, to Moscow in 1927 for a meeting of the executive committee of the International. He became world-famous during World War II for his anti-fascist novels and was nominated for the Nobel prize for literature. After the war, Silone detached himself from the PCI and became one of the most important voices within libertarian socialism (outside of any political party), collaborating also with the *Volontà* group.

expressions); the dimension of will is also necessary. The dimension of will is that of creative intelligence, of planning intelligence, and leads us to the two last definitions/functions of utopia: utopia as an intellectual model and as a project.

Here we are entirely within the space of reason and experimental science. Utopia, as put by Carmela Metelli di Lallo (translated from 1969: 10),

> is 'a mental experiment', formally analogous to that which contributed to the sudden advancements of contemporary science, whereby 'science' is not an accumulation of facts but rather a challenge to the world as it is experienced phenomenologically, through a theory-informed design. A design that does not rest on the already known, but is driven by creative intelligence to discover meanings of the world that would otherwise remain unchartered.

Or we can turn to George Kateb (1968: 269): 'many Utopian books are, in effect, comprehensive sociologies and improve our understanding of social relations in much the same way as large-scale studies of real societies.'

Just as social sciences can represent and study real systems through models, we can use utopian models to *rationally* explore the space of the 'impossible', to discriminate the relative from the absolute and try and deduce elements for a *rational* critique of the false necessity of the existent. In providing models, utopia widens out the space of the imaginable, beyond that of the immediately possible, and allows for a further logical *screening* [in English in the original] for coherences and incoherencies within projects for change, with respect to the values which this change aims to realise.

If the desired social transformation is informed by will and planning (i.e. of people who construct their own future), then it is perfectly appropriate to make a – critical – use of utopian models, not only positive models but also the negative ones, that is, those which sketch out the scary consequences of certain models. The reformer or revolutionary can perhaps go without proposing detailed projects and models, but they cannot omit the intended direction of change. In order to indicate such a direction, it is not enough to pinpoint pursued values (freedom, equality, justice, etc.) because they remain mere words with a hundred meanings, if not interpreted within a specific social context, whether real or planned, which gives them a more precise meaning.

Only a narrowly deterministic conception of social change can do without models, as it follows the idea that the new does not need to be planned and built, but lies entirely within necessary mechanisms belonging to history or providence.

To be sure, dialectical historical materialism itself has not been able to fully abandon such models. As is well known, Marx was extremely cautious in describing a communist society. Time and time again he was on the verge of describing this society, only to then step back and stick to some generic formulae which he adopted very early on (in *The Manifesto*) and which often reappear (from *The German Ideology* through to *The Critique of the Gotha Program*). His barely sketched model proved to be detailed enough for Marx and his followers to build an identity that was not exclusively 'scientific' . . . and for anarchists to denounce its authoritarian character and totalitarian tendencies. Indeed, the model proved to be insufficient to his epigones, who were dealing with a movement in need of knowing a little more about where it was going, and later on with the challenge of building a socialism which did not give birth to itself alone. It is an irony of history that they did let in through the back door many of the 'inventions' of utopians. Perhaps not the best ones, given the results. Otherwise, they carried out live experiments – that is, on the backs of millions of people, whereas they could have been weighed up conceptually.

Paradoxically more scientific than 'scientific socialists', utopian socialists proposed less vague models that could have been more easily discussed, accepted or rejected. I do not mean to say that the content of their proposals was necessarily more scientific (or more desirable) – it was often the contrary – but they were more scientific in their method, as Martin Buber (1949) has rightly observed. Also, when the utopians or their followers went from a model to a project, and eventually to its realisation, they did not carry out experimentations on unaware guinea pigs in the name of history, but through voluntary communities.

The results, whether positive or negative, of the thousands of 'utopian' experiments, of these realised 'utopias' (whether ephemerally or more stably, on a larger or smaller scale, from the American 'Icarians' to the Israeli Kibbutzim, from French industrialist communities to Spanish agrarian collectives),* provide extraordinarily rich scientific materials, equal to – and perhaps even greater than – the colossal 'historical' experiments of the USSR and China, a swathe of material which for the most part is still ignored by the adolescent 'science of freedom'.

We shall now make a couple of general observations on utopia before moving on to the specificities of anarchist utopia.

First: all or part of the definitions/functions that we have distinguished in our 'classification' might very well be considered as aspects of a *single utopian function*, once the necessary specifications are coherently made. This has emerged quite clearly from our analytical discussion of the shifts from one meaning to

---

* On the American communities, see Creagh (1983); on the Spanish collectives, see Peirats (2011) and Semprún Maura (1978).

another. In other words, we can establish logical links between the various facets of utopia and bring them together coherently.

For example, one might assume that from an 'objective' tension for change – due to the 'objective' contradictions of a determinate social system – might arise an image of the future that negates the present and can translate into 'impossible' – in a relative sense – models and projects, which in their turn, through a feedback on to the collective imaginary, increase the tension towards breaking the boundaries of what exists. In our case, this means that whilst the different aspects of anarchist utopia can be studied separately, they must be considered as necessarily connected to each other.

Second: certainly, the utopian function belongs to any social movement pursuing radical transformation, yet this fact in itself says nothing about the meaning of this transformation. We can observe that an amoeba, a fish, a butterfly and a horse can all move within space, but our understanding of locomotion is still nascent: we must go beyond the observation that it is present in (almost) all animal organisms and absent in (almost) all vegetable ones. That is to say, what further defines and qualifies individual utopias are the values on which they are founded, the expectations and interests of which they are expressions, the content explicitly or implicitly proposed, in the models, the nature of their means and strategies . . . In our case, this means that the utopian function of anarchism must be read from *within* its *specific* theoretical-practical context.

Even a careful scholar of utopia like Mannheim fails to grasp the specific character of the anarchist utopia: he sees in it only the most recent expression of the chiliastic or millenarian utopia. To be sure, paraphrasing Mannheim's writings on Bolshevism, many of the central traits of the millenarian attitude have been transferred and transformed into anarchism (especially in popular anarchism in Latin America and Eastern Europe) in order to accelerate and catalyse revolutionary action. Yet before, after, at the margins of, and even within these millenarian expressions of anarchism we also find other expressions which, on the contrary, present a strong affinity with two of Mannheim's other forms: the 'liberal-humanitarian' (or Enlightenment) utopia, and the 'social-communist' utopia.

In truth, if we are to interpret the utopian function in its entirety and in relation to the *essential* traits of anarchism, the anarchist utopia cannot be reduced to any of the other forms. If we fail to recognise its extraordinary character, whether in good or bad faith, we reduce it to a caricature, a variant or a combination of the late-millenarian, late-Enlightenment or proto-socialist versions of utopia.

The axiological base of anarchism, the 'primary' value from which its theory and practice derive, is freedom. As we are not concerned with freedom as a philosophical category but as a sociological one, we heuristically define it as absence of power. A negative definition seems more useful in this context than any positive one (such as 'the maximum development of personal potential'). As encapsulated by the etymology of the word 'anarchy', anarchists believe that the absence of power is the social condition allowing for maximum development and so on.

'Absence of power' is in turn an insufficient definition, if we do not also define power itself. With another heuristic simplification, we define power as the faculty (attached to specific social roles) to emanate norms and apply sanctions; to issue orders and enforce them. Power as a series of authoritarian and permanently asymmetrical social relations. Let us explain: by authority we mean, with a slightly heretical twist with respect to traditional anarchist semantics, the asymmetrical nature of a social relation in terms of the faculty to make decisions. Hence, we must recognise that authority is present in more or less centralised and explicit forms in all societies, whether real or imaginary. Authority is an ineliminable social function, at least as collective function (the assembly, public opinion, etc.). In highly differentiated societies, to imagine an undivided form of collective authority is not enough: there is clearly a wide range of choices that go beyond the individual sphere and cannot be carried out collectively by all of the interested parties in a strict sense, that is, according to rigorous unanimity and parity, for reasons of both functionality and competence, and so on. *Single* relations can thus be expressed through asymmetric forms, among individuals themselves, and between them and the community. But this asymmetry is still not power if, *taken as a whole*, social relations comprise a substantial equivalence of authority between all individuals, if there is what we might call a general and equitable 'symbolic exchange' of authority, through which no one is defined by their behaviour any more than defines the behaviours of others.

When the asymmetry between individuals is made permanent, when the asymmetry between single individuals and the community is no longer characterised by the voluntary acceptance of its limits and authority becomes a separate function of society, mediated and imposed by specific social groups, when asymmetry is institutionalised in hierarchical structures and codes of behaviour, power arises.

Power derives from authority – but *not necessarily*, just as inequality can arise from diversity but *not necessarily*. To avoid any misunderstanding, we reiterate that the meaning we attach to the terms 'authority' and 'power'* does not match

---

* I delve deeper into the question of 'power' and 'authority' elsewhere [see Chapter 4], providing a different and more specific definition (to my mind at least, a more useful

their current usage among anarchists (who generally merge the terms into a single and indistinct negative value) nor that of the apologists of hierarchy, who deliberately confuse authority with power in order to justify the former through the latter (see Engels' obvious example of the ship captain, but also Dahrendorf's more sophisticated arguments). Making our own distinction between the two terms, we might say that, for anarchism, the more freedom endures and develops, the more it prevents authority from becoming power and diversity from becoming inequality. With one substantial difference: while authority presents by its very nature the high risk of transforming itself into power, that is, of contradicting and limiting freedom, diversity is perfectly congenial to freedom. The first needs to be reduced to its physiological 'minimum', including as a collective function,[*] while the second has to be unrolled in all its richness, right up to its physiological 'maximum'.

The social *freedom* of anarchism thus necessarily also entails *equality* and *diversity*. Or, if we prefer, anarchist freedom – which is to date the most extreme and coherent interpretation ever conceived and planned – can also be read as the most extreme and coherent form of equality (as it denies authority's transformation into power, i.e. into unequal authority) combined with the most extreme and coherent diversity.

Indeed, far from being contradictory, the concepts of equality and diversity are in fact complementary: it is, paradoxically, inequality that leads to uniformity, levelling, massification. Guiducci (translated from 1980: 115) writes:

> Even today one hears the relentless and tired repetition of the idea that equality means violating human nature and its diversity, when in truth it simply means grasping that differences only become possible – and deprived of conflict – in situations of equality, and tend to disappear in the oppressive flattening-out of classes and layers when everybody is interchangeable.

and convincing one) by connecting them with two other terms ('domination' and 'influence', belonging to the same sociological 'constellation') as well as with a different conception of 'freedom'. Nevertheless, I maintain that the terminological and conceptual distinctions made here still work for the proposed aim, i.e. a synthetic outline of anarchism's specific character.

[*] Anarchists are quite aware of the danger that collective authority can transform into that 'tyranny of society' of which John Stuart Mill (2003: 8) wrote, i.e. the 'tendency of society to impose, by other means than civil penalties, its own ideas and practices as rules of conduct on those who dissent from them; to fetter the development, and, if possible, prevent the formation, of any individuality not in harmony with its ways, and compel all characters to fashion themselves upon the model of its own.'

As we have written elsewhere in relation to autogestion: 'Diversity does not need to be simply accepted but continuously praised, searched for, created and re-created – because diversity is a basic *need* of mankind and a value in and of itself. *Different is beautiful*' (translated from Bertolo 1979: 27). Freedom, equality and diversity at their highest peaks, with a necessary coherence between them – this is the kernel of anarchist specificity from which descends the specific character of the anarchist utopia.

Anarchism is thus the hope and will for a social transformation that is so radical, so much in contradiction to the existing order, as to make a strong utopian tension *possible*. This very tension is also *necessary* to direct social action towards a mutation that is so exceptional as to imply a qualitative leap: the bigger the difference between the existent and that which negates it, the bigger must be the tension itself, to allow for the 'future' to act upon the present and transform it, to allow for the impossible to become possible. Incidentally, this perhaps also explains the presence of certain millenarian elements within mass anarchist movements.

An anarchist mutation implies a qualitative leap in culture (a 'cultural mutation' we might say). An anarchist utopia plays the revolutionary role of nurturing the hope and will to change society up to the point at which it not only overcomes the boundaries of a given system of power, but even breaks through the cultural membrane that separates the symbolic space of power from the symbolic space of freedom. This membrane has been formed from the sediment and layering of thousands of years of authoritarian-herd behaviour and hierarchical values passed down through the generations into the very structure of character and the social imaginary, of ghosts and myths, constructed through and by societies fundamentally divided into the dominant and the dominated.

In such *cultural fracture* lies the true sense of anarchist revolution, which is not the *grand soir*, the apocalypse, but a cultural 'mutation' of unprecedented magnitude and effects, composed of structural ethical and behavioural transformations, both individual and collective. As the State exists above all in people's heads – and in those of the slaves more than the masters – the utopian function is a revolutionary function in an anarchist sense above all *if and to the extent to which* it manages to dissolve this 'unconscious State' (Lourau 1978), thus freeing vast potential energies, opening up the much-feared – by both masters and servants – 'cataracts of anarchy'.

Nevertheless, the utopian tension of anarchism is not limited to its revolutionary role as enabler of this cultural leap. It does not proceed from one closed system to another, as is the case for utopias that move within the space of power.

The anarchist utopia is a permanent utopia, perhaps the only utopia that cannot become ideology in Mannheim's sense, that is, a justification of the existent. One can certainly imagine a drop in tension after a revolutionary breakthrough, but the libertarian specificity of the anarchist utopia *nevertheless* guarantees the permanence of an irreducible tension for change. This is because the space into which it shifts society is one of infinite possibilities to be explored. Libertarian society is open society. The anarchist utopia is a horizon that can never be reached: perhaps you can claim to have arrived in India when in reality you have reached America, and build a whole ideology on this – but no one can claim to have reached the horizon. No one can ever claim that the infinite forms of freedom have been exhausted.

The anarchist utopia is thus the space of a thousand utopias, which can follow one after another, as in Wilde's image, but can also coexist in different societies simultaneously or even within the same society. The anarchist utopia has nothing to do with those change-deprived monolithic and homogeneous constructions feared by Dahrendorf (1971). This might prove true for single utopian constructions, for particular utopian *models*. Indeed, we have little difficulty in admitting that the vast majority of utopian models are characterised by suffocating conformism and dead stability (it is not by chance that so many utopias – almost all of them – were authoritarian, models of power). This does not apply to the utopian *function*, which is dynamic, as we have seen, and its disappearance, if it were to occur, would lead to a 'static state of affairs in which man himself becomes no more than a thing' implying 'the decay of the human will' (Mannheim 1979: 236). Even more at odds with the specificity of the anarchist utopia is the image of egalitarian society given by Dahrendorf (translated from 1971: 426), in which he mistakes inequality and diversity: 'A completely equal society is not only an unrealistic idea but also a terrifying one: freedom does not reign in Utopia . . . instead it is ruled by the perfection of terror and absolute boredom.' Anarchism presupposes a *choice of freedom*, which is the greatest possible guarantee of the *freedom of choice* which concerns liberal democrats like Dahrendorf so much.

The anarchist utopia is the space of a thousand utopias, the space of thousands of models that explore forms of freedom, with the double function of acting subversively upon the social imaginary (by pointing at the possibility of the 'impossible', giving credibility to the 'incredible') and of mentally experimenting with projects for libertarian and egalitarian societies. As discussed earlier, the construction of models and their comparison are logical operations that allow for the rational exploration of the future that one wants to build, and keep at a minimum live experiments, failed attempts and errors. Perhaps many of the errors and fatal uncertainties of the Spanish Revolution could have been avoided if the anarchist movement had had a less simplistic vision of emancipated society, its decisional mechanisms, and the enormous problems of transition.

Some anarchists refuse to engage with this kind of mental experimenting and discuss the problems of egalitarian and libertarian social organisation. Such refusal is unreasonable, whether it derives from the fear of 'acting prematurely' or from the idea that to build freedom is the task of the masses, not their own, of the collective protagonist of the social revolution, and hence, only the destructive moment pertains to them. The errors behind these arguments can be traced back to a misunderstanding around the utopian function, or to a narrowly deterministic conception of history, or a naturalistic conception of humanity, or even a mystical, apocalyptic vision of the revolution. This kind of refusal mortifies subversive creativity and impoverishes the intellectual legacy and emotional charge of anarchism, and thus risks leaving libertarian theory and praxis unarmed before the immediate problems of destruction/construction, and above all before the formidable strength of social inertia through which power reconstructs itself after every revolutionary breakthrough.

'If the old Master were to die', Guiducci (translated from 1980: 29) writes, 'the Slave would finally manage to win, but he would not know how to build a new society. In fact, he had always exercised refusal but had never developed a project for an alternative society able to democratically function in each and every aspect.' A project for a society without a State, as an anarchist might say more explicitly.

Today more than ever, the State embodies the hierarchical principle in itself. If yesterday it was only the organisation of political power, today the State – de facto or tendentially – absorbs and justifies (and is justified by) a wide range of social functions (economic, pedagogical, logistical, cultural, welfarist). The utopia of the State – a techno-bureaucratic utopia – represents the structuring of society as a whole along hierarchical lines. True absolute power. If this utopia were to be realised, it would mean the death of society and paradoxically it would also be suicide for the State itself.

Like a cancer replacing cellular nuclei, cell after cell, tissue after tissue, right up to the point of killing off the organism, the State progressively invades society, ever more deeply and pervasively. The anarchist utopia is the antibody that society must produce in increasing volumes, if it wants to survive.

The *society against the State* of the anarchist utopia is the revolt of dominated social groups (exploited classes, women, oppressed minorities . . .) against the principle of domination, against the logic of power as embodied by the State.

However, for society to move against the State it must first be able to imagine itself – as a real possibility and not only as a dream – without police officers, priests, judges, bosses, bureaucrats, leader-comrades . . . It must be able to concretely imagine itself without positions of power, without hierarchical structures. It must think through – and, so far as is possible, experiment with – forms of autogestion and direct democracy, of decentralisation and federalism. It must think through and experiment with non-hierarchical relations between men and women, between adults and children, between the city and the countryside, between manual and intellectual labour . . . It must think through and experiment with anarchist utopian models.

Bakunin (2002: 135–6) wrote:

We have neither the intention nor the least desire to impose on our own people or on any other an ideal social organization that we have drawn from books or thought up on our own . . . We believe that the people can be happy and free only when they create their own life, organizing themselves from below upward.

What is rejected here is not so much utopian planning in general, but the unquestionably anti-anarchist claim of imposing global plans from above on to the present and into the future; it is the dreadful technocratic dream of all too many wannabe social engineers who want to force reality into the straitjackets of *their own* rationality; it is the pre-packaged 'happiness' imposed on the people by 'enlightened princes' (or even 'revolutionary' dictatorships), the 'happiness' of authoritarian utopias built upon their authors' idea of happiness.

Anti-authoritarian utopias, on the contrary, as Marie Louise Berneri (1982: 8) observes, 'did not present a ready-made plan but daring, unorthodox ideas . . . they demanded each of us to be "unique" and not one among many'; they propose 'an ideal life without becoming a plan, that is, a lifeless machine applied to living matter'.

Entirely different from the authoritarian-utopian model is planning [*progettualita*] understood as individual and collective creativity and experimentation; planning that develops alongside social struggle, within revolutionary movements, within a continuous interaction between theory and praxis, science and ethics. Indeed, as Malatesta (1929) makes clear: 'I believe that the important thing is not the victory of our plans, our projects, our utopias, which in any case need the confirmation of experience and can be modified by experience.' Here it is apparent that he coherently refuses the dogmatic rigidity of models, but not their existence, nor their utility. Malatesta himself provided a fairly explicit model for a libertarian society in *Anarchy*; before him we have Kropotkin's *The Conquest of Bread** and afterwards Besnard's *The New World*.

Alongside many other well- and lesser-known anarchists, they contributed to destroying the bases of the system of domination and exploitation and laying the bases for a society without power, outlining some of the thousands of faces of the anarchist utopia, which are sometimes written down but more frequently expressed through their behaviour, choices, their lives . . .

By their words and example – in daily life and in struggle, through the enthusiasm of revolutionary periods or the fatigue of the retreat [*riflusso*], in the factories of Barcelona and in Stalinist gulags, with a hundred contradictions but nevertheless with an indestructible fundamental coherence – anarchists have kept alive an image of an im/possible community of free and equal persons. Possible because this lies entirely within human 'nature'; impossible because it lies entirely outside of dominant culture. Possible because human beings can think and choose freedom for themselves; impossible if slaves continue to think of themselves as slaves, or dream of being the master.

Anarchists have given concreteness and awareness to an image that, whether as a dream or a project, cuts across the history of domination, usually latent but at times emerging in individual and collective revolts. Anarchists – along with social movements that have, in one way or another, both spontaneously and through their influence, tried to enact this libertarian and egalitarian image – have shown that the anarchist utopia, far from generating 'imaginary subversives', produces and nurtures a subversive imaginary.

References

Alberoni, Francesco (1980), 'Una società senza futuro', *Corriere della Sera*, 22 December.

Bakunin, Michael [1873] (2002), *Statism and Anarchy*, Cambridge: Cambridge University Press.

Berneri, Marie Louise (1982), *Journey through Utopia*, London: Freedom Press.

Bertolo, Amedeo (1979), 'La gramigna sovversiva', *Interrogations* 17–18: 9–37.

Besnard, Pierre (1936), *Le monde nouveau*, Paris: CGT-SR.

---

* See the same author's *Fields, Factories and Workshops Tomorrow* (Kropotkin 1998), which is at least as utopian and propositional as it is descriptive and scientific.

Bloch, Ernst [1923] (1980), *Spirito dell'utopia*, Florence: La Nuova Italia.

Bookchin, Murray (1971), *Toward an Ecological Society*, Montreal: Black Rose Books.

Buber, Martin [1946] (1949), *Paths in Utopia*, New York: Routledge.

Cattarinussi, Bernardo (1976), *Utopia e società*, Milan: Angeli.

Cavallari, Alberto (1981), 'La real-utopia', *Corriere della Sera*, 18 March.

Clastres, Pierre [1974] (1989), *Society against the State: Essays in Political Anthropology*, New York: Zone Books.

Creagh, Ronald (1983), *Laboratoires de l'Utopie. Les communautés libertaires aux États-Unis*, Paris: Payot.

Croce, Benedetto [1908] (1913), *Philosophy of the Practical: Economic and Ethic*, London: Macmillan and Co. Ltd.

Dahrendorf, Ralf (1971), *Uscire dall'utopia*, Bologna: Il Mulino.

Dumont, René (1974), *Utopia or Else. . .*, London: André Deutsch Ltd.

Evans-Pritchard, Edward Evan (1940), *The Nuer: A Description of the Modes of Livelihood and Political Institutions of a Nilotic People*, Oxford: Oxford University Press.

Guiducci, Roberto (1980), *La società impazzita*, Milan: Rizzoli.

Kateb, George (1968), 'Utopia and Utopianism', in *International Encyclopedia of the Social Sciences*, ed. David L. Sills, New York: The Macmillan Company & the Free Press, pp. 267–71.

Kropotkin, Peter [1899] (1998), *Fields, Factories and Workshops Tomorrow*, ed. Colin Ward, London: Freedom.

Kropotkin, Peter [1892] (2007), *The Conquest of Bread*, Edinburgh: AK Press.

Landauer, Gustav [1907] (2010), 'Revolution', in *Revolution and Other Writings: A Political Reader*, trans. Gabriel Kuhn, Oakland: PM Press.

Lourau, René (1978), *L'État-inconscient*, Paris: Éditions de Minuit.

Malatesta, Errico (1929), 'Reply to Nestor Makhno'; available at <https://www.marxists.org/archive/malatesta/1929/12/makhno.htm> (last accessed 3 June 2021).

Malatesta, Errico [1891] (1974), *Anarchy*, trans. Vernon Richards, London: Freedom Press.

Mannheim, Karl [1929] (1978), *Ideologia e Utopia*, Bologna: Il Mulino.

Mannheim, Karl [1929] (1979), *Ideology and Utopia*, London: Routledge.

Marcuse, Herbert [1967] (1970), 'The End of Utopia', in *Five Lectures: Psychoanalysis, Politics, and Utopia*, trans. Jeremy Shapiro and Shierry Weber, Boston: Beacon Press, pp. 62–9.

Metelli di Lallo, Carmela (1969), 'Scienza e utopia per l'educazione di domani', *Formazione e lavoro* 39, September/October.

Mill, John Stuart [1859] (2003), *On Liberty and Other Writings*, Cambridge: Cambridge University Press.

Montagu, Ashley (ed.) [1978] (1981), *Learning Non-Aggression*, Oxford: Oxford University Press.

Mumford, Lewis [1922] (1971), *The Story of Utopias*, New York: Viking Press.

Peirats, José [1971] (2011), *The CNT in the Spanish Revolution*, vol. 2, Oakland: PM Press.

Riesman, David (1947), 'Some Observations on Community Plans and Utopia', *The Yale Law Journal* 57 (2): 173–200.

Semprún Maura, Carlos (1978), *Revolución y contrarrevolución en Cataluña: 1936–1937*, Barcelona: Tusquets.

Silone, Ignazio [1968] (1971), *Story of a Humble Christian*, trans. William Weaver, London: Harper & Row.

Wilde, Oscar (1891), *The Soul of Man under Socialism*; available at <https://www.marxists.org/reference/archive/wilde-oscar/soul-man/index.htm> (last accessed 3 June 2021).

10 The Source of the Nile:
In Search of the Origins of Male Domination
Rossella Di Leo (1983)

First published in *Volontà* 37 (3)

A FRIEND ONCE told me about his visit to a large agricultural community in Northern Somalia living by the principle of 'Islamic communism'. Having listened to his hosts' long explanation of their egalitarian principles and structures, this friend (who was comfortably lying on a carpet drinking tea and chewing 'khat' leaves with some men of the community) asked about the role of women (who had humbly served their tea in silence). Caught off guard by the unusual question, the charismatic chief and religious leader replied with an expression exuding both irritation and 'man to man' complicity: 'Well, you know, even the Prophet says it, women are *similar* to men, but not equal.'

Spurred on by a concept so candidly expressed, I would like to travel backwards into the history of humanity in search of the origins of the idea, informing the most deep-rooted human cultures for millennia, which we can define here with the general term of patriarchal culture.

Before I set out to complete this gruelling task, some clarifications are required. First and foremost, a necessary declaration of modesty. As I embarked on this research I somewhat boldly set myself the aim of arriving at the origins of sexual inequality. Yet, as the research unfolded, my audacity was frustrated. I felt, if I may be allowed the comparison, something similar to what Livingstone must have felt when, moving up the Nile, he found only bifurcations fading into uncharted territories, and never the source he had hoped for. Once more we are reminded that there are more things in Heaven and Earth than are dreamt of in our philosophy. There are many more expeditions to be organised, trails to be explored and disappointments to be suffered before we can reach its mythical source. But the adventure loses none of its fascination. Just as Livingstone in his long and troubled search could not benefit from the cold precision of satellite images, so must we work without any sophisticated technical equipment, accepting the intrinsic limits of human knowledge. Humanity is fully immersed in its own culture and cannot hope to view itself objectively from sidereal heights. We are left with no choice but to accept the unease of a long research, armed with some certainties and many questions.

One of these certainties is implicit in the statement of our intentions: if one sets out to look for the origins it is to be taken for granted that such origins exist, that sexual asymmetry is not a fact of nature but a fact of culture. Without going into the details, which will be provided in the next pages, it is enough for now to note that if sexual asymmetry were a fact of nature, stamped on human biology, we would be caught in an inexplicable paradox: woman's refusal of her 'natural' condition. If female subordination were *genetically* determined, woman would be totally and unarguably identified with her nature, her consciousness and her being perfectly superimposed one upon the other. Quite in contrast, today (a today which began with the birth of the movement for the emancipation of women at the end of the eighteenth century) we are witnessing woman's inconceivable refusal of her 'nature'. In the very act of rebellion, conceiving of the inconceivable, women are declaring that female 'inferiority' does not arise from nature, but is a product of culture. As such, it has an origin and can be modified.

Before embarking on the search for these origins, I would like to briefly outline the forms assumed by sexual asymmetry in societies with a patriarchal culture. That is to say, those societies which have a hierarchical social structure split into a public sphere and a domestic sphere, the former shaping and determining the latter; in which women are relegated to the domestic sphere and are excluded from political power, whatever their economic roles may be, and must submit to male domination in the domestic sphere as well; in which an inegalitarian culture orders the meanings attributed to male and female attitudes and activities along hierarchical lines. Societies with a patriarchal culture are therefore societies which, while exhibiting some difference between them, are situated within the space of domination and are characterised by two intertwining divisions: the public sphere and men on one hand, and the domestic sphere and women on the other. By public sphere, I mean those institutions, activities and forms of association that exist over and above the family unit and in which domination develops, providing a hierarchical model on which the entire society is then moulded. This is the area of male competence in society. By domestic sphere, I mean those 'minimal institutions' formed around the basic social unit (that of the family, extended or otherwise) predominantly determined by the public sphere. This is the area of female competence.

How and why these divisions come into being we will consider later. For the moment it is enough to outline the general profile of this disharmonic society which combines a hierarchical social structure with a culture ordered around concepts of 'superior' and 'inferior' and, obviously, attributes the superior values to the dominating male sphere and the inferior values to the dominated female sphere.

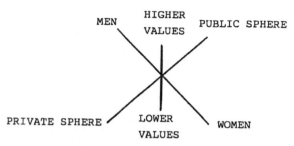

Figure 10.1 The three figures in this chapter were drawn by Amedeo Bertolo.

On the basis of this inegalitarian social order, we have antithetical images of two prevailing sexual genders. On the one hand, there is the Man, the central, determining element of society, thanks to his supposedly abstract, rational, active, assertive 'nature'. All decision-making power is in his hands; it is he who chiefly develops cultural values (including the very definition of woman); it is he who occupies the most prestigious social positions, whatever these may be. Then there is the woman, a peripheral, marginal element of the social body because of her supposedly practical, impulsive, passive, subordinate 'nature'; she occupies social positions of little or no prestige. While man, the social actor, is defined in terms of his role, profiting from the plurality of choice offered him by society, woman, the social object, is defined in terms of her relationship to a man, subjected to the only socially accepted model of life: marriage (that is, the legal passage from parental authority to marital authority) and maternity.

In patriarchal cultures, representations of social roles rely on two abstract definitions. First is the common conception of the social structure as a pyramid in which the upper part is occupied by the masculine gender, and the lower by the feminine gender.

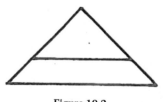

Figure 10.2

This simplification is theoretically forced and in no way does justice to the much more articulated asymmetrical relationship between the sexes. This could be better illustrated by two semi-pyramids, split along the vertical median in such a way that the vertex and every successive level of the feminine semi-pyramid is lower than the vertex and each corresponding level of the masculine semi-pyramid. Thus, *under equal conditions*, the social status of the woman is always inferior to that of the man.

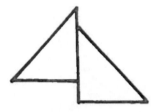

Figure 10.3

For this reason, it is preferable to use the term sexual 'asymmetry' to define this more complex configuration of society, avoiding the term 'inequality', which brings to mind the abstract dichotomic vision of the simple pyramid.

The second abstraction to be found in the above images is also due to the fact that these are generalisations, ideal models, and do not coincide perfectly with the dynamic reality of the different patriarchal cultures. This lack of alignment is evident in contemporary Western society in which such conceptions seem to be, partly, out-of-date clichés, extreme cases which are no longer fair representations of social reality. To be sure, it seems quite unthinkable to maintain that the woman in Western countries today is a mere social object, marginal and without influence.

While it is undeniable that, until the last few decades, the ideal model coincided with the reality in society, it is equally undeniable that the female condition is changing rapidly and widely. Even if a large number, possibly the majority, of women today still fall within the bounds of the above definition, a substantial minority show this definition to be, fortunately, obsolete. In the Western world the forms of sexual asymmetry are becoming ever more blurred and its very existence ever more opposed so that it is now possible to talk about the 'crisis' of the patriarchal culture. This crisis forms part of a more general subversion of the system of values on which Western society is based, a process which is too complex to be included in this study. For our purposes now it is enough to state that the problem of sexual asymmetry in Western society must be considered with an analytic lucidity that sweeps away all those clumsy theoretical simplifications which it has undergone. This lucidity will also allow us to consider an idea which is inherent to the libertarian point of view: sexual asymmetry may be modified and even disappear without causing any substantial modification to the overall inegalitarian structure of society.

Returning to the core of the problem, the first macroscopic fact to consider when reflecting on sexual asymmetry is that its presence is so widespread as to give credence to the hypothesis of its *universality*. The vast majority of anthropologists have already expressed such a belief. This presumed universality does indeed seem to be confirmed on a first analysis, as Michelle Rosaldo (1974) tells us, by both a synchronic investigation of existing societies and a diachronic investigation of known ones. While Rosaldo, and most anthropologists with her, do not ignore the myths and archaeological evidence which would seem to prove the greater social importance of women in some prehistoric societies, they believe that the highly speculative theories interpreting such myths and evidence cannot be verified. This prudence seems further motivated by the fact that societies which seemed to have reversed the man/woman relationship, on deeper analysis reveal the 'classic' asymmetry, delegating the ultimate power to a male member of the mother's family rather than of the father's.

Human culture seems to be characterised by this homogeneous trait, which is repeated over time and space in otherwise widely different societies. Countless myths explain the origins of the asymmetric relationship between the sexes and they are surprisingly similar despite the thousands of years or miles separating the cultures which produced them.* It does not therefore seem far-fetched to proclaim that the universality of sexual asymmetry is a necessary fact of human culture.

In order to verify the validity of this hypothesis we can accept the unintended assistance of Claude Lévi-Strauss (1969: 8), who declares that

> it is easy to recognize universality as the criterion of nature, for what is constant in man falls necessarily beyond the scope of customs, techniques and institutions whereby his groups are differentiated and contrasted ... Let us suppose then that everything universal in man relates to the natural order, and is characterized by spontaneity, and that everything subject to a norm is cultural and is both relative and particular.

If this definition is accepted, the supposed universality of sexual asymmetry would endow man/woman domination with the biologically inexorable

---

* One can note for example the extraordinary resemblance between the myths of various Amerindian tribes such as the Yámana-Yaghan or the Selk'nam (Bamberger 1974) and the Babylonian myth of Tiamat and Marduk (Stone 1978).

character that we have already challenged. On the other hand, Lévi-Strauss himself declares that where there is the Norm, there is culture. It only remains for us to determine whether sexual asymmetry is constant, uniform and uncodified, and thus natural, or if it is diversified, not constant, codified and thus cultural.

It seems clear that in no civilisation is the social behaviour of the sexes left to chance, to the realm of 'spontaneity', but is instead the subject of meticulous social regulations. In fact, once certain biological determinations have been fixed, nature withdraws, leaving sexual behaviour unspecified. This open space is immediately invaded by culture, whose primordial role, again in the words of Lévi-Strauss (1969: 32), 'is to ensure the group's existence as a group, and consequently, in this domain as in all others, to replace chance by organization', when in fact 'it is impossible for culture not to introduce some sort of order where there is none'.*

We are hence dealing with culture, not with nature, as is confirmed by the astonishing variety of gendered behaviours and roles across human civilisations: if in all societies we find a gendered division of social work, what are to be considered feminine roles and behaviours and what are considered to be masculine varies greatly across societies. This is yet another confirmation that the social behaviour of the two sexes is not based on instinctual factors which impose universal models of behaviour but rather on cultural elaborations which vary greatly across societies. After all, not only is sexual asymmetry explained by myths (which implies the necessity of providing some justification for it) but every society meticulously codifies the particular form it assumes in that cultural context. This excludes the hypothesis of a uniform and uncodified sexual asymmetry. We have yet to clarify why a large part of anthropology (feminists included) has seen sexual asymmetry as a universal phenomenon.

I shall briefly anticipate the discussion of the following pages and say that this ostensible universality is the fruit of a distorted reading, widespread in anthro-

---

* There are few roles that do not seem to be interchangeable between the sexes and these are apparently determined by biological factors: woman's ability to procreate and man's greater physical strength. The former seems to determine the maternal role, transforming a biological fact into a social function. The second seems to determine those male roles related to the use of violence, such as war and hunting. To us it seems, nonetheless, that, despite the apparent universality of these role attributions, they are in fact cultural elaborations of simple biological facts. The biological fact of procreation, for example, does not imply all the complex and protracted social, affective and economic relationships making up the mother-child relationship. And, equally, it does not seem at all obvious that man's *average* greater physical strength necessarily implies the monopoly of violence.

pology, which assumes as general a given fact that is in fact partial. Such an error of perspective is quite typical of Western culture's arrogant aspiration to reduce the world to 'its own image'. Imbued with ethnocentric philosophy, Western culture projects hierarchy, its organising principle, on to all other human societies, thus reducing reality to its societal model of domination.

It is for this reason that sexual asymmetry, like every other cultural trait of the society of domination, becomes universal, in the same way that domination does. Thus, the partial reality of patriarchal culture, that is, the coexistence of a hierarchical social structure with sexual asymmetry, is transformed into an absolute reality when it is in fact *a universal cultural trait of societies of domination.*

Having clarified the origin of the misunderstood universality of sexual asymmetry, we will later explore the still little-known societies without domination and without history (to use Pierre Clastres's definition) in order to verify whether the absence of domination brings about, per se, the disappearance of sexual asymmetry.

It would be as well to pause for a moment on the problem of ethnocentrism before continuing with a deeper analysis of the relationship between power and sexual asymmetry. Clastres (1989: 16–17) declares:

> The still robust adversary was recognized long ago, the obstacle constantly blocking anthropological research: the ethnocentrism that mediates all attention directed to differences in order to reduce them to *identity* [my emphasis] and finally suppress them ... Ethnology, on the other hand, wants to situate itself directly within the realm of universality without realizing that in many respects it remains firmly entrenched in its particularity, and that its pseudo-scientific discourse quickly deteriorates into genuine ideology.

We have just seen how this perspective has brought a good part of anthropology to consider as universal those societies with coercive political power (again Clastres's definition), and their specific cultural traits, such as sexual asymmetry. The rejection of this formulation has gained further critical depth in what we can define as 'feminist' anthropology, originating in the United States in the 1970s. Feminist anthropology's major contribution lies in the detection of a specific facet of Western ethnocentrism which is key for the analysis of sexual asymmetry: androcentrism.

By androcentrism, as the word itself shows, we mean Western anthropology's male-centred vision of reality. It imposes an asymmetrical reading of the relationships between the sexes on to its description of other societies, while marginalising the role of women in society by subsuming it into that of men or ignoring it altogether. Thus, the history of the human species becomes the history of man while the 'second sex' sinks into an undefined world, a mere backdrop to the 'true' protagonist in the human adventure: the Man.

Evans-Pritchard's (1940: 7, my emphasis) declaration in his classic research into the Nuer can be seen as paradigmatic in understanding the androcentric approach of traditional anthropology: 'The Nuer, like all other peoples, are also socially differentiated according to sex. This dichotomy has a very limited, and negative, significance for the structural relations which form the subject of this book. *Its importance is domestic rather than political* and little attention is paid to it.'[1] The whole problem of women's absence from the political sphere is dismissed here in a few words, to the point that it no longer appears as a problem, but rather as the given, unchallenged reality which is shared by both the person who writes and those he writes on.

Feminist anthropologists have risen up against this androcentric approach, putting the entire methodological framework of traditional anthropology on trial with the declared aim of bringing the social world of women out of the depths to which the male-centred culture has relegated it. There are two problems of particular urgency for this research: to address the startling lack of data left by Western anthropology and to critically reassess the existing data so as to extract from this history of men written by men a truer and more complete image of women, and so of the human species. This must be the preliminary aim of any definitive research into sexual asymmetry.

The enthusiasm necessary for this challenging task comes from the women's liberation movement, which has undeniably influenced the development of feminist anthropology. The need to reconstruct the unknown identity of the second sex was born within the women's liberation movement, and in feminist anthropology this need becomes the attempt to rewrite the history of the human species freed of the androcentric prejudices that have characterised it up to now.

Nevertheless, while we have to credit the feminist movement for imitating this revolutionary turn in anthropological research, it has also passed down some of its limits, or, better, those of the mainstream feminist movement.*

---

[1] See Chapter 9, footnote 2.

* It is incorrect to speak of the women's liberation movement as one monolithic structure and sharing a single analysis. We are in fact dealing with an extremely multifaceted movement which legitimately contains opposing positions. In particular, we cannot overlook the existence of a minority with a libertarian practice and analysis (the anarcha-feminist tendency) whose positions are far from the ones to be criticised. All the same, it is undeniable that the majority of the feminist movement shares those positions.

First of all, the movement continually falls prey to the analytical simplification that we identified earlier in the horizontal stratification of the sexes (see Fig 10.2 above).[2] This is an optical-theoretical illusion which reduces reality to a false dichotomy in which the female element is laden with positive qualities while the male element, demonised, is laden with purely negative traits. This dichotomy gives us two images which are overly idealised and abstract, and of very little use in reaching any deeper understanding of sexual asymmetry. In fact, on a closer look, we can easily recognise the traits of a very specific historical and social category – the man and woman of the white middle class in Western countries. These social models are undeniably mainstream in Western culture (that is to say that they are the most widely represented in the body social and have determining influence on the cultural models of the lower classes), just as the Western culture is the mainstream culture (in the sense of the most influential) in the world today. Yet, within a discussion on sexual asymmetry, this particular model cannot be promoted as encompassing all the fundamental characteristics of a far more diverse concept of man and of woman.

Even more fundamental is the second analytical limitation of the women's liberation movement, which also pertains to an abstract view of the sexes. The movement lacks an in-depth analysis of power and of the resulting hierarchical structure. *Male power* and the structure of the *sexual* hierarchy have been analysed down to the deepest, darkest recesses, down to the slightest shades of meaning. But power without qualifications, power as an absolute social category, has not been discussed. Virtually unchallenged, power appears to be more or less a 'natural' fact of human society which is questioned only because of its degeneration into male power. Imprisoned in its own logic, the feminist critique moves all around that ideological space defined by hierarchy, without succeeding in connecting the rejection of a particular asymmetry with the overall rejection of the principle behind it.

This limitation in theory was unfortunately inherited by feminist anthropology which follows traditional anthropology in considering the society of domination as *the* human society. This complacent acceptance of power as an inexorable event in society reopens the way to that ethnocentric perspective which feminist anthropology has so deeply criticised: the phantasm is exorcised only to reappear again.

Moving further along in the analysis of sexual asymmetry we find ourselves at a theoretical crossroad. On the one hand, we are directed towards the identification of the mechanisms through which social asymmetry is reproduced

---

[2] The three figures in this chapter were drawn by Amedeo Bertolo.

in contemporary society. On the other, we pursue our search for the mythical source.

The first road is undoubtedly the most concrete and fertile and, unsurprisingly so, also the most trodden. Feminism, in particular, has pushed on in this direction, convinced that *whatever* may be the origin of sexual asymmetry, if we, today, wish to modify it, we must first identify and act upon those mechanisms which reproduce and perpetuate it. This entails that sexual asymmetry, having lost over time its original motivation, keeps on reproducing itself by inertia, through the persistence of its mechanisms.

Without resorting to a detailed analysis – we point at the vast existing literature on the topic, like the 'classic' work of Simone de Beauvoir (2010) – we will limit ourselves to a brief identification of the most important mechanisms.

The first, in both time and importance, is definitely the differentiated socialisation of the sexes, which, generation after generation, trains males and females to conform to the asymmetric sexual model from early childhood. This diversified socialisation deeply affects the psyche, contributing to the formation of the male and female personalities according to the psychological attributes which each culture considers to be 'inherent' in the two sexes. The rigid sexual division of labour then continues to deepen the division between the female and male roles in society, thus delineating the limits of two separate worlds which are crystallised thanks to the separation of society into a public sphere with a male stamp and a private sphere with a female stamp.

Even if we recognise the validity of this choice, we can still object that the act of defusing the mechanisms overseeing the reproduction of asymmetry is not in itself sufficient to eliminate it. If the root causes are not identified and eradicated, it is likely that other mechanisms will replace those that have been stopped, so perpetuating sexual asymmetry.

This type of approach is usually justified with an argument that we have already encountered: due to the impossibility of validating our hypotheses, we risk projecting our own desires on to the origins, in a veritable act of 'mythical narration'.

The risk is real. But isn't it inevitable, a risk intrinsic to human knowledge? Aren't 'rational' and 'objective' explanations of reality – and of human reality in particular – all imbued with the founding myths of the culture they belong to (including the myth of objectivity and rationality forged by Western culture)? Myth and reality are inextricably intertwined: they form the inevitable weft on which human knowledge is woven.

Following these thoughts and spurred on by some crucial questions that still await an answer, we remain firm in our intentions and choose to go down the second road, fully aware of its problems and perils.

Let us, first of all, delve deeper into the existing hypotheses. The first great division between the interpretations of the origins of sexual asymmetry is based on the binary Nature/Culture. On one side we can classify those theories which seek to explain sexual asymmetry in terms of biological motivations and on the other we can group together those theories which see the human species as a chiefly cultural phenomenon, and so place sexual asymmetry within the field of human choice. The second major division, which partly overlaps the first, is concerned with power, and divides the field into those who recognise a causal link, or at least a correlation, between the two social phenomena, and those who do not see any such nexus. All the 'naturalistic' hypotheses, which obviously do not recognise power as a determining factor in sexual asymmetry, fall into the first group, while the second includes its 'culturalistic' interpretations. The first group contains those theories (rapidly declining today) which see no origin for sexual asymmetry, holding it to be a fact of nature. These are the theorists who see in the passive and subordinate 'nature' of woman – as opposed to the active and dominating one of man – a hierarchical order dictated, inexorably, by biological factors.

Even if this crude instinctual determinism (sociobiology apart) seems to be losing credibility, it was the founding concept of sexual culture for thousands of years. Such a 'naturalist' conception proves to be essential in analysing the purely cultural argument that man has built upon biological difference. Patriarchal culture interprets the indisputable biological differences in an antagonistic light, reducing them to that fundamental pair of concepts around which the human species revolves: Nature and Culture. Man appropriates for himself that which is human *par excellence* – culture – and relegates woman to the realm of nature, to an almost pre-human stage of the species. This assimilation is justified by the all-invasive presence of biology in the life of the female, whose cyclical existence seems to move to the same rhythm as the cycle of nature. Man considers himself to be immune to that biological determination so obvious in woman and elects himself as the sole representative of the species, capable of transcending nature and of embodying the peculiar trait of our species – the symbolic capacity. Taking for himself the role of the sole producer of culture, man condemns woman to immanence. The social sphere, thanks to its intrinsically transcendent character, becomes the privileged zone of male activity. The female world is delimited by a domestic sphere which is determined and limited by biology. 'Humanity is male,' declares Simone de Beauvoir (2010: 26), and

> man defines woman, not in herself, but in relationship to himself, she is not considered as an autonomous being . . . She is determined and differentiated in

relation to man, while he is not in relation to her; she is the inessential in front of the essential. He is the Subject; he is the Absolute. She is the Other.

Objectifying the woman and making her into the Other, man creates the terms of another inseparable pair: 'Once the subject attempts to assert himself, the Other, who limits and denies him, is nonetheless necessary for him: he attains himself only through the reality that he is not' (Beauvoir 2010: 193). Woman is therefore the object that allows man to define himself. The definition of woman handed down to us by the patriarchal culture is therefore of more use in understanding man.

The reason why man initiated this process of cultural dispossession, depriving woman of her symbolic capacity and condemning her to a state of immanence, calls for deeper consideration. We can, in part, accept the not entirely satisfying thesis that this sense of revenge in man was born out of his envy of woman's reproductive capacity. As Ida Magli[3] affirms, man sees a power of life and death in this procreative capacity that must be controlled by culture.* As biology excludes man from procreative capacity, he can assert his superiority over woman only by appropriating for himself the capacity of intellectual creativity, then going on to proclaim the superiority of Culture over Nature, and thus of the One over the Other.

In fact, the widely proclaimed symbolic incapacity of woman, which relegates her to nature, is nothing but an invention of patriarchal culture, aimed at justifying her dispossession. It is patriarchal culture that prevents woman from developing her capacity for abstraction, as Merlin Stone (1978) demonstrates in her excellent book on the predominantly female religious culture which reigned for thousands of years before patriarchal culture appeared. This is yet another confirmation that female 'nature', as proposed by asymmetric culture, had a definite date of birth confirming its cultural origin.

Before we leave the field of 'naturalistic' hypotheses, there is a second and more insidious current proposing a more subtle interpretation of the biological fact. Woman is no longer considered to be 'naturally' inferior but is rather the victim of a 'biological destiny' that constrains her to a marginal role in society

---

[3] Ida Magli (1925–2016), Italian anthropologist and philosopher. Some of her key texts are available in English, including *Cultural Anthropology: An Introduction* (2001); *Women and Self-Sacrifice in the Christian Church* (2003); *Taboo and Transgression: Jesus of Nazareth* (2009).

* For others, like Clastres, man, taking the exclusive right to the use of violence, rises in the eyes of society as the dispenser of death to himself and to others, putting up this (cultural) power of death against woman's (natural) power of life.

and, in the longer run, to her subordinate condition. Maternity, the neoteny of the human infant, her inferior physical strength, all exclude woman from fundamental human activities, like hunting, around which the species developed. Thus, although the source of woman's social inferiority is no longer written in female 'nature', it is nonetheless biologically determined. In this case, the origins of society would coincide with the origins of sexual asymmetry.

This is an extremely ethnocentric reading of human evolution, one that projects the asymmetry of our hierarchical and inegalitarian culture on to radically different socio-historical formations, like nomadic hunter-gatherer societies, thus overestimating the male contribution to evolution. Sally Slocum's essay (1975) destroys this theory by demonstrating how those evolutionary events associated solely with hunting (that is, with men) are to be equally found in the sphere of female competence. The need for greater cooperation is to be found in both the male organisation of hunting and female domestic organisation. The sophistication of language, which leads to the development of symbolic capacity, is equally indispensable to the hunt and to the socialisation of children, which is allotted to women; the invention of new tools, which leads to the development of technological capacity, is required by both man for his hunting weapons and woman for her domestic tools and the transport of food.

Once we lay bare this shamelessly androcentric vision of human evolution, we must ask why woman's biological functions, by determining her role in society, *force* her into a subaltern position. It is by no means obvious why the bearing, rearing and socialising of children, a task essential to the survival of the species, or the management of the domestic sphere, which is essential to the survival of the community, should be inferior *in itself*. And it is equally hard to understand why hunting should be socially superior *in itself*, or, widening our perspective, why are *all* men's activities in society, whatever they may be, always socially superior, and women's social activities socially inferior? Clearly it is not the intrinsic value of a particular role in society that determines its placing, but rather the gender that personifies it: masculine is superior, feminine is inferior. The origin of woman's subordination lies neither in her 'nature' nor in her 'biological destiny', but rather in a cultural interpretation of sexual differences and related social roles.

For Margaret Mead (1977: xv) it is startling to see how 'human imagination has been at work, re-evaluating a simple biological fact'. In reality, the biological fact is, in itself, neutral, assuming a positive or negative value only in the framework of a culturally defined system of values. This is not to say that the importance of the biological fact should be denied but, while this does differentiate between the sexes, it does not decide their social behaviour. The culturalist interpretation of sexual asymmetry goes so far as to overturn the cause-effect link between cultural and biological facts. Indeed, with the concept of 'cultural plasticity' this relationship is inverted: it is man's cultural capacity which elaborates the biological factors and not vice versa. A certain culture, writes Mead (1977: xiv), 'may bend every individual born within it to one type of behaviour, recognizing neither age, sex, nor special disposition as points for differential elaboration'. The strength of this cultural fact, which is capable of forcing most human beings into the suggested models over and above their individual temperaments, serves to explain not only the diffusion of 'female' characteristics among women and of 'male' characteristics among men, but also that characteristics considered to be 'female' in one culture become, in an equally diffuse and 'natural' way, the 'male' characteristics of another culture.

Claude Lévi-Strauss's (1969) position on the problem of sexual asymmetry, as far as one can infer from *The Elementary Structures of Kinship*, is contradictory. Even if he does not deal directly with this theme, it provides the background to his theory on the prohibition of incest. There, Lévi-Strauss maintains that the prohibition of incest marks the precise 'place' of passage from nature to culture, thus constituting the founding act of society. The aim of this prohibition 'tends to ensure the total and continuous circulation of the group's most important assets, its wives and its daughters' (ibid. 479). Thanks to this generalised exchange 'the bond of alliance with another family ensures the dominance of the social over the biological, and of the cultural over the natural' (ibid.). But women, who are defined as the group's most precious good, are also a rare good. In fact, 'this deep polygamous tendency, which exists among all men, always makes the number of available women seem insufficient' (ibid. 38). Polygamy (or rather polygyny), being biologically unfeasible on a universal scale because of the demographic equilibrium between the sexes, becomes a privilege reserved to chiefs: 'the reward for and the instrument of [their] power' (ibid. 44).

Although Lévi-Strauss's overall discourse is about the pre-eminence of culture over nature in human evolution, when we consider the underlying problem of sexual asymmetry, such pre-eminence appears to be contradictory. This feeling arises from the lack of a convincing explanation of why women (and only the women) must circulate in order to weave the structure of kinship on which society is grounded. One has the impression that the groups overseeing this exchange identify with their male element, while women become the objects of this generalised exchange between men. If the woman is the good *par excellence*, the man is the possessor of this good. It remains unclear why man's 'polygynous tendency' is not mirrored by an equally logical 'polyandric tendency' of the woman. In fact, no sexual tendencies at all are attributed to her; she is assigned an implicit passivity which makes her adaptable to the sexual choices of her male counterpart. Equally unclear remains the reason why polygyny should be the distinctive mark of power. This implies not only the existence of a monopoly of power when society is birthed, but also that power itself is gendered at birth (needless to say: male). Woman seems to participate at the founding moment of society – the incest taboo – the 'place' of passage from nature to culture, already laden with cultural meanings that paradoxically exist prior to the birth of culture. This suggests that woman's subordinate condition and her social value are not a fact of culture but of nature, that is, universal. We have already addressed this with the words of Lévi-Strauss.

Lévi-Strauss sees the existence of domination as an undisputed fact in human society, taking a very clear stance on sexual asymmetry. This is hardly surprising, as such is the view of mainstream anthropology. As mentioned, feminist anthropologists have put on trial only 'male' power, forgetting to extend their critique beyond gender. Only libertarian anthropology can hope to undertake an investigation of power as an absolute category, as the cultural unconscious that needs to be made explicit in order to identify the ideological underpinnings of knowledge.

Here, we refer to the work of French anthropologist Pierre Clastres and, more recently, of the American ecologist Murray Bookchin. While they pave the way to a lucid libertarian analysis of human evolution, much is left to do, especially with respect to the problem of sexual asymmetry.

The first theoretical challenge facing libertarian anthropologists was the need to move away from the ethnocentric vision which allows Western culture to project its own hierarchical structure on to all societies, and consider itself as the *only* model of present and past society. To abandon the ideological space of domination in order to understand other societies: this is the categorical imperative of libertarian anthropology. Thanks to this ability to recognise and analyse difference, libertarian anthropology can begin to formulate hypotheses about the origins of domination.

Before embarking on a closer examination of this perspective, let us conclude our review of the existing theories on the origins of sexual asymmetry by touching upon a 'classic' topic: matriarchy. Is it myth or reality?

The controversy around matriarchy has been brought back into sharp relief by the women's liberation movement, which has shown the full utopian scope of the idea of female superiority. Feminist anthropology has taken a more 'scientific' approach to an emotionally loaded topic. All the same, when faced with the ritual question as to whether matriarchy was a myth or an historic reality, feminist anthropology is divided into two opposing camps, like traditional anthropology. One camp declares that there is no concrete historical proof of an archaic gynaecocracy; the other replies with archaeological evidence of a higher status of women, whose implications for the overall social structure are yet to be verified. Already in 1935 Margaret Mead (1977: xviii) wrote that 'there had been and still were matriarchal institutions which gave to women a freedom of action, endowed women with an independence of choice that historical European culture granted only to men'. Far from proclaiming the indisputable existence of a matriarchal regime, Mead supports the idea that the whole archaic matricentric culture (the greatest proof of which is that female-oriented religiosity to which we have already referred) had to be reflected in its related social structure. This hypothesis is strengthened by the fact that, even limiting ourselves to matrilineal societies in history, it is easy to see how the status and the value of women in society are already higher, on average, than in patrilineal societies.

The myriad myths of matriarchy in primitive and archaic societies, demonstrating how the world moved from chaos and social iniquity under women's domination to the order and justice of men's domination (we can easily guess the gender of their unknown authors), are proof of a *new* social order brought by male domination; such order was in need of cultural legitimisation through the production of a justifying myth. This is considered to be the birth of 'male power', as a fact of human history, in contrast with the assumptions of those who consider male supremacy to be a timeless fact (including scholars who think that matriarchy is purely mythical). In reality, those scholars are themselves prisoners of the 'myth of patriarchy', that is, the illusion that patriarchal culture is the only historical reality known to the human species.

For the Italian anthropologist Ida Magli (1978), who can be taken as representative of this trend, matriarchy is not only a myth, but in fact a sexist one. Such a myth is useful for understanding the deep-seated motivations of the society which has created it, less so for increasing our overall knowledge of history. Magli here has in mind anthropologists who, like Bachofen, have revived the myth of matriarchy in our culture, giving it a markedly patriarchal interpretation.*

We recognise some merits to Magli's thesis, yet it seems reductive to dismiss as a sexist myth important evidence pointing toward the existence of a society with a different gendered culture. As many reduce the 'difference' to a matriar-

---

* It was, in fact, Bachofen who first brought the hypothesis of matriarchy back into view with an interpretation that was far from feminist. He interpreted it as a 'state of nature' which was to be followed by patriarchy, identified as the 'state of culture', thus restating the same explanations of archaic myths in modern terms.

chy that perfectly mirrors patriarchy, thus restating the inevitability of domination in social life, we concur with Bookchin (1982: 79) when he says 'here, I must reiterate the point that a "matriarchy", which implies the domination of men by women, never existed in the early world simply because domination itself did not exist'. This statement brings us back to the heart of the problem.

As promised, we have now reached the point where we must untangle the knot of power to come as close as possible to an explanation of sexual asymmetry. We have already seen how sexual differences have assumed asymmetric values under an inegalitarian culture such as that of hierarchical society, and how, due to a methodological approach tainted with ethnocentrism, this society, this culture and this asymmetry have come to be seen as universal realities. We must turn to Clastres to subject this distorted vision to a critique which opens the door into an unknown universe: society without domination.

> We cannot think of western society's ethnocidal inclinations without linking it to this characteristic of our own world, a characteristic that is the classic criterion of distinction between the Savage and the Civilized, between the primitive world and the western world: the former includes all societies without a STATE, the latter is composed of societies with a STATE. And it is upon this that we must attempt to reflect. (Clastres 2010: 107, my capitalisation)*

The absence of a formal, hierarchical political structure had always relegated savage societies to the limbo of apolitical societies, to a primitive stage in human evolution, which is seen as moving inexorably towards the appearance of the State, the symbol of the political maturity of the human species, of 'civilization'. Clastres pits himself against this arrogant conception of evolution, rejecting the apolitical nature of savage societies and showing how they in fact demonstrate a *different* way of conceiving politics. While, in fact, the society of the State 'shows

---

* Clastres laments that these societies are defined in negative terms as societies *without* the State, societies *without* economy, as stated by certain anthropologists that fix these societies at the level of mere subsistence, a hypothesis that has been brilliantly contested by Marshall Sahlins (1972). In reality, these definitions in negative terms denote a limit intrinsic to Western culture rather than any real 'lack' in the societies described; Western culture does not in fact succeed in understanding and defining other societies except by starting from its own reality which is that of domination. The forms of the existing inevitably determine the ways of knowing. For the same reason we should not marvel at the negativity of the term 'an-archy'. Since this doctrine of equality and freedom was born in the cultural reality of domination it is only logical that it hypothesises an alternative that *negates* the present, the existing.

this *divided* dimension unknown to the others', for in societies without a State, 'power is not separated from society' (Clastres 1976: 3).

Political power, far from being absent, escapes the logic of coercion peculiar to divided society and resides in the social body.*

This analysis gives us a new political figure which Clastres paradoxically calls 'the chief without power' – a chief who does not command, whose words do not have the force of law. If the social body is the realm of actual power, we must see him as the realm of virtual power. He personifies social power without possessing it, while society as a whole keeps him under control, aware of the implicit threat that lies in domination and in the division it brings. The thirst for prestige, which is the moving force of the 'chief with power', is held in check by society through a series of obligations, the first of which is a generosity, close to economic self-spoliation, that represents the 'debt' which the 'chief without power' has to society for his particular function. The political significance of this new figure cannot therefore be understood as falling into the category of 'domination' but rather into that of 'social prestige', a concept to which we will return later.

Let us pause to consider the terms 'power' and 'domination' (up to now used as synonyms) in order to avoid their misleading conceptual and terminological confusion. We can refer to the definitions proposed by Amedeo Bertolo in Chapter 4 of this volume. The aim is to disaggregate the 'nebula-power' into its different and often contradictory meanings. Bertolo proposes that the term 'power' be reserved for the social regulatory function (a neutral function in itself). It signifies the totality of the processes through which society regulates itself, producing, applying and enforcing norms. This function is 'necessary, not only to the existence of society, culture and of humanity itself, but also to the exercise of freedom as freedom to choose between determined possibilities' (Bertolo, Chapter 4, p. 73).

By domination, on the other hand, we can understand those hierarchical social relationships which are characterised by relationships of command/ obedience and which distinguish the 'social systems in which the regulating function is exercised, not by the collectivity on itself, but rather by one part of

---

* Let us leave to a later date the evaluation of the complex relationship between social power and tradition in savage and primitive societies. This 'desire to repeat the cosmic order', to use Clastres's words, seems to paralyse the self-regulating capacity of these societies, compelling the entire body social to passively conform to roles and behaviours that it hasn't elaborated. As Bertolo (Chapter 4) says, this is a situation of 'socially diffuse totalitarianism', the influence of which on the problem of sexual asymmetry has yet to be investigated.

the collectivity (generally, but not necessarily, a small minority) over another (generally the great majority); that is, systems in which the access to power is the monopoly of one part of society (individuals, groups, classes, castes . . .)' (Bertolo, Chapter 4, p. 76).

If we apply this fundamental distinction to both historical and primitive societies identified by Clastres, we can define the former as *societies of domination*, in which a part of the social body has ensured its monopoly of power – that is, of the social regulatory function – expropriating it from the other part, and thus dividing society. And we define the second as *societies of equality*, in which power is spread throughout the entire undivided social body. The former are hierarchical societies formed around the relation of command/obedience; the latter are egalitarian societies formed around relationships of reciprocity.

It is implicit that the 'universal' sexual asymmetry found in the society of domination is not a cultural trait of egalitarian societies. In those societies that Bookchin (1982: 44) defines as 'organic', 'notions such as "equality" and "freedom" do not exist. They are implicit in their very outlook. Moreover, because they are not placed in juxtaposition to the concepts of "inequality" and "unfreedom" these notions lack definability.' The idea of difference exists but it is not yet ordered along a vertical axis, as it is in hierarchical societies: 'To such communities, individuals and things were not necessarily better or worse than each other; they were simply dissimilar' (ibid.). Both societies – of domination and of equality – perform the human act *par excellence* by 'patterning bare existence with meaning' (Mead 1977: xvi), but one follows hierarchical values, whereas the other values every person and every thing on the basis of its own uniqueness.

Thanks to Bookchin's work, the fragmentary vision of societies of equality is reassembled into an intelligible organic system, in a comprehensive picture. In particular, with regard to the man/woman relationship, what was implicit in Clastres becomes more detailed and articulated in Bookchin.

Bookchin's image of an egalitarian society (which he situates in the historical epoch of transition from the nomadic conception of life, typical of hunter-gatherers, to the sedentary one of horticultural communities) is one bound together by the blood oath, a society based on the absolute parity of individuals, sexes and age groups; on usufruct and the principle of reciprocity; on the rejection of social relationships based on coercion; on the 'irreducible minimum' (the right to receive that which will allow one to survive, whatever one's own contribution to the life and wealth of the community may be); a society which develops the ideal of *homo collectivus* instead of the concept of *homo economicus*. 'Home' and 'world' are one and the same in this organic society, which is devoid of that fatal split between the public and the private spheres, whose appearance marks the end of a single, undivided community. Both sexes are sovereign, autonomous and independent in their respective spheres of competence which are based on the gendered division of labour. This functional division reflects an economic complementarity and has neither positive nor negative meaning, since an essential role for the survival of the community is attributed to both sexes.

This is a culture of gender parity in which Bookchin (1982: 58), in fact, discerns a prevalence of the female element, to the point of defining it as matricentric.*

> By using this term, I do not wish to imply that women exercised any form of institutional sovereignty over men or achieved a commanding status in the management of society. I merely mean that the community, in separating itself from a certain degree of dependence on game and migratory animals, began to shift its social imagery from the male hunter to the female food-gatherer, from the predator to the procreator, from the camp fire to the domestic hearth, from the cultural traits associated with the father to those associated with the mother.

Ultimately, social asymmetry is alien to this culture, as it is the principle of hierarchy which reshapes society in a pyramidal form, transforming diversity into inequality.

While considerable progress has been made towards explaining how the hierarchical principle has made its mark, that is, in describing how we move from an egalitarian society to one of domination, we are still far from fully explaining why domination originated in the first place. This is uncharted territory, where we must move cautiously, from one hypothesis to another, from one uncertainty to another.

It is worth considering Bertolo's (Chapter 4, p. 86) exploratory idea that '[d]omination could be seen to be a mutation, that is to say, a cultural innovation which, in certain conditions, proved advantageous, in terms of survival, for those social groups who adopted it – for example, for greater military efficiency – and was subsequently imposed as a model either by conquest or by imitation for defensive purposes'.

This cultural mutation slowly invades and conditions the psychology, language and the very unconscious of humankind, reshaping it along inegalitarian

---

* Clastres (2010: 314) agrees with the attribution of an overall feminine stamp to this nonetheless egalitarian culture. 'To state it more clearly: in primitive societies, often marked by masculinity in certain aspects, indeed by a cult of virility, *men are nevertheless in a defensive position in regards to women.*'

lines. Each and every role, behaviour, person or thing is assigned a value, which will determine its position in the hierarchy.

Paradoxically, it is within egalitarian society that we must seek the origin of the process of social transformation leading to domination.* There are at least four phenomena which have, over the course of millennia, broken the unity-totality of egalitarian society, bringing it to the point of crumbling. All form part of the vast and tormented process of *social differentiation* within the single and undivided primeval community, which will eventually give rise to the concept of the individual as opposed to the collectivity. This process does not necessarily lead to the society of inequality, but in combination with the accidental 'cultural mutation' represented by hierarchy, it brought about that society of domination which still prevails today.**

The first phenomenon (without any given order in time or importance) is economic in nature. Demographic growth and increases in productive capacity led to differing degrees of wealth among members of the community. The danger inherent in this individual accumulation of wealth is very clear to egalitarian society, which consciously seeks to prevent it through the practice of usufruct, the gift and the principle of reciprocity (the 'institutional generosity' of the chief without power must be understood in the context of this lucid awareness).

Secondly, egalitarian society is slowly eroded by the progressive crystallisation of social roles. Based on sex, age and descent, sexual roles define individual responsibilities towards the community and fundamentally shape the division

---

* Clastres is of a quite different point of view, denying that there is a necessary logical continuity between the figure of the chief without power and that of the chief as privileged possessor of power and warning not to fall prey to a clumsy, evolutionist logic. On the other hand, it seems to me that it is through just such a process (perhaps not inevitable – but this too has yet to be shown) that humankind found itself prisoner of its own disastrous invention, domination. If it is right to contest the logic according to which the existing is the only possible reality, we must also avoid the reversal of this logic whereby seeing the events of human culture in causal succession is always dire evolutionism.

** One further consideration in this respect: these primitive or savage societies do *not* correspond to the anarchist ideal of the egalitarian society. They do not represent a mythical golden age, the original anarchy to which we must return. And, furthermore, it is unthinkable to propose, in this day and age, a single and undivided community in which the individual would once again disappear. Far from cancelling out the millennia of cultural evolution of the human species, the anarchist conception of the egalitarian society is an attempt at a harmonious synthesis of the binomial individual/collectivity that, throughout the history of the human race, has always seemed unbalanced towards one or other of the poles.

of labour which seems to characterise all human societies. The origins of this division are uncertain,* but they do arise from the need for rational organisation of life and work in the community. We have already seen that the attribution of roles is entirely cultural (with a few well-known but contested exceptions) and so varies enormously. Nevertheless, in every culture, the perpetuation of the same division of roles over long periods eventually ends up crystallising the two sexes and their respective spheres of competence. Such a process of differentiation is institutionalised and inherited through new forms of socialisation. This differentiation also affects the very character structure of the sexes thanks to thousands of years of selection of those traits compatible with the assigned roles (without, however, arriving at a cultural cloning, as the persistence of deviation shows). This crystallisation of roles entails the permanent gendered attribution of certain social activities, like mobility, that play a fundamental role in determining the exclusive appropriation of previously shared social fields.

A third key phenomenon destroying the unity of egalitarian society is the emergence of a public sphere as distinct from the domestic one. This is perhaps the most dramatic split that organic society was to undergo. The emergence of a public sphere does not imply that egalitarian society lacked a social dimension. The public sphere does not come about by parthenogenesis, but by splitting from the sphere that can be defined as domestic only *a posteriori*. As we have seen, in the egalitarian society 'home' and 'world' are one and the same; society is undivided. As differentiation progresses, the unity is broken into two spheres which slowly become estranged until they reach the point of antagonism and disequilibrium that characterises them in the society of domination. Thus 'home' becomes the private sphere of female competence: the sphere of nature, of immanence, of the inessential; the 'world' becomes the public sphere of male competence: the sphere of culture, of the transcendent, of the essential.

---

* Taking up an idea mentioned by Bertolo (Chapter 4), one can put forward the hypothesis, yet to be demonstrated, that the division of roles arises through *cultural imitation* of the instinctual behaviour of those social animals which most closely resemble the human species. Such imitation would also explain why the procreative capacity of the woman and the physical strength of the man have been associated respectively with the maternal role in society and with those roles connected with the monopolistic use of violence. The surprising resemblance between the so-called 'maternal instinct' of the woman and that of the female of many animal species and between the aggressive behaviour of man and of the males of those species could be seen as the result of this process of imitation. It is by no means unthinkable that the human species, having to invent all its cultural forms *ex novo*, turned to the world of nature in search of models to imitate and reproduce.

This is not the place for an in-depth analysis of the chain of phenomena causing the split between public and private. Such a process deserves careful consideration, if we wish to answer fundamental questions about the origins of sexual asymmetry which remain unanswered. Why was it men who appropriated the public sphere? One hypothesis is that by assigning the greater share of domestic work and childcare to the woman, primitive societies left the man free for social activity. Furthermore, conditions such as the greater mobility of men may have favoured extra-community relationships. But we are still far from having found a comprehensive and satisfying answer. And why did the women passively accept a process that made them marginal, ultimately interiorising a conception which undervalued them? We could perhaps resort to Simone de Beauvoir's concept of female 'complicity',* but even this proves insufficient to explain such disconcerting acquiescence. We are faced with crucial and complex questions whose answers can only be found through a collective effort.

In conclusion, when this process of social differentiation comes into contact with domination, the latter will absorb into its hierarchical conception all differences at place in egalitarian society, transforming them into inequalities. When usufruct and reciprocity are replaced by exchange, when political relationships are set against natural ties, when undivided society is succeeded by one ordered around concepts of superior and inferior, egalitarian society and its organic and symmetrical view of the world are dead. Not one but hundreds, thousands of asymmetries will develop within the social body, some tied to biological factors (sex, age, etc.), others to socio-economic factors (artisan against agriculture, intellectual work against manual labour, urban against rural . . .). In short, the society of domination will slowly take shape, and with it the ideological space in which we still live and think today.

---

* In Simone de Beauvoir's (2010: 30) view, there is a certain element of psychological 'complicity' in the subordination of women: refusing to be the Other, refusing complicity with man, would mean renouncing all the advantages an alliance with the superior caste confers on them. Lord-man will materially protect liege-woman and will be in charge of justifying her existence; along with the economic risk, she eludes the metaphysical risk of a freedom that must invent its goals without help. This is an unpleasant and perhaps extreme view of female subordination but nevertheless contains an element of truth. However, as Kathy Ferguson (1983) also maintains, those traits which are often defined as 'female' are those which are typical of subordination, that can be found in all social categories, regardless of sex. Thus the psychological 'complicity' is no longer to be seen as a typically female attitude but rather as a psychological characteristic which is intrinsic to all relationships based on command/ obedience.

The last of the four phenomena contributing to social differentiation is of particular importance: *social prestige*. As a category which is frequently confused with domination, social prestige inhibits the understanding of societies that do not fall within this logic:

> We detect here the rather widespread confusion in ethnological literature between prestige and power. What makes the big-man run? What is he sweating for? Not, of course, for a power to which the people of the tribe would refuse to submit were he even to dream of exercising it, but for prestige, for the positive image that the mirror of society would reflect back onto him celebrating a prodigious and hard-working chief. (Clastres 2010: 202)

We can define prestige as a different, higher valuation that society attributes to certain individuals and/or roles. As such, it is a 'positional good', a privilege in its own right that, in primitive societies, is not connected with other social privileges (economic, political, etc.). Individual prestige is tied to certain personal abilities or gifts, while the prestige attached to certain roles involves the possession of those abilities that are connected with the role itself. Ultimately, what allows us to distinguish domination from social prestige is the relationship of command/obedience, which shapes the former but forms no part of the latter.

Thus any asymmetry of role that, even if informal, involves a command/obedience relationship falls within the realm of domination, while any asymmetry of role, even if formal, which does not involve the command/obedience relationship falls within the ideological space of social prestige. Referring to Bertolo's definitions, we could say that individual prestige, manifested through personal relationships, falls into the category of *influence*, while prestige attached to a role, manifested through functional relationships, falls into the category of *authority* (see Chapter 4). While they are distinct and interact differently with the social body, individual prestige and the prestige of certain roles are two successive moments in the same process of individualisation. However, while the former, which is chronologically first, does not involve the shattering of the egalitarian social order, the latter, which does not cause the absorption and disappearance of individual prestige, goes a step further, succeeding in shifting prestige from the person to the function and thus institutionalising the difference.

Having broadly defined the concept of social prestige, we can now see its relationship to sexual asymmetry. Yet, however convincing and acceptable the picture of egalitarian society outlined here may be, there is one fact which requires deeper examination: when individual prestige is transformed into the prestige attached to certain roles, the high-prestige roles are all male. Two opposing hypotheses are possible here: either the very exclusion of women from these roles implies the existence of domination, or else sexual asymmetry comes about in egalitarian society and precedes the rise of domination.

The analysis of egalitarian society clearly reveals how woman loses social prestige as man acquires it: from a single, undivided society where prestige was equally divided, but in which the culture was predominantly female, to a differentiated society with a predominantly male culture. While initially the groups that 'invented' a prestigious position for themselves, such as the oldest age groups or the shamans (see Bookchin 1982), are made up of men and women indifferently, over time the female element tends to disappear. There is no clean-cut separation in this process, so that even today the social prestige of the old woman is still considerable in certain matricentric societies, just as woman shamans existed in many primitive societies. Nevertheless, in societies preceding that of domination, women disappear from the most valued roles.

The social figures that assert themselves – the chief without power, the shaman and the warrior (see Clastres 2010) – are all male, and when hierarchical culture begins to assert itself, women are excluded from those roles which monopolise political, magic-religious and military power. We could almost say that when prestige is individual, both men and women enjoy it, but when prestige is connected with roles and is formalised, it is exclusively male. Nonetheless (and with this we exclude the first of the two hypotheses), if we accept the fundamental difference between domination and prestige – that is, the presence or absence of the command/obedience relationship – we must admit that the relationship between the sexes is not one of domination. But it is equally clear that we are not faced with a situation of perfect equality. Thus the second hypothesis seems more reasonable.

Turning once again to Bertolo's (Chapter 4) definition, within societies without domination we can find *social asymmetries of authority* which do not fall within the category of domination but still contradict social equality. The man/woman asymmetry of authority seems to fall into this category.

Our expedition has come to an end. Like Livingstone, we have not succeeded in discovering the mythical source. Even if many questions remain unanswered, a map of the explored area is beginning to take shape, if imprecisely. In identifying those social asymmetries of authority between the sexes that precede the appearance of domination, we have cautiously entered the currents of the river Kagera, towards what has conventionally been defined as the source of the White Nile. However, unlike those geographers who have bestowed on the Kagera the honour of being proclaimed the source of the White Nile, we remain convinced that this honour shall go to all the tributaries feeding Lake Victoria.

Leaving aside the metaphor, we do not believe in a single origin of sexual asymmetry. On the contrary, its sources are complex and ramified, just like those of the Nile. And we must search for those sources. Their discovery will provide an essential contribution to the drawing of another fundamentally important map which remains incomplete: the genesis of domination.

To conclude, let me quote a scathing observation attributed to Saint Augustine by Beauvoir (2010: 141) which greatly motivated me during this research: 'A woman is a beast who is neither firm nor stable.'

References

Bamberger, Joan (1974), 'The Myth of Matriarchy: Why Men Rule in Primitive Society', in Michelle Zimbalist Rosaldo and Louise Lamphere (eds), *Woman, Culture, and Society*, Stanford: Stanford University Press, pp. 263–80.

Beauvoir, Simone de [1949] (2010), *The Second Sex*, London: Vintage Books.

Bookchin, Murray (1982), *The Ecology of Freedom*, Palo Alto: Cheshire Books.

Clastres, Pierre (1976), 'La question du pouvoir dans les sociétés primitives', *Interrogations* 7.

Clastres, Pierre [1974] (1989), *Society against the State: Essays in Political Anthropology*, New York: Zone Books.

Clastres, Pierre (2010), *Archaeology of Violence*, Los Angeles: Semiotext(e).

Evans-Pritchard, Edward Evan (1940), *The Nuer: A Description of the Modes of Livelihood and Political Institutions of a Nilotic People*, Oxford: Oxford University Press.

Ferguson, Kathy (1983), 'Bureaucracy and Public Life: The Feminization of the Polity', *Administration and Society* 15: 295–322.

Lévi-Strauss, Claude (1969), *The Elementary Structures of Kinship*, Boston: Beacon Press.

Magli, Ida (1978), *Matriarcato e potere delle donne*, Milan: Feltrinelli.

Mead, Margaret [1935] (1977), *Sex and Temperament in Three Primitive Societies*, London: Routledge & Kegan Paul.

Rosaldo, Michelle Zimbalist (1974), 'Woman, Culture, and Society: A Theoretical Overview', in Michelle Zimbalist Rosaldo and Louise Lamphere (eds), *Woman, Culture, and Society*, Stanford: Stanford University Press, pp. 17–42.

Sahlins, Marshall (1972), *Stone Age Economics*, Chicago: Aldine Atherton, Inc.

Slocum, Sally (1975), 'Woman the Gatherer: Male Bias in Anthropology', in Rayna R. Reiter (ed.), *Toward an Anthropology of Women*, New York: Monthly Review Press.

Stone, Merlin (1978), *When God Was a Woman*, New York: Harvest Books.

Luciano Lanza in Venice, September 1984, as he prepares a press release in the temporary office set up in the bookshop Utopia/2, which also contributed to the organisation of the event.

Giampietro 'Nico' Berti at Venice 1984. Berti was one of the key organisers of the conference.

Amedeo Bertolo (1941–2016) in Campo San Polo, during Venice 1984.

Francesco Codello at the end of the 1970s.

Eduardo Colombo (1929–2018) during the session on 'State and Anarchy' at Venice 1984.

Rossella Di Leo in the 1980s.

Tomás Ibáñez as he intervenes during the session 'Which Revolution?' at Venice 1984.

Roberto Ambrosoli speaking at the session 'Living Anarchy', Venice 1984. To his right are Roger Dadoun (France) and David Koven (USA).

The Venetian designer Fabio Santin designed this lion/Bakunin image as a possible logo for Venice 1984. In a letter sent to Bertolo and Di Leo in September 1983, he explains his idea of morphing Bakunin into the symbol of Venice, the Lion of Saint Mark. While the lion is an 'imperialist symbol' of the Republic of Venice, he ironically explains that he prefers the so-called lion *in moleca* (in the form of a crab) over the military pomp of the lion in full (of which he attached a draft nonetheless).

Part IV: The Pride in Being Anarchists

'I'll do my worst.' Anarchik's paradoxical motto has accompanied the experience of the GAF and all their subsequent initiatives, including *A/Rivista Anarchica, Volontà* and the Centro Studi Libertari. The motto was widely used by Italian anarchists.

11   Towards an Historical and Ideological Appraisal of Anarchism

Giampietro 'Nico' Berti (1984)

First published in *Volontà* 37 (3)

ANARCHISM FINDS ITSELF at a turning point. The forces that birthed it and encouraged its development have faded away, and this cycle seems to be irreversible. Anarchism has lost many of its historical and ideological characteristics with the end of the era in which these grew and took shape. This presents us with a fundamental problem: does the exhaustion of this historical cycle throw doubt on the very identity of anarchism? What is left of anarchism? Is what we are left with still anarchism as we knew it? Provided that these are relevant questions, can we act according to *The Leopard*'s lesson 'For things to remain the same, everything must change'?[1] Can we fully change in order to fully preserve?

I believe that these questions deserve an appropriate answer. What is at stake is the future of anarchism, our own future. These questions provide the 'speculative' background to the utterly arrogant task I have set myself: to trace, in however partial a fashion, an historical and ideological appraisal for anarchism in order to discover a meaning and direction for its future.

The first issue pertains to the very nature of anarchism, as no appraisal is possible without having defined what we mean by anarchism. This is an 'ontological' question, as we are concerned with the *being* of anarchism, with its ultimate and irreducible essence. And here we step into a challenging historiographical problem, as we must identify the origins of anarchism – its original constitutive elements – and its historical phenomenology (not all that has called itself anarchist was in fact anarchist). Hence, defining the kind of anarchism at stake

---

[1] Berti refers here to Giuseppe Tomasi di Lampedusa's novel *Il Gattopardo* (posthumously published in 1958). There, the character Tancredi pronounces the famous sentence 'For things to remain the same, everything must change'.

means to outline quite neatly both its concrete historical form and its ideological nature. This calls for a kind of circular reasoning. On the one hand, we must
'choose' what we want to see in history, and on the other we want to extract
from this history that specific history of anarchism which can ideologically
prove the criterion governing our initial choice. The *essence* of anarchism is not
up in the sky but in the bowels of history: to tell the real history of anarchism,
to point at its historicity, means precisely to uncover its true nature, its essence.
The ontology of anarchism unfolds as a coherent synthesis of historical concreteness and ideological nature.

The ambivalent oscillation between history and ideology – within which the
'ontology' of anarchism unfolds – delimits our methodology, but not yet its
propositional contents. Here comes the first fundamental assertion: we can gain
clarity on the essence of anarchism only by making a fundamental distinction
between anarchism and the anarchist movement, between historical concreteness and its ideal model understood as complete, inclusive and replicable. This is
a necessary epistemological distinction. We are aware of the complexity of these
passages, but I insist on crossing these stormy waters beyond which – the reader
can be assured – safer ground awaits.

To pose the problem of a fundamental distinction between anarchism and
the anarchist movement, between the potentiality of a universal model and the
specific factuality of the real, means to liberate all our capacity to think the universality of this model, as we would like it to be, and simultaneously introduce a
hermeneutic criterion to guide our evaluation of the history of anarchism, that
is, the real history of the anarchist movement.

Let's be clear: we don't want to trample on the most elementary norms of the
most elementary historicism, because we do not crudely place an abstract model
of anarchism out of history. More simply, we build a universal 'ideal' model with
its real constitutive elements – which are, mind you, the constitutive elements
of its origin.

Anarchism

As a schematic outline, we can say that anarchism is the result of multiple inter-
sections between the long wave of secularisation processes and the advancing
'disenchantment of the world'[2] and its two compounding historical events:
the Industrial Revolution and the French Revolution. Anarchism is, and could

---

[2] Berti is hinting at Max Weber's concept of disenchantment ('Entzauberung der Welt')
introduced in his 1917 essay 'Science as Vocation'.

not be otherwise, the cultural peak of this process, marked by a continuously revolutionary dimension, in the widest sense of the term: the total rejection of all authority, human or divine; the critique of the principle of authority at all levels of its historical forms, both given and possible; the critique of both the status quo and its future incarnations. Anarchism is hence situated on the thin frontier separating the extreme fringes of the revolutionary critique from the problematic and ineffable no-man's-land of nihilism.

The origins of anarchism are to be found in the revolutionary dimension inherent to the historical process as it unfolded in Europe in the eighteenth and nineteenth centuries, the beginning of the contemporary era. More precisely, we can see anarchism as the child of the most radical form of the Enlightenment. By its very nature, therefore, it cannot be reduced to this or that starting point, as it was only the concurrent emergence of all these elements that permitted its appearance. In other words, *it is only when secularisation exhausts all its logic* that anarchist culture can appear in its fullest sense. This is why anarchism as we know it was born in Europe at the end of the eighteenth century and the beginning of the nineteenth century. Herein lies its universality too: once the human spirit goes down the path of secularisation, anarchism becomes a completely logical point of arrival. Born at the level of culture, as a universal human creation, anarchism, in its final essence, bears this 'mark of origin'. Thus, the decisive moment in its historical formation came long before the birth of anarchism as a specific social and political movement. *Unlike the anarchist movement, anarchism itself has no class origins.* Its birth, and thus its primary characteristics, cannot be reduced to those historiographic explanations that seek to identify it with the birth of the anarchist movement, deducing in some way its nature and ideological features from the compound and contradictory features of the latter.

What, then, is the 'propositional' content of anarchism, understood as a moment of universal human creation and, specifically, as the logical point of arrival of secularisation? The same content underpins liberalism and socialism, which were equally born out of secularisation. To explain the 'propositionality' of anarchism we need only direct our attention to that *historical genesis of a synthesis* gradually eradicating those elements which proved to be incompatible with their own authentic logic.

Anarchism was born out of the desire to bring together two great principles – freedom and equality. To be sure, it has sought to position itself at the logical confluence of the fundamental questions of liberalism and socialism. It was not by chance that it appeared in the late eighteenth and early nineteenth centuries for it coincided with a consideration of the theoretical, historical and logical limits of the liberal idea and the socialist idea and an ideological elaboration aimed at overcoming the partiality of their principles. From an anarchist stand-point, individual freedom can only be realised through the complete extension of social equality, and social equality can only be truly realised through the complete extension of individual freedom. Thus, in order to realise equality, we must leverage freedom, while to realise freedom we must leverage equality. In order to achieve one, we *must leverage the other*. This necessitates bringing the respective assumptions to their ultimate consequences. In other words, anarchism blames liberalism for being only a partial doctrine of freedom and socialism for being a partial doctrine of equality. This partial nature lies in the fact that both doctrines aim to realise their principles by means of laws – and so of a particular power – whereas anarchism seeks to show that it is only by overcoming the sphere of law that their proposals gain real validity. Anarchism maintains that the shared path to social equality going from the collective to the individual (the idea of social equality) must not be interrupted half-way when equality tends to turn de facto into freedom. When such freedom is extended through the *conditions of equality*, it leads to the establishment of human relations that are no longer dictated by laws of equality, but by the *effects and consequences* descending from everybody's freedom. The path going from the individual to the collective (the idea of individual freedom) must not be interrupted when freedom tends to become de facto equality. When such equality is extended through the *conditions of freedom*, it leads to the establishment of human relations that are no longer dictated by laws regulating the principle of freedom, but according to the *effects and consequences* descending from everybody's equality. The power relations are established through the full development of the conditions (and not dictated by the law) that make their realisation possible. The principles must become facts, and only thus can they exist as principles. However, to become facts, all the consequences of these self-same principles must be fully accepted.

The merging of the two principles in a single, coherent, organic whole is the 'ideal formula' of anarchism. Here we can see how its theory is equidistant from both liberalism and socialism, thanks to the two-fold nature of its doctrine, which is epistemological and ethical at the same time. This is an enormous ambition: anarchism in fact maintains to have forged the epistemological key to complete and real human emancipation. The ethical conditions of freedom and equality – and here the secret lies – *when activated at one and the same time* are intrinsically revolutionary.

In conclusion, we can say that what is to be seen as anarchism in its fullest realisation – what we have called the *essence* of anarchism – is given by the process of secularisation at its highest degree. This process generated the two great ethico-political movements of the contemporary era: liberalism and socialism;

the coherent and radical synthesis of these two has produced anarchism. It is not, however, a simple synthesis, as the two great principles of freedom and equality are to undergo *a radical genetic mutation*, thus becoming libertarian and egalitarian principles. The revolutionary dimension of anarchism and its intimate and irreducible ideological nature is due to the logical and ethical adoption of the two principles of freedom and equality taken, shall we say, by their *roots*.[3] By becoming libertarian and egalitarian principles, they give birth to something different, a revolutionary ideology, that is, anarchism. The intimate and irreducible ideological nature of anarchism lies in this genetic mutation triggered by the logical and ethical endorsement of the principles of freedom and equality, from the perspective of their contemporary activation in a revolutionary sense.

What we have outlined above could be termed the necessary *formal* condition for the definition of what is and what is not anarchist. It is a necessary formal condition – to use an analogy – in the Kantian sense of the term. Just as for Kant knowledge is only possible through the pure, *a priori* forms of space and time, so can we only talk of anarchist ideology if this satisfies, *a priori*, the formal condition of a coherent balance between the demands of freedom and those of equality.

Pivoting around our model, which is both hermeneutic and ideal, we can outline the map of the positive doctrine of anarchism as it unfolded in history and, thus, as it has been propounded and elaborated by thinkers and militants. Without going into a detailed analysis, which would be out of place here, we should remember that the various tendencies produced by libertarian thought in different times, places, traditions and circumstances must rotate on this orbit if they are indeed to be considered libertarian. All of them – through the many possible gradations and variations from the ultra-communist to the ultra-individualist – must partake of this formal condition or they cannot be included in anarchism. On the basis of our 'hermeneutic' and 'ideal' model, we can measure the degree to which the doctrines of Malatesta, Bakunin, Kropotkin, Proudhon and so on were coherently anarchist or not, through formal, *a priori*, distinctions.

The Anarchist Movement

Just as I have extracted the *essence* of anarchism as a universal human creation from its origins, so shall I now draw out the primary historical characteristics of the anarchist movement, understood as a specific social and political movement,

---

[3] The word 'radical' comes from the Latin *radix*, meaning 'root'.

from its origins. Our model provides us with a criterion for discerning what we can consider to have been anarchist. These historical characteristics will allow us to explain the fundamental phases in the concrete history of the anarchist movement.

Here we encounter the first fundamental question. How can we explain the huge discrepancy between anarchism's 'perfect' ideological equidistance from both liberalism and socialism and the anarchist movement's 'objective' historical presence in the wider socialist workers' movement? Does this contradiction obscure the connection between anarchism and the anarchist movement? We could answer with the usual line, with its own merits: history is in itself a contradiction and the translation of a 'perfect' model into reality is not of this world. Such a translation is always imperfect and – as it is in our case – unbalanced. However, it is this very relationship between anarchism's 'unrealised' history, understood in its fullest sense, and the actual history of the anarchist movement that fully reveals the 'ontology' we were looking for, situated at the frontier between ideology and history. To be sure, the connection between anarchism and the anarchist movement is indeed historical and can be summarised as follows: the anarchist movement was born out of the socialist milieu, because in Europe at that time it was the socialist movement which – in theory and in practice – operated in the historical wake of secularisation. But we must be careful: in the wake of secularisation, but with its particular revolutionary version of social transformation.

It is here that we can find a convincing explanation of the troubling connection binding anarchism to the anarchist movement, and the latter to the socialist movement. Let us see how.

Liberalism, socialism and anarchism are historical products of secularisation, and anarchism represents the logical confluence of the fundamental demands of freedom and of equality, and thus the logical point of arrival of this historical phase. Anarchism is ideologically equidistant from liberalism and socialism and we can further substantiate this argument by considering the different attitudes of the three movements towards the process of modernisation sprung by secularisation. While liberalism and socialism have uncritically absorbed the logic of capitalist rationality produced by secularisation (as is universally known, Marxism is nothing but inverted capitalist rationality),[4] anarchism has a more ambivalent stance. It is both the extreme limb of secularisation and its most

---

[4] Berti evokes the critique that Marxism too closely inverts (and thus reproduces the logic of) what it seeks to dismantle. See for instance Jean Baudrillard's *Mirror of Production* (1975) on this.

extreme and radical answer. Indeed, the anarchist movement proved this, as its entire history is nothing but a radical, unambiguous reaction to the disintegration of meaning brought about by secularisation itself.

What is the fundamental character of the anarchist movement, arising out of its origins and surviving unchanged up to the present day? Undoubtedly, this character consists in its ineradicable and contradictory double nature: the anarchist movement is the only movement that has been historically political only in order to satisfy its fundamental ethical demands. The origins of the anarchist movement – born in Saint-Imier in September 1872[5] – mark the origins of a firm yet contradictory denial: anarchism constitutes itself as political, as it denies doing so. The entirety of the political action of the anarchist movement is aimed at negating the political, in the sense that it rejects, *a priori*, any possible management of it. Anarchism, under the influence of the Enlightenment, shares the desecratory and dissolving 'spirit' of secularisation, while the anarchist movement provides secularisation with an answer: a radical, historical break with the Machiavellian tradition resting on the separation of ethics and politics. We might even argue that the secularisation process which began during the Renaissance here comes to an end. The disintegration of meaning produced by the separation of ethics and politics ends with the birth of the anarchist movement, which reacts to this disintegration by re-signifying all politics in an ethical register.

The fundamental 'tablets' of its act of foundation – the famous resolutions of Saint-Imier – are a clear expression of the 'logic of supersedence' produced by the process of secularisation (the political vanguard of the proletariat is rightly seen to be the new vehicle of mystification and domination; the real revolution lies in a 'logic', not in a particular historical subject). On the other hand, they also perfectly expose the major limit of this logic beyond which, evidently, only an ethical dimension can re-give meaning to politics.

In conclusion, we can say that the anarchist movement could only be born within the socialist workers' movement, as this latter operated in the wake of secularisation towards social transformation, in its specific revolutionary version. To be precise (and we must be careful here), with respect to the objective modernisation spurred on by the process of secularisation, the socialist workers' movement was more of a reaction than a revolutionary phenomenon. Indeed, modernisation caused the dissolution of every former social, political,

---

[5] This is a reference to the 'Congress of the anti-authoritarian Sections and Federations of the International' (the First Anarchist International) which was held in Saint-Imier, Switzerland, after the expulsion of Mikhail Bakunin and James Guillaume at the Hague Congress (1872).

economic, ethical codification, and triggered a reaction to such disintegration. The anarchist movement was born within the socialist workers' movement because it was part of this reaction, *although its participation has a double meaning*. Pushing secularisation to its ultimate consequences, it nullifies the Machiavellian divide, thus re-investing politics with an ethical dimension, re-imbuing it with meaning. *Inevitably, such a process of re-signification was based on the 'logic of supersedence' which is typical of secularisation, so that what had been a social and political phenomenon of reaction to modernisation (the socialist workers' movement) became with the anarchist movement a radically revolutionary phenomenon.*

The historical comparison between liberalism, socialism and anarchism will be outlined along these lines. Liberalism and socialism are mirror images of one another because they are unequivocally in the wake of secularisation: the former personifies the rationality of the Enlightenment as it is manifested in the capitalist logic; the latter is a social reaction to the disintegration of meaning caused by the process of secularisation, and later, in its Marxist form, fails to achieve a new meaning, but simply turns that logic upside down. Both are irremediably only a part of history. And anarchism? What about anarchism?

Anarchism released the secularising logic of the Enlightenment into the body social of the socialist workers' movement. As an anarchist movement, it resolved the political in the ethical, thus giving *an autonomous* meaning (not a dialectical necessity) to the social reaction triggered by modernisation and transforming it into radical revolution. As far as it takes full part in the events of history, it divides and re-divides, sometimes presenting a radical critique of secularisation itself, and other times unceasingly activating secularisation's own desecratory logic. Anarchism is *in* history, yet *against* history. The link between anarchism and the anarchist movement and between the latter and the socialist movement is laid bare in the above-mentioned duplicity, which far from being a dialectical ruse is the actual historical nature of anarchism as it materialises in the anarchist movement. Within it, anarchism's equidistance from both liberalism and socialism turns into a dramatic and conflictual division. This very division is key to the 'ontology' set out at the beginning of this chapter, whose development can now be seen as an explanation of its real history.

The Socialist Phase of the Anarchist Movement

Our discussion so far has unveiled the difficulty of applying only pure political categories to the complex historical experience of the anarchist movement. In order to grasp its meaning, we must resort to a variety of disciplines and logics.

Primarily, in order to understand why anarchism has lost (as the entire history of the anarchist movement as a political movement with ethical intentions is the history of a loser devoid of any other destiny), we must evaluate all possible consequences of its structural 'ontological' duplicity, which has, in turn, originated a paralysing division between the ethical and the political.

From this historical-interpretive perspective, an appropriate definition of the anarchist movement could be as follows: the anarchist movement is an ethical subject that moves in a political direction within a social body. It was thus that, for all its multiformity, it existed through the first phase of its history from 1872 to 1917 without major contradictions. The anarchist movement was born as a 'heresy' within the First International (but the internationalist vocation was more anarchist than Marxist) and retained the following fundamental prerogatives up to 1917: internationalism remained revolutionary insofar as the political struggle did not encroach upon and dominate social struggle; revolution – by its very definition – could not be 'postponed' or 'diluted' as neither a 'principle' nor a 'logic' can be postponed or diluted, being an existential posture and way of life; thus it cannot be political, but only social (we are tempted to say universal); there can be no mediation between the 'bourgeois world', with its God, its State and its capital, and the world of the proletariat. What matters in this historical phase are two fundamental characteristics, the first subjective and the other objective. The subjective characteristic pertains to the anarchist movement whose action in history can be reduced to a precise meaning: the application of a particular version of the logic of secularisation whereby social revolution supersedes political revolution. This casts anarchism ever more in the role of the *guardian of an image* (in its own eyes as well as in those of the proletariat) and this image was, naturally, the revolution. The progressive multiformity of the historical process, while nurturing and adding to it more ideological and practical options (mutualism, collectivism, communism, individualism, anti-militarism, communitarianism, pacifism, syndicalism, etc.), did not change its ultimate essence, which remains revolutionary *tout court*. Paradoxically, as anarchism gradually mediated and distilled itself as pure anarchism and revolution (as guardian of its ever 'purer' image in the face of reformist and authoritarian mediations and betrayals), its space in society tended to shrink (with the exception of Spain and, partly, Russia). It emerged prominently when social antagonism got rid of political mediation and became open rebellion (as with various insurrectional or strongly conflictual movements in Italy, France, Spain, Russia, the United States, etc.).

The anarchist resolution of the political into the ethical, the social revolution as universal, human and internationalist, as political and economic, sexual and anti-authoritarian, pedagogical and participatory, Enlightened, planetary and imbued with ethical pathos, did not exhaust its historical possibility, although it reduced it to a 'chance' (this being the precise meaning of insurrectionalism). The key moment is the moment of revolution itself and not its contingent forms, which are imposed by the historical process as mediated through the emergence of new subjectivities.

The objective characteristic can be summed up in a few words; throughout this phase the battleground was divided into two opposing fields: the world of the proletariat and the bourgeois world. Society, as a sociological system, is a single entity, the bourgeois capitalist society which is in turn opposed by one single antagonist, the workers' movement. Within the latter, the anarchist movement and the Marxist movement came into confrontation. Even though the Marxist movement – particularly in its reformist and social-democratic guise – had gained much ground over the years, the struggle remains open and victory does not irreversibly lie in the hands of the authoritarians.

Bourgeois society has yet to be brought down and socialism has yet to be realised. The historical-strategic significance of this entire phase can be summarised in the fact that there were two main subjects, socialism and capitalism, and two subjects competing within socialism, anarchism and Marxism. However, the historical conjuncture never becomes a duel to the death: Marxism and anarchism are subjectively enemies but objectively allies.

The Russian Revolution and its Effects

It was the October Revolution that changed everything, in that it assigned to each the historical role best suited to its genetic character. With the October Revolution the skirmishing between Marxism and anarchism became a duel to the death (to put it simply, anarchism was exterminated) and their radical social and political difference clearly emerged. The anarchist movement found itself displaced on to a new historical ground, with its de facto exit from the socialist camp, although it remained ideologically anchored there. Finally, the overall global balance of power was altered: the battlefield was no longer divided into two but into three – the socialist world, the capitalist world and the revolutionary anarchist movement. From the moment that Marxism won by being the first in the world to realise socialism, anarchism was reduced to a mere distant hope. It is not necessary to state the influence that this victory had on the struggle between Marxism and anarchism; in Russia the proletariat could see the realisation of socialism being transformed from a vague utopia into a concrete reality. The myth was to last for decades, influencing tens of millions of proletarians and cutting the ground from under the feet of the anarchist movement, which lost, in a few years, much of the ground it had won with blood and pain. All Marxists working outside Russia benefited from a status that is yet to be exhausted.

These considerations descend from an historical-strategic point of view. Now we must ask: what was the significance of the Russian Revolution from the point of view of socialism seen as integral human emancipation, that is, from the anarchist point of view?

I believe that this disastrous experience, the true historical ruin of socialism, exemplifies both the meaning of the conflict between Marxism and anarchism and the internal contradictions of the latter (the other and perhaps even more significant example is the Spanish Revolution). The Russian Revolution brought to light socialism's total lack of a political theory suited to its needs. Marxism overcame this lack with the dictatorship of the proletariat which, being unable to declare itself to be what it was, became an ideological demagogy rather than an operational political theory well-suited to its desired end. For anarchism, on the other hand, this was the very reason for the existence of the anarchist movement, which was born out of this very rejection (the secular 'logic of supersedence', in a revolutionary direction, of the universal social revolution which overcomes political revolution, and became the vehicle of a new power). Thus, it cannot be superseded. The Russian Revolution fell prey to the Marxists because the anarchists did not know how to oppose the former's ideological demagogy with an anarchist form of political action. The anarchists' only response to the Bolsheviks' Machiavellian organisation and manipulation of the soviets was to propose a simple generalisation of the self-same soviet system, which is to say virtually nothing. In other words, they did not know how to defend the methodological principle (or one of the principles) of social revolution.

Here, for the first time, anarchists had proof of the deleterious practical effects of a complete resolution of the political into the ethical. Paradoxically, this came at the very moment at which anarchism became the overwhelming victor from a theoretical point of view. Such victory was due to the confirmation of the anarchists' analysis of the primacy of the political over the economic that the Russian Revolution provided: the revolution did not break out in the heart of the capitalist system but in its periphery.

More specifically, it highlighted the decisive importance of political will as a determining factor in a revolutionary rupture. It underscored the relationship between subjective willingness and the historical possibility of realising socialism, a possibility which is independent of the degree of capitalist development and modernisation (as every so-called socialist revolution since the Russian Revolution has infallibly confirmed). Anarchism was also victor for its forecasting of the irremediably totalitarian nature of Marxist socialism as a vehicle of domination of a 'new class' (the 'red bureaucracy') whose power is based not on a juridical-privatist ownership of the means of production but on an intellectual ownership of those means. Finally, anarchism is victor because this power of bureaucracy, which is founded on the totalitarian character of the State, does not come from the elimination of capitalism (as liberal historiography would have it) but from the particular political form assumed by this elimination. It is this 'politicalness' which was the decisive cause of the failure of socialism and the success of the State: Marxists set up the most totalitarian regime in the twentieth century as they obstinately delegated all the chances of socialism to the power of the State.

Hence, for anarchism, the victory of its theoretical reason is directly proportional to the defeat of its practical reason, almost as if everything had been betted on this tragic, paradoxical relationship. To summarise, the matter is as follows: the anarchist movement cannot transform its revolutionary will, which is morphologically political but ethical in its intentions, into an entirely political will that is able to lead the whole revolutionary process (the risk of doing so is to end the spontaneous social dimension of the soviets on which relies its own subjectivism). It is therefore incapable of moving from the negative moment of the revolution-insurrection to the positive moment of its organisation [*gestione*]. It was, furthermore, incapable of successfully inhibiting the Jacobinist/Leninist direction because to do so, in view of the less than favourable balance of power, it would have had to ally itself with other social and political forces that, in the revolutionary context of advanced and almost irreversible socio-economic transformation, were markedly more moderate than either the anarchists or the Bolsheviks.

As we can see from the degree to which the 'spontaneous' social revolution requires 'voluntary' political revolution (the historical condition which proved anarchism to be theoretically right and Marxism wrong), the anarchist movement ended up being its own prisoner. If too great an emphasis is placed on the political (provided that it has had the capacity to do so), it tends to replace social spontaneity (and so, with this substitution, comes into conflict with its own ends). If, on the other hand, the social forces are given free rein and no attempt is made to disengage with political determination (as effectively happened, except for the Makhnovist experience), this ends up, as in Russia, favouring the Bolshevik expansion which was based on the political determination to take over the direction of the whole revolutionary process. Any attempt to halt this Bolshevik advance by an alliance with other forces requires acceptance or at least mediation of a politics aimed at stopping or turning back the revolutionary process. This is obviously repugnant to anarchists as revolutionaries. All in all, to be able to act effectively, anarchism should somehow manage to put aside, at least temporarily, its 'revolutionary extremism', thus renouncing a part of its identity. It should become much less 'ideological' and more 'unscrupulous', that is to say, less ethical and more political.

From Democracy to Totalitarianism

Over the twenty years from 1917 to 1937, all the historical possibilities of the 1872 anarchist movement had been exhausted. An era came to its end. In the socialist world the anarchist movement was physically exterminated; it no longer offered a valid alternative. In the capitalist world it had to face up to the growing totalitarian reaction spreading through Europe (Italy, Spain, Germany, Hungary). The rise of various fascisms or authoritarian regimes severed the anarchist movement from its social base, forcing it into the diaspora of exile and consequently into its organisational disintegration.

Alongside the relentless advance of fascist reaction was the disastrous myth of the Bolshevik Revolution. It was disastrous from a pedagogical point of view, as the working and socialist masses, spurred on by indisputable concrete evidence (the realisation of socialism), wanted to 'do it like the Russians'. Thanks to communist propaganda, the catastrophic idea that the realisation of socialism was combined – indispensably – with the practice of an authoritarian political will was born in the collective popular imaginary. Rather than appearing as a horror, Stalinism became the crystal-clear confirmation of virtue, and the extermination of adversaries, rather than being seen as the destruction of freedom, was ultimately considered to be the indubitable sign of an incorrupt and intransigent revolutionary will.

This myth was disastrous also from a strategic point of view, as it encouraged the proletariat to model its actions on the basis of repetition, rather than acting in accordance with the given historical conditions, as well as with the times and the means suited to its traditions and circumstances. Here too the communist movement played its part by exporting strategies and programmes from Russia in accordance with the dictates of a hegemonic design. As a consequence, the revolutionary action of the masses became more fragmented. The socialist workers' movement split, sometimes irremediably, on these very questions of strategy and modes of operating, all to the good of bourgeois reaction.

In these circumstances the anarchist movement either folded back in on itself under the blows of reaction or became a de facto victim of isolation. By remaining anchored to its firm critical stance on the totalitarian socialism realised in Russia (and what else could it have done?), it had to sever many of its organic ties with the socialist workers' movement. On the other hand, it could not seek support or alliances in the liberal-democratic camp as, while critiquing socialism as it had been realised in Russia, it continued pursuing its revolutionary end. The internal and external effects of the Russian Revolution alongside the mounting fascist reaction in Europe put the anarchist movement in an almost desperate strategic situation: if it wished to remain what it was and preserve its identity, it could neither join the bourgeois camp nor avoid a definitive uprooting from the socialist one. The price it paid for its progressive isolation was all the higher the more it stressed its own 'anarchistness', that is, its 'ontological' duplicity which places it *within* history yet *against* history.

Had the anarchist movement tried to graft itself on to the liberal camp, it would have had to abandon its socialist demands, renouncing its role in that process of re-signification which only socialist culture, with its communitarian, mutualist and communist aspects, could create as a social-revolutionary response to modernisation. By abandoning the socialist workers' movement, anarchism left the wake of secularisation as social transformation.

On the other hand, the price of avoiding total uprooting from the socialist camp was the abandonment of its secularising Enlightenment legacy. This would have meant renouncing the logic of 'revolutionary supersedence' which underpinned its critique of the advent of socialism in Russia as advent of a new power.

In both cases it would have lost its 'ontological' duplicity. By moving towards the liberal camp it would be prisoner of a logic of modernisation devoid of re-signification; it would have remained *within history* by participating in the course of history, but would have been unable to be revolutionarily against it. By remaining within the socialist camp it would have to renounce combining the process of re-signification of the old bourgeois world (the critique of its exploitation and alienation) with the revolutionary logic of the Enlightenment which now situated anarchism *against history*, with respect to the new socialist world.

This is the key to understanding the progressive 'historical erosion' of the anarchist movement in the 1930s, during which it was caught between communist and fascist totalitarianism and liberal democracies. This process of 'de-historicising' the international anarchist movement, which not by chance coincided with the progressive decline of anarcho-syndicalism and revolutionary syndicalism (from France to Brazil, from Argentina to the USA, and from Portugal to Germany), was due to the anarchist movement's progressive return to the core of anarchism. The movement did not take sides because it could not. Thus its revolutionary nature slowly but surely became ideological immobility.

It is in such necessary yet sterile conditions that the movement faced the devastating effects of the Second World War.

The Spanish Revolution

Our interpretation of the relations of anarchism, totalitarianism and democracy in the 1930s does not, of course, apply to Spain. There, this historical situation did not arise, as the anarchist movement prevailed over the virtually insignificant communist element. It was, however, the Spanish Revolution that raised this logic to its highest level, thus bringing the era that began in 1917 to an end.

A great and unique chance – this is what we could call the Spanish Revolution. True. It was equally a chance to bring to light, in a tragic scenario, the historical and tactical problems of the struggle for emancipation without any of these having been resolved by the end. Spain between July 1936 and May 1937 was the peak of the century-long struggle for human liberation; at the same time, it was the tragic confirmation of anarchism's inability to resolve the problem of the relationship between ethics and politics. Such inability is responsible for the split within Spanish anarchism between its *political representatives*, sitting in the Catalan and Madrid governments, and the living *social formations* of the autonomous collectives. While one part of anarchism became pseudo-State (an anarchist surrender to politics without a suitable political theory or strategy), the other became social revolution (yet without a viable political strategy for defending the achievements of the revolution). From here, a tragic, paradoxical situation arose: the anarchist political involvement in the government merely served to give 'revolutionary' legitimacy to the State, while at the same time, and for the same reasons, destroying anarchism's own legitimacy. Similarly, the immense social force of Spanish anarchism, especially in Catalonia, proved to be incapable of political action in defence of the social revolution.

At this point, we may well ask why the anarchist movement in Spain was not fully revolutionary (had it been, its representatives could never have joined the government) whereas the Russian movement was 'too much' so. In 1936 we see a primacy of 'historical times' (that is, the 'realistic' consideration of the given social conditions, with the principle of reality prevailing over that of utopia) over 'revolutionary time(s)' (a revolutionary evaluation of reality), whereas in Russia it was the opposite. Yet, the result in both cases was the same, as Marxist counter-revolution triumphed. Why so?

It seems to me that the answer lies in the fact that, in Russia, the anarchist movement was not majoritarian, hence it could not even think of managing the overall revolutionary process. In Spain, on the contrary, the movement was majoritarian and hence in a position to take on that responsibility. What had already emerged in Russia emerged even more clearly in Spain: the lack of political judgement entails the lack of historical judgement; the inability to use one's force strategically with 'unscrupulousness' does not bring about the victory of ethics over politics but rather the contrary. Moving immediately from an ideological evaluation to a political one – an automatism that implies an evaluation which is 'indifferent' to the various forms of power, be it liberal, communist, democratic, Fascist, Nazi and so on – is never a winning strategy.

How, then, coming back to Spain, should we explain the anarchist participation in the government? The only way that I can see is to go back to political categories.

Spanish anarchism became the State because it inherited the unresolved question of the political in a politico-military context which offered no alternative. The anarchist presence in the government was a compromise, one which clearly revealed the political impotence of the anarchist movement born in 1872. To be more exact, it is the fear of bringing the logic of social revolution to its end. This implied a radical and irreversible break with all existing political forces. Such a break could be actualised only by resolving the immense social force of Spanish anarchism in a self-determining political will ready to take on the direction of and the responsibility for the whole revolutionary process. From 20 July 1936 onwards, the anarchists in Catalonia could have done it, but they did not. They did not because they did not know where they should politically begin.

The dilemma 'anarchist dictatorship' or 'democratic collaboration' is a false dilemma to the ends of social revolution. Without a political theory and strategy for either situation, that is, neither for the complete direction [gestione] of the revolution nor for defending its gains, anarchism was doomed to defeat. Without a political theory and strategy for the revolution, 'anarchist dictatorship' would have become a 'revolutionary totalitarianism' with one of two results: the return of the moderates or communist takeover. The result of the 'democratic collaboration' in 1936–37 is well known: the moderates were manipulated and the communists eventually took over.

To the question 'could it have ended differently?' we must answer: no. It could not have been different for the same reason that the relationship between anarchism, totalitarianism and democracy could not have been different.

The anarchist movement in Spain was caught between the political moment of its pseudo-presence in the government (I repeat 'pseudo' – because the 'anarchists' in the government remained, after all, anarchists) and the social movement of collectives. If the social element were decisive in determining the effective productivity of a revolution (which it is not), we have to ask why the anarchists of the collectives did not prevail over political anarchism sitting in government. The answer is simple: in the end it is always the political (the concentrated use of the collective force for a certain end, as Proudhon teaches us) that decides, rather than the 'social' (the spontaneous but inconclusive expression of the 'collective force' itself). All forms of human will, including the revolutionary one, are expressed through politics above all else. So it can be said that at that very moment when, in September 1936, the anarchists entered the government in Catalonia, the revolutionary image of anarchism in the collective popular imaginary died, and it was not, or hardly, reborn in the revolutionary action of the heroic anarchism of the collectives in Aragon, in the East and in Catalonia itself.

To complete our explanation of Spanish anarchism's division into its political and its social moments, we must return to the relationship between totalitarianism, democracy and anarchism. The increasing 'anarchistness' of the anarchist movement in the 1930s – which, as we have seen, affected its relationships with totalitarianism and democracy – did not occur in Spain, or only occurred marginally. Who would wish that Spain had undergone an integral process loyal to the anarchist core of anarchism, and acted with revolutionary intransigence in the face of communism and liberal democracy? Who considers the 1937 anarchist surrender to the communist counter-revolution to be sheer folly, as it indeed was? It was not the Spanish anarchists (with a few exceptions) but the diaspora of anarchists who were exiled by the split between totalitarianism and democracy. Spanish anarchism never became anarchist to its core, as it suffered from the disastrous myth of the popular front, the strong religious anti-modern element of its social base. It hampered the extension and assimilation of the secularising logic which is essential if anarchism is to be *in* history and yet *against* history, that is, if anarchism is to be revolutionary despite any imbalance between its Enlightenment-liberal and socialist-communitarian components.

The tragedy of the Spanish Revolution was also the tragedy and the end of the anarchist movement born in 1872. The years up to the 'turning point' of 1968 brought no substantial changes to the irreparable situation caused by the defeat of the Spanish Revolution. The anarchist movement did not undergo a real generational shift because its isolation grew even bigger after 1945; it was solely *against* history and with such sterility as to be placed *outside of* history.

The Anarchist Analysis of Power

As we have seen, anarchism's 'ontological' duplicity, its being both *in* and *against* history, explains the origins of the anarchist movement which was born on a wave of revolutionary, secularising 'supersedence' of Marxism, in which it sees the creation of a new history through a new power. Ultimate power, in its pure form, was founded on the intellectual ownership of the revolutionary process: within the radical immanence of secularisation, Marxism re-deifies the revolution, endowing it with the principle of authority through the party, which became the source of a new political power (as Leninism, the inevitable result of Marxism, demonstrates).

We must equally stress that anarchism's 'ontological' duplicity – as criterion for the historical explanation of the origins of the anarchist movement and, conversely, the authoritarian nature of Marxism – underpins its scientific thought and ideology. From a theoretical standpoint, being *in* history and yet *against* history means to enable the scientific analysis of history in order to oppose it. We can see here the structural difference of the two levels – to be in history (which means to analyse a given historical process) and the being against history (which means to elaborate, if necessary, ethico-ideological ends in contrast to that process). It recalls, by analogy, the heterogeneity between the 'ethical nature' of the end that is sought and the 'political nature' of the means employed to achieve it, a heterogeneity which feeds its revolutionary tension. The revolutionary dimension of anarchism, which is *revolutionary insofar as it is ethical*, lies entirely in this tension/conflict: to inform the means with ethics.

However, while in praxis anarchism seeks to integrate its means and ends ideologically – and this has been the cause of its recurring subordination and political impotence – in its theory it rejects the idea according to which ideological ends are deducible from scientific analysis and vice versa. On the theoretical and ideological planes, anarchism has won over both Marxism and liberalism thanks to this difference between theory and praxis and to the epistemological division within its theory. We can only hint at this point here, so we shall limit our analysis to anarchism and a few comparisons.

The epistemological division within anarchist thinking does not stretch throughout all anarchist thought: we can certainly find anarchist or libertarian writers who, consciously or unconsciously, mix the two planes. Nor is it always possible to think scientifically without any ideological interference. Still, the search for this dividing epistemological tension is destined to remain open, as it lies at the core of anarchist thought. It is through this duplicity that anarchism becomes radically free and universal. It is radically free because it has no form of integralism: the ethical and the historical planes are not required to coincide, neither is freedom required to coincide with scientific truth, nor scientific truth with the totality of human experience. The logic of freedom prevails. Anarchism is also radically universal because it is through this epistemological divide that it establishes what we can call 'revolutionary transcendence', that is, its infinite renewal. If ethics is not necessarily deduced from historical experiences of power, it can be continually reformulated according to a new revolutionary will.

Thus the division between ideology and science brings anarchism to a decisive point: it allows the continual reformulation of its ethical outlook and at the same time the continual scientific reformulation of its theory. Anarchism can abandon its former scheme of scientific analysis if it considers it to be outdated, without renouncing its ideal ends. Here the divide between science and ethics has brought us forcibly to the very core of anarchist thought around which pivots the relationship between the analysis of power in its individual historical formulations and the analysis of power as such. Once again, its 'ontological' duplicity emerges strongly because, while the analysis of particular historical forms of power reflects a use of scientific analysis *in* history, the analysis of power as such is 'metaphorically' *against* history.

The difference between the scientific critique of a particular historical power and the scientific and ideological critique of power as such recalls, respectively and analogically, the diversity between the analysis of exploitation and that of inequality. The former is always the analysis of a precise historical reality whereas the latter is an inquiry into the structural causes of the reproducibility of power. Just as a specific historical power is a particular and mutating expression of the logical reproducibility of power as such, so is the historical form of exploitation a particular and variable expression of the reproducibility of inequality. From a theoretical point of view, this explains anarchism's radical difference and opposition to Marxism. From this standpoint, anarchist thought developed its view on capitalism as one of many historical variables of inequality. Capitalism is not the structural cause of inequality and oppression, but the most recent and historical form of it, descending from the economic logic of modernisation.

For anarchist thought, bourgeois ownership is a phenomenological form of power. Even better, every form of ownership expresses one of the many phenomenological forms of power. Thus all the possible forms of ownership – from the economic to the intellectual – express all possible historical forms of power, while this latter reproduces itself as inequality. Hence, if property is an historical variable of inequality as reproduced by power, in order to understand the root causes of exploitation we must develop a science of the reproducibility of power and its fundamental laws, rather than an analysis of property in its capitalist form. Now we can better understand why a branch of anarchist theory specialising in political economy is missing (except for Proudhon, although he too prioritises a sociological understanding of power), as well as the deep-seated difference from Marxism (which remains a mere revolutionary critique of political economy).

At this point we can equally make a comparison with liberal thought with regard to the effective realisation of freedom. For anarchism, economic ownership as embodied in capitalist relationships of production can always be reduced to an historical phenomenology of power, as every form of property is a phenomenological expression of power as such. When property is identified as a form of power, it takes on this essential nature, that is, it is a social relationship, an intrinsic power relation. As a balance of power, property (and here the liberals are right) cannot be eliminated. The balance of power can be modified and adjusted but, short of bringing society to an end (as utopian Marxism and the naive undercurrent of anarchism would like), it cannot be overcome.

For freedom to be realised, property must be 're-distributed' (as Marxism argues in the guise of elimination), but in order to 're-distribute' property we must also 're-distribute' the power which is attached to property. This is why the *actual* redistribution of property, in its connection with an *infinite redistribution of power* – up to the limits imposed by the attainment of equilibrium in the balance of power freed from any legalistic dimension – is unacceptable to either Marxism (revolutionary critique limited to political economy) or liberalism (contradictory and de facto impossible extension of 'classical' political economy).

Freedom: Cause or Effect?

Thus we come to the issue of the governing principle of socialist, liberal and anarchist thought. Even if briefly, we maintain that the difference between anarchism, liberalism and socialism lies in the fact that only the first treats freedom as the governing principle of its entire theory, whereas for the remaining two freedom is the effect of an historical cause.

For liberalism, freedom is realised by the degree to which it serves the growth of civil society, yet freedom is not its governing principle. The governing principle of liberal civil society derives its epistemological premises from classical political economy, which asserts that freedom is attained through the preservation of property. Since property cannot be extended to everyone, it follows that freedom cannot be made universal. On the contrary, the inevitable necessity arises to defend the freedom of the holders of property by means of political power, that is, the State. The division between civil society, where freedom exists through property, and the State, where freedom is brought back to its 'functionality', therefore remains impossible to bridge.

With socialism, things change only marginally. For socialism, the realisation of freedom goes hand in hand with the extension of the socialist economic bases and their ability to overturn and overcome the bourgeois ones. In communism, the final stage of socialism, the contradictions which liberalism poses between citizen and bourgeois are declared to be resolved. Still, also here the governing principle is not freedom, as the epistemological premises of socialism lie in the revolutionary overturning of classical political economy. Communism postulates the realisation of freedom in the irreversible overcoming of the economic, in transcending economic laws *tout court.*

Thus, in a deep-reaching analogy between them, socialism and liberalism see freedom as an historical achievement and, specifically, as the final product of a process of modernisation. *For socialism and for liberalism, freedom is an effect of causes which are not 'ontologically' intrinsic to freedom itself.* The epistemological premises underlying the 'constructive' strategies of both socialist and liberal societies differ in nature from their theory-informed end goal. This explains why, in both socialism and liberalism, the nature of the means ends up in deep-seated contradiction with their end, and subsequently why the Political dimension, that is, the State, domination, is unavoidable to them.

At this point the abyss separating them from anarchism becomes clear. They are very far from seeing the realisation of freedom as an end in itself, to be pursued for itself without any other justification (historical, economic, political, social, etc.). They are therefore light years away from conceiving of and practising freedom as *the criterion for discriminating everything and between everything* and thus as governing principle of all human conduct, whether individual or social, political and economic, ethical and aesthetical, productive and recreational, sexual and amorous. They are in no way 'fanatical lovers' of freedom, as is anarchism by its 'ontological' nature.[6] Socialism and liberalism place freedom *in* history, as an effect of modernisation, whereas anarchism places it *against* history, as a cause of modernisation. They are 'univocally in this world' while anarchism is 'doubly' so; this is why, in short, they can never be downright revolutionary. At most, they can vaguely indicate, from the camp of authority, the borders beyond which the ground of freedom stretches away into infinity. But they cannot, without annihilating themselves, cross the 'threshold' which divides the authority principle from that of freedom.

Anarchism remains the supreme guardian of freedom in the modern world. In the last century, only anarchism has unceasingly identified the principle of

---

[6] Reference to Bakunin's (1998: 17) famous description of himself as a 'fanatical lover of liberty'.

authority as the governing principle of society and as the root cause of every defeat of human emancipation (over and above those social, economic and political gains achieved), if emancipation is taken to mean the realisation, to the highest possible degree, of freedom and equality. Only anarchism has identified the State – which incorporates in its very principle all existing authoritarian forms of any historically given society – as the great obstacle in the way of emancipation, the rock on which any intentions of regeneration are shattered, regardless of whether they are motivated by a passionate utopian dream or by a cold scientific project. Only anarchism with its dual theory – on the one hand the critical analysis of a particular historical power and on the other the ideological induction of power itself (the latter 'orienting' the former) – has declared that freedom is a 'metaphysics' before being the object of a possible economic, social or political science. This opens up its value to a double use: to a scientific use, because the theory of freedom, not being ultimately anchored to any theory, has been able to be corrected and recorrected *ad infinitum*, à la Popper; and to a human use, because it has given a voice to all the 'rebels' of this world, all those who reject any conformity, to the 'unsettled' ones of every generation (it is thanks also to this human 'abuse' of freedom that there has remained an historical possibility of freedom in this world in defiance of every massifying totalitarian tendency).

In the end, what has been easily dismissed as anarchism's naive and inexperienced 'idealism', its 'scientifically simplistic' theories, and the 'extremism' of its proposals, has won hands down, as the 'harsh reply of history'[7] has confirmed,

---

[7] In the Italian context this phrase was popularised by the philosopher Norberto Bobbio (1909–2004). The section 'The state as an unnecessary evil' in his book *Democracy and Dictatorship: The Nature and Limits of State Power* (University of Minnesota Press, 1989, first published in Italian in 1978) reads: 'The most popular of the theories that supports the realizability and even the necessary advent of a society without a state is Marx's, or rather Engels's on the reasoning which, reduced to its barest, can be laid out like this: the state develops from the division of society into classes opposed (because of the division of labour), with the intention of allowing the class on top to dominate the class below; when, following the conquest of power by the universal class (the dictatorship of the proletariat), class divided society will disappear, so will the necessity of the state. This is perhaps the most ingenious theory amongst those that defend the ideal of society without the state but it is no less debatable for that. Neither the major premiss of the syllogism (the state is an instrument of class domination) nor the minor premiss (the universal class is destined to destroy class society) have resisted that formidable argument which is, as Hegel would have said, "the harsh reply of history"' (1989: 131). Bobbio is citing the Italian translation of Hegel's (translated from 1954: 389) *Elements of the Philosophy of Right* – 'words are silence before the earnest

over every other well-intentioned proposal of emancipation which has never-theless featured the principle of authority.

This is the issue around which anarchist thought has always struggled. An almost paradoxical contradiction seems to permeate its logic: the ethical foun-dation of its ideology, and its near obsession with the problem of the Political. Indeed, the explanation of reality always ends up being subsumed under this category, as anarchism always relates the complexity of reality to one univocal, decisive explanation: domination. In their pure states, politics and domination can be reduced to one another: there can always be economic, social, cultural, racial, psychological and religious domination, but *domination as domination* (that is, the *fact of dominating* and of *acting to dominate*, over and above its specific economic, social, cultural, etc. forms) is always, and above all, political. What was – and still is – theoretically crucial for anarchism is the obsessive reflection on the relation between politics and domination. Such reflection has led anarchism to synthetise the two 'concepts' under the notion of the 'authority principle' and to identify this notion with an existing and logically coherent reality, as it is personified in the supreme image, the ultimate essence, the fun-damental function of the modern world: the State.

Just as the anarchist movement is an ethical subject which moves politically within the body social, so we can equally say that anarchist theory is ethical thinking that reflects on the Political with the aim of overcoming it within the broader solution, which is called freedom. This is, however, extremely diffi-cult because of the 'ontological' differences between domination and freedom. Domination, being the governing principle of the existing reality, is finite in the sense that a description of what exists suffices for a description of all its possible ways of being. Freedom, on the contrary, does not enjoy this 'physical' prerogative. It remains the governing principle of an ethical will which seeks to overturn, or, better, overcome, the existing reality. Thus, it can never be fully described. The immediate description of freedom is in fact negative, as by freedom we mean the absence of domination. Furthermore, freedom is in itself 'incommensurable' as it has, and can have, no end, be the exploration of freedom economic, social, religious, racial, sexual, amorous and so on.

repetitions of history'. The difference between the Italian and English translations is due to the fact that the Italian translation used by Bobbio renders the German word *Widerholungen* ('repetitions') with the Italian word *repliche*, meaning both 'replies' and 'repetitions', or copies, with an intended ambiguity. Special thanks to Luca Albani for helping to solve the puzzle of the translations.

The lack of a political theory of anarchism as positive anarchism (federalism is not yet anarchism) is directly related to the understanding of the nature of domination, which is political. It seems that anarchism can have no political theory, as this would cancel its *raison d'être*. This is its past and current impasse. Yet, this has not prevented anarchism from emphasising, through this difficulty, the historical problem of emancipation.

Indeed, we have seen how important the unresolved relationship between ethics and politics has been in the history of anarchism. The fact that this cannot be solved – the trait of being unresolved is the *raison d'être* of the anarchist movement – is the reason why anarchism became the anarchist movement. Looking deeper, it is necessary to say that this contradiction, which has so far proven insoluble, has been part of both the anarchist movement and the idea of freedom itself. As the Spanish experience teaches us, the unresolved relationship between ethics and politics is nothing but the hard problem of defending freedom by means of freedom. While anarchism as a universal theoretical model is a balanced play of the needs of the individual and those of society, anarchism as a system of thought reflecting on the historical problem of human emancipation is an immensely difficult theorem which seeks to extract from an ethical end those and only those means that are coherent with it, in form, logic and content. This theorem is immensely difficult, *almost impossible*, because while the end is, by definition, purely ethical, the means are, and cannot be otherwise, always and above all historical, which is to say 'political'. Means and ends are thus structurally heterogeneous. However, should anarchism seek to even partially attenuate or renounce the ethical nature of its end, it would fall inexorably into one of the two parts of its positive doctrine, according to the historical context. In other words, it would end up being either a more radical form (or a further stage) of socialism or a more extreme form (or a further stage) of liberalism, because in attenuating or renouncing the ethical nature of its end, *it would lose that revolutionary tension* which makes it radically and 'genetically' different from both.

The reason for anarchism's historical defeat has also been the reason for its ideological victory: as it sticks to its objective of full human emancipation, against history, it was and is left with no choice.

To be sure, the reasons for its ideological victory are the same as for its theoretical victory, as the conditions of its historical defeat must be explained by an obstacle, or rather a 'self-made political obstacle'; the anarchist movement could not be totally political because this would have weakened its ideological rightness. And, on the other hand, its ideological rightness has shown, through its political defeat, that the historical problem of emancipation can only be resolved through the elimination of politics. Human emancipation means the overcoming of politics, which means the elimination of power, which, to be epistemologically more precise, means the elimination of domination. Either way, we are left with the problem of politics. Anarchism was proven right by its defeat, provided, of course, that we truly aim at emancipation.

References

Bakunin, Michael (1998), *Marxism, Freedom and the State*, London: Freedom Press.

Baudrillard, Jean (1975), *The Mirror of Production*, St. Louis: Telos Press.

Bobbio, Noberto [1978] (1989), *Democracy and Dictatorship: The Nature and Limits of State Power*, Minneapolis: University of Minnesota Press.

Hegel, Georg Wilhelm Friedrich [1820] (1954), *Lineamenti di filosofia del diritto*, trans. F. Messineo, Bari: Laterza.

12 Banality and Iniquity: Some Objections to Anarchism

Rossella Di Leo (1996)

First published in *Volontà* 3 (4)

THE OTHER DAY, while waiting my turn at my local bakery, I had an exciting close encounter with Signora Maria herself,[1] one of the major 'opinion makers' [in English in the original] of the (very virtual) television democracy established by late modernity. The aforesaid lady entertained a small but engaged public with comments on foreign policy which, needless to say, concerned the Albanian situation,[2] quickly identified as one of the few existing forms of 'anarchy'. Abandoning my inveterate habit of avoiding these daily talk-shows, I tried to remind Signora Maria and her audience that the Albanian events have very little to do with an ethical-historical-socio-political-etc. definition of the term 'anarchy'. Never have I regretted my actions so quickly. Feeling myself like an unwanted 'migrant of thought', I hastened away from the embarrassed and perplexed agora, baguette under my arm.

---

[1] 'Signora Maria' is an expression used to signify mainstream opinions.

[2] Following the collapse of communism in Albania in 1990, many Albanian people decided to leave the country. Given the geographical proximity, and the fact that many Albanians could speak Italian (mostly thanks to television), Italy was the most popular destination. In the weeks following the overturn of the regime in March 1991, thousands of people reached the harbours of Puglia on overcrowded boats, fuelling the proliferation of discourses on an 'invasion'. Those arriving in March 1991 were granted the status of refugees thanks to a special provision of the Martelli Law. A different scenario occurred for those arriving in August 1991, as by that time Albania had a democratically elected government and it was argued that they could no longer be treated as refugees fleeing a repressive regime. The Italian government classified them as illegal immigrants and initiated several repatriation operations.

This is the way of the world, I told myself. Yet that mixture of clichés, enervating banality and bestiality is the mainstream idea of what anarchy is about. How could such a strong ethical conception, a sophisticated social theory, a grandiose utopian vision, be so ignored and distorted to end up being identified with its opposite? Signora Maria (and the press with her) define as 'anarchic' a society characterised by a weak or absent central power – we could agree to this to some extent – and at the same time a constant struggle between subjects for the conquest of power. This interregnum phase, this struggle between competitors operating within the same social conception – that of hierarchy – is labelled in the crude political language of Signora Maria (and the press) as 'anarchy'. It is with this interpretative key that, in the specific Albanian case, we should explain statolatry-bureaucracy,[3] ultraliberal lobbies, the emerging drug cartels and traditional bandits, the tribal clans of the South and those of the North . . . In short, it is truly ludicrous to identify semblances of anarchy in the Albanian situation (if not for some questionable and dubious traces of direct democracy), while what we are witnessing is a classic feature of human history from the Neolithic onwards: a conventional hierarchical dynamic for the appropriation of exclusive social power.

Of course, I am only pretending to be surprised by the misinterpretation of anarchy as chaos, a distortion so established that it is an etymologically codified meaning. This has originated a rather funny linguistic paradox: in our dictionaries two opposite and legitimate meanings coexist in the span of a few lines, from a social doctrine based on self-government to one of chaos due to the absence of a constituted central power. What a semantic jump! As if under the term 'Catholicism' we could find the secondary meaning 'systematic persecution of the non-conformist', or for communism 'mass prison system'. Unthinkable, isn't it?

Yet, from this etymological paradox descends the most common objection to anarchist social theory: 'if no one is in charge, how do you make things work?' The question is ostensibly pertinent, and therefore requires an answer.

The Authority of the Steam

The subheading refers deliberately to a well-known exponent of 'scientific socialism', Friedrich Engels, who in 1872 wrote a critical essay on anarchism

---

[3] Statolatry (a compound word combining *state* and *idolatry*) is a word used by Antonio Gramsci in his *Notebooks* in 1932. It was popularised in the essay 'Doctrine of Fascism' published in 1931 and attributed to Benito Mussolini, but in reality ghostwritten by the philosopher Giovanni Gentile.

entitled 'On Authority'. It was the time of the First International, when social-ism had to choose between authoritarian and libertarian paradigms. Many things have changed since then, and today, when the only remaining 'scientific' thing is *scopone* [a variety of the Italian card game *scopa*, named 'scientific scopone'], it might seem superfluous to wander among these relics of modern-ism. And, indeed, it would be, if in the socialist vulgate (and beyond) Engels' shoddy considerations had not been metabolised as common knowledge. Truly common because, right and left, statists and liberals, spiritualists and materi-alists and so on all share the same view, one that confuses – terminologically and conceptually – heterogeneous social criteria such as power, domination, authority and influence.

For Engels (1972), the 'authority of the steam' was an appropriate metaphor to expose those 'objective' limits against which libertarian frenzy can do noth-ing, limits that dictate the exercise of authority. But what is authority? Let's go into detail, into that dark night where all cats are grey: grey is social hierarchy, indistinguishable from thermodynamics; grey is the command/obedience rela-tionship, as inexorable as the force of gravity. In this primordial darkness, power and domination are synonymous, and so are deciding and commanding.

So, let's try lighting a match and see if all cats really are grey. As someone has already done this (Bertolo, Chapter 4, p. 79), I quote:

> To sum up, I have identified four conceptual categories which both common and scientific language put or can put under the same umbrella-term: *power*. I then proposed to limit this term to the first category: the social regulatory function, the sum of those processes through which a society regulates itself by producing and enforcing norms. If this function is carried out by only one part of society, that is, if one privileged (dominant) sector has a monopoly of power, it gives rise to a second category, to a set of hierarchical relationships of command/obedience, which I propose to call *domination*. Finally, I proposed the term *authority* for those asymmetries of roles which cause asymmetries of reciprocal determination, and *influence* for those asymmetries arising from personal characters.

Light enough, therefore, to notice that cats are only grey in darkness. A com-fortable darkness, if one wants to pass off as analogous very different social functions. This deliberate confusion of terms and concepts has been (and is) necessary for imparting the hierarchical principle – that is, the principle inform-ing society and the collective imaginary, including representative democracies – justifying (and concealing) it behind functions and skills and abilities that are necessary and desirable for social functioning. 'Taking decisions' is intrinsic to any social entity: without this regulatory function, no society – whether large or small – exists as such. But to infer that the decision-making process can only move along a socially determined vertical axis takes a step too far. To accept that a role is useful – usually symbolised in hierarchical iconography by the notorious figures of the orchestra conductor or the 'technical expert' – does not mean accepting the sacredness of this role and the privileges attached to it. And if skills are welcome – as already stated by a 'founding father' (Bakunin 1970): who questions the authority of the bootmaker in the matter of boots? – they do not justify the establishment of a political arena separated from society and managed by an autonomous class of experts with their own goals (and who may well decide who should wear boots and who should not). Furthermore, stepping into the interplay of *temporary* asymmetries – adult-child, teacher-student, or those linked to personality traits – does not legitimise the enforcement of *permanent* asymmetries such as those that exclude from privileged knowledge or access to power when this regulatory function is the monopoly of one part (whether the majority or minority) of society.

I insist: it is laughable to justify domination on the grounds of the second law of thermodynamics, or to invoke the expertise of the engineer in carrying out his duties to justify the delegation of the social decision-making process. It is equally laughable to theorise, as some do, a sort of social original sin that finds its remedy in the institution of a hierarchical order. Behind these effective honey traps hide specific choices dictated by opposing worldviews: those (most) who accept the hierarchical principle and those ('there is not one in one hundred, and yet they exist'[4]) who reject it.

This peculiarity has placed anarchism outside modernity, despite it being its bastard son; at its beginning anarchism was accused of being pre-modern, only to be rediscovered as postmodern later. Anarchism has been modernity's great repressed, a ghost that has accompanied its entire history while remaining both a stranger and a point of reference, because its new paradigm constitutes the alterity against which modernity has defined itself. Modernity has developed around the two pairs order-disorder and rationality-irrationality, attributing in each instance the former to itself and the latter to the libertarian paradigm. The project of modernity, deeply imbued with authoritarianism (in both its totalitarian and democratic forms), aimed at the construction of a rational social order that placed in the State-form, the modern paradigm of hierarchy, the centre of its organisation and imaginary.

---

[4] Reference to the line of Léo Ferré's song 'The Anarchists' (*Les anarchistes*).

All those 'enemies of the State' who have criticised (and mocked) this rational social order cannot but be identified as bearers of chaos, prophets of disorder threatening the social order. It is precisely for this reason that they must be purged from history, for being 'incompatible' with the hierarchy identified by modernity (though with differing ethical contents) as the *modus operandi par excellence*, the pure machine that, run expertly by trained operators, would have efficiently driven an increasingly complex society in a 'fair' (albeit inegalitarian) fashion. Such positivist faith in the rational project has often resulted in horrors and disillusions; such disillusion has generally spared the machine and scapegoated its 'incompetent' operators.

Anyway, this is not the place to discuss the centrality of the State in the collective imaginary. Here it is enough to say that its myth persists because State and community are treated as synonyms. This explains the continuous appeals to strengthen and extend the 'sense of the State', a ghastly expression that aims to replace a communitarian sense of identity with its bureaucratic representation, direct participation with delegation, citizens with tax-payers and voters.

No Limits[5]

I shall now move on to the second most common – and equally classic – objection to anarchism, known as the traffic light objection. As recently formulated by a sociology professor: 'How could society work if everyone is free to do whatever they want and drivers no longer respect red lights?' This objection, equally deploying simple and misleading metaphors, pertains to another crucial issue: the assimilation of anarchy with anomie. Here we see a double cross of concealing the hierarchical principle behind the 'law and order' formula, postulated as the only possible rule of social coexistence. First of all, there is the attempt (a successful one, as shown by Signora Maria) to pass off anarchism as the formulation of a structurally anomic society, that is, one based on the 'institutional' breach of the norm. Then there is the attempt (so successful that even some naive anarchists buy it) to make anarchism overlap with a 'no limits' theory, that is, the reign of the individual free will, where the individual can legitimately act ignoring social interaction.

To be sure, anarchism has never theorised a society without rules, institutions or social interactions. It never has simply because such an entity would not be a society, while anarchism is chiefly concerned with human sociality, and a form of 'being together' built around egalitarian and libertarian rules and

[5] In English in the original.

values. Within societies of domination, anarchism certainly pursues a 'creative chaos', the destruction of institutions and the transgression of norms, against the homogenisation of hierarchy. It also theorises a 'right to transgression' that prevents societies of freedom from institutional tightening by preserving their distinctive trait of 'openness'.This said, anarchism's social project cannot be considered as a form of anomie. Behind the simple breach of an unacceptable rule – not in itself a viable social proposal – lies a complex project of social self-organisation, based on a horizontal decision-making process. Such a process makes sure that the normative social function (power) is an act of the community as a whole, and not a privilege exercised by a part of it (domination). Ultimately, rules are useful, not sacred; choices are shared, not imposed; and institutions are flexible and not eternal. Most of all, there are limits. The myth of absolute individual free will as an anarchist principle is in open contradiction with the anarchist theory of freedom, which is relational and posits that my freedom enhances other people's freedom (rather than limiting or erasing it). Bakunin's brilliant intuition: freedom is a social relationship, for my freedom can only exist in relation to that of others, and not in a social vacuum, where it would be completely superfluous. It is only when the individual exists in a social vacuum, as an atomised entity that does not recognise itself as part of a community, that his absolute will can find its longed-for expression, that of nihilism.

'It is sweet and fitting to die for the homeland',[6] while crossing the red light is just stupid. I can guarantee that if anarchists abide by the traffic regulations as exerted through the 'authority' of traffic lights, they are not also bound to accept, for the sake of an alleged coherence, political domination, subordination, the unequal distribution of wealth, or the division between intellectual and manual labour. I must reiterate: some relish such misunderstandings.

Beautiful and Impossible[7]

Objections are not always so malicious and lazy. Some of them are indeed starting from an opposite standpoint, which we can summarise as 'wonderful ideas, but unachievable, as people are stupid and evil. They are just beautiful utopias.' This certainly sounds like a fairer objection compared to the others (and, in all

---

[6] Translation of the Latin *'Dulcē et decōrum est prō patriā mōrī'*, from the Odes (III.2.13) by the Roman lyric poet Horace.

[7] The Italian title alludes to Gianna Nannini's popular song *'Bello e impossibile'* (1986). Di Leo changed the gender of the adjective from masculine to feminine ('bello' becomes 'bella'), as the word 'anarchy' in Italian is feminine.

honesty, in moments of the greatest discouragement it does not seem so far-fetched). This said, we shall offer some thoughts, albeit with a slight dizziness caused by the unusual role in which we have found ourselves, for we are now the 'good guys' rather than the usual 'bad guys'. In this objection, in fact, anarchism is recognised as a radically innovative and strongly ethical vision of the world. No longer the evil chaos-makers, anarchists become the knights errant of utopia,[8] the pristine heroes of a social vision so great to project them well above the drab pettiness of mankind. Captivating, isn't it? But don't fall for it: anarchism is considered complex and refined, yet completely unfeasible, and anarchists become some nice but pathetic Don Quixotes.

Undoubtedly, the professional utopianist does not carry a reputation for pragmatism, but this view overstates it, indeed, mystifies it. The goal here (stained with guilt) is to take this social and ethical conception that is 'exorbitantly'[9] egalitarian and libertarian and make it alien; anarchism is alien as its values and methods are presented as if they did not belong to human social history, but were instead abstract creations, dreamlike hallucinations, at odds with a credible anthropological theory.

In reality, this is an attempt to de-historicise anarchism, depriving it of its past and present (and also, we shall see, of its future). Too beautiful to be true, anarchism is left floating into thin air, as if it had crossed time and space without contaminating itself with base reality. It is celebrated in the realm of non-history only to deny its key role in the history-making of fundamental concepts for human (or at least 'Western') culture: freedom, autonomy, direct democracy, equality, solidarity, diversity . . . Together with anarchism, the millions of men and women who embodied it are also dematerialised. Real, tangible flesh, true feelings and hopes, born in the here and now of concrete existences that have embodied, in the literal sense, what is held to be a ghost, an abstraction. In reality, anarchism is alien only to the society of domination.

---

[8] Di Leo is recalling the phrase 'the knights errant of anarchy', from Pietro Gori's song 'Addio Lugano Bella'. Written in 1895 to commemorate the expulsion of anarchists from France, it remains a popular political song in Italy. Di Paola's (2017) book of the same name offers an interesting look into the lives of those exiles in London.

[9] The author here alludes to the slogan of the Centro Studi Libertari group, elaborated by Nico Berti. Berti is referring to Karl Popper's evaluation of anarchy. In an interview with Franz Kreuzer, Popper states that 'Anarchism is a kind of exaggeration of the idea of freedom' (translated from Popper and Kreuzer 1986: 19). Berti exploits the double meaning of exaggerated in Italian, which can be used both as a pejorative and in the hyperbolic and positive sense of 'overly good'. It can be translated as 'an exorbitant idea of freedom'.

Even more dangerously, this objection tries to deprive anarchism of its future. This attempt at dematerialisation is redolent of the classic political realist critique of all utopian thought: it is not a project but a dream, a fantasy (as if humans were not motivated as much by desires as by needs). These are the strenuous supporters of reality as it exists, those who consider it as the only legitimate reality from which to extrapolate the future.

There is little doubt that the weight of reality, the drift of the existent, is very strong and does shape customs, mentalities, even desires. But it seems to me that one or two things have changed since the Palaeolithic era. We went through less obvious and predictable evolutions – unexpected changes here, radical breaks there – that we can easily trace. In short, history marches on, things change, the universe expands . . . and utopias become history.

To better understand, let us play a little mental game with an historical background. Let's try to identify ourselves with the mindset, habits and expectations of an industrious craftsman in the late Middle Ages, with his sober life and his protective guild (but it could as well be an arrogant feudal gentleman or an unlucky, goitred peasant). Now, enter his world and with clear and plain words try to explain how capitalism works. Some problems? I have the same issues in the bakery.

Heart-Less Capitalism

The name 'capitalism' was not invoked by chance. We must move on to the last of the objections considered here, one that goes more or less like this: 'Your ideas, however appealing, are only good for simple, indeed primitive, social entities. Current society is way too complex for your embarrassingly inadequate proposals.'

Here, the problem is the inadequacy of anarchism to cope with the challenge of complexity. Anarchism is a nice idea, if we are talking about a Yanomami tribe, but if it's about our complex Western society then, for heaven's sake, let's be serious . . . Fine, let's try and be serious.

On closer inspection, the current 'complexity' comes from an overlapping of quantities: quantity of living beings to be coordinated, social needs to be met, administrative functions to be carried out, mass consumption to be managed . . . Putting all these quantities (and others) together and making them work properly is certainly not simple; it involves big ideas, means, institutions . . . Or at least this has been the only social vision deemed capable of containing such a quantitative proliferation. So let us not be surprised if we again come across the all-encompassing social planning, the all-pervasive bureaucratic apparatus, the omnivorous mega-institution, that is, the constitutive characteristics of modernity.

Faced with these grandiose visions, corroborated by the myth of infinite progress, thinking 'small' has become petty, reductive, certainly incompatible with the great invention of modernity: the masses (whether people or consumers is irrelevant – the subjects of so-called complexity). Those who do not embrace this grand dimension, those who continue to talk about individuals and communities and their relations, cannot aspire to manage the new mass society.

But why define this as 'so-called' complexity when institutional elephantiasis is there for all to see? The logic by which all this happened led not to making society more articulated and diverse, but rather to making it more simplified and standardised. The massification of the social body, of consciousness, consumption and desires, has become a synonym for homogenisation. Stratified homogenisation, of course, even if no longer the traditional pyramidal representation of society but – here in the 'rich' world – according to a new configuration that we could define as egg-shaped, to account for the colossal expansion of the middle class along with the permanence of an apex and a base. But beyond these para-geometric representations, the concept of the mass (fit for the electoral system, large retailers, television shares, for the school, for huge rallies and for anything else that implies quantity over quality) only holds if diversity is no longer of value but merely a fraction to be reabsorbed, an additional cost to be cut, an extravagance to be penalised. Human plurality is in fact incompatible with a massified social vision; it is not manageable by any 'big project' that, in order to work, must constrain plurality by reducing society into 'big' categories. This is not due to some abstract philosophical matter: mass society is not against diversity per se, it is just beyond its budget.

And yet if, by thinking 'big', modernity has reduced human complexity (and its anthropologies), it has, however, produced a complexity of its own that is passed off as important and necessary: institutional complexity, that is, that pile of bureaucratically regulated functions that modernity has had to invent to manage mass society. Thus the institutional octopus infiltrates its slimy tentacles into all social interstices to regulate, administer and ultimately 'complicate' social coexistence. An artificial complexity, therefore, as it is produced and exists only within its own frame of reference: the centralist paradigm.

Establishing an operational centre, a social 'heart' to which all information flows, reworked to be recirculated to the whole society, seems to be the most suited mode of functioning for complex (complicated) societies. Without invoking utopia, let us try and imagine another scenario and see if a centre is really necessary to manage complexity. If you take even a cursory look at the world of nature, it is not that uncontainable complexity needs a centre to function, or that this complexity is reduced in the absence of central coordination (which is exactly what happens when there is human intervention to interfere with or control natural processes). And if the comparison with nature does not convince, because its 'nature' is too different, we can remain within the human sphere and take into consideration another primary phenomenon of our age: capitalism.

Where is the centre of capitalism? I have some difficulty identifying it. Of course, the intrusive, invasive Western Empire oozes capitalism: multinationals and stock exchanges are its macroscopic concentrations; investors, entrepreneurs and techno-bureaucrats are its microscopic embodiment . . . but where is the centre towards which everything converges and from where everything departs? Where is its 'grand old man'? In my view, he is nowhere, because capitalism is (notoriously) heart-less; it does not abide by the centralist paradigm, but rather a different mode of functioning: the network. That is, a much more articulate and dynamic relational structure, with multidirectional flows that intersect and branch out through the knots of the reticular structure (which resembles that of the brain).

I must admit that it is sly to let your arch-enemy support your argument, but it helps in summarising an operating model traditionally put forward by anarchists and dismissed as 'simplistic' by the proponents of a centralist paradigm. There is concrete evidence, in both nature and society, that the network model does work, and in a more dynamic and sophisticated fashion. Look at capitalism!

And here the analogy ends because capitalism, beyond its opportunistic use of networks, is one of the most perfect social pyramids that we know, structured around values that are antithetical to those of an egalitarian and libertarian vision. (This should make us ponder – and this is not the place to do it – on modalities and values: some modalities are clearly incompatible with libertarian values – the centralist paradigm – while others are indeed compatible – the network structure – but do not constitute *the* libertarian method per se, as they can work with different ethical categories.) Nonetheless, the analogy made is a nice shortcut to our conclusion, which can also be read as a warning against the centralist paradigm: it is not the only but certainly the best available way of coordinating complex societies, if under the garb of managing flows, the hidden agenda is to control them.

And here we close this non-exhaustive review of the most common and foolish objections to anarchism. Foolish, mind you, because they are usually due to crass ignorance or made in bad faith. To be sure, there are less common and more refined objections to anarchism, which deserve to be taken into serious consideration. From Godwin to Kropotkin and Malatesta (but also, more recently, Goodman and Ward), anarchists have always found themselves in the position of having to respond to these kinds of objections, the legitimate children of the prevailing culture. And I shall refer you to them for far more articulate and convincing answers. The problem of Signora Maria remains mine. Perhaps I should change my bakery.

References

Bakunin, Michael [1882] (1970), *God and the State*, New York: Dover Publications Inc.

Di Paola, Pietro (2017), *The Knights Errant of Anarchy: London and the Italian Anarchist Diaspora (1880–1917)*, Edinburgh: AK Press.

Engels, Friedrich [1872] (1972), 'On Authority', in *The Marx-Engels Reader*, ed. Robert C. Tucker, New York: W. W. Norton & Company, pp. 730–3.

Popper, Karl Raimund, and Frank Kreuzer [1982] (1986), *Offene Gesellschaft/ Offenes Universum*, Munich: Piper.

13   *Volontà*: Workshop of Anarchist Research
Francesco Codello

VOLONTÀ (MEANING 'WILL' in Italian) represents a particularly significant editorial experience in the landscape of Italian and European anarchist publishing (Masini et al. 1996). Giovanna Caleffi Berneri (who co-founded the journal with Cesare Zaccaria in 1946) was its main driving force and an important figure in Italian anarchism, with strong international connections between the immediate post-war years and her disappearance in 1962.* *Volontà* was the most important Italian anarchist journal in this difficult period for anarchism in Italy. Like other radical movements, anarchism emerged weakened from the rubble of war, its strength mutilated by the fascist dictatorship. It was difficult to reorient and renew anarchist thought at a time when the dominant economic and cultural logic was strongly conditioned by the Catholic Church and the parties of post-war reconstruction, Christian Democracy and the Communist Party. This mirrored the international climate, polarised into two opposing blocks: one governs whilst the other hegemonises the opposition. A dual dialectic was imposed that gave little space to other possible paths or to secular and libertarian cultures. In this context, leafing through the journal's pages from the period, we can appreciate the enormous effort made by its editors and collaborators, including the

---

* Giovanna Caleffi (1897–1962) was an Italian anarchist. She was forced to leave the country with the rise of fascism and spent the years of the dictatorship in several European countries with her partner, the anarchist philosopher Camillo Berneri. Berneri died in Barcelona in 1937 and after the end of World War II Caleffi returned to Italy, engaging in several cultural and educational projects until her death. For further information on her life and activism (in Italian), see De Maria (2010, 2019) and Berneri Family Archive (2012).

fundamental role of Pio Turroni,[1] to renew anarchism without repudiating its classical tradition through an open process of 'cross-contamination' with those cultural and political expressions of a secular and libertarian culture present and active in Italy.

The journal's pages were enriched by international collaborators (George Orwell, Albert Camus, Paul Goodman, Vernon Richards, Alex Comfort, Herbert Read, Louis Mercier Vega, George Woodcock, Gaston Leval, Luce Fabbri, Giovanni Baldelli, Colin Ward and others) who offered the Italian reader a complex view of the economic, political, social and cultural realities in different countries. The Italian contributions were no less impressive, if we consider the quality of the various articles that appeared in *Volontà* (authors included Gaetano Salvemini, Ignazio Silone, Danilo Dolci, Giancarlo De Carlo, Carlo Doglio, Pier Carlo Masini, Ugo Fedeli, Armando Borghi, Guido Tassinari and Luigi De Marchi). Each issue also contained selected pieces by classic anarchist authors who, in the editors' opinions, had contemporary resonance and could outline the broad contours of a renewed anarchist thought.

In an attempt to take a more proactive and practical stance, compared with more traditional orientations on identity, the journal carried accounts and analyses of concrete experiences across diverse areas of social life that could be characterised as libertarian. We find, for example, alternative educational experiences (such as Alexander Neill's Summerhill, Ernesto Codignola's didactic experiments in Florence with the Pestalozzi school-city, Giovanna Caleffi's Marie Louise Berneri summer colony for the children of comrades and the poor, the educational renewal of pedagogical activism, the activity of Aldo Capitini); anarchist communities' experiences of production and the overall organisation of society during the 1936 Spanish Revolution; the problem of housing and urban planning; life in the *kibbutzim* first in Palestine and then in Israel; the promotion of a secular conception of motherhood and issues relating to birth control and contraception; support for initiatives and struggles over the secular-

---

[1] Pio Turroni (1906–1982) was known as the 'bricklayer of anarchism'. He was an important figure both in Italy and internationally. An autodidact, he became an anarchist as a teenager and was forced into exile in 1923 to escape fascist repression (first to Belgium and then to France). Turroni knew and visited (among many others) the Ukrainian anarchist Nestor Makhno and Camillo Berneri, with whom he became close friends in Barcelona in 1936. At the end of the war, after having fled to Mexico and England, he returned to Italy and became one of the most active militants in the reconstruction of the Italian anarchist movement. Thanks to his countless international anarchist connections (especially in the United States), Turroni represented the thread that provided Italian anarchism with an internationalist and critical vision (see Sensini 2004).

isation of culture and social and welfare organisations; support for workers' and peasants' struggles; anti-militarism and conscientious objection, pacifism and the struggles against the war industry; Italian and international current affairs, cultural and artistic experiences and so on. In short, a variety of issues and an open-minded approach characterises the pages of *Volontà* in its early years, to the extent that it can be considered an example of how to conceptualise and write a journal that remains loyal to the core of the classical anarchist tradition while exploring emerging anti-authoritarian social and cultural movements. The clear purpose was to stimulate thinking beyond existing militant circles, a thinking that otherwise risked being excluded from the attention of the wider population.

The death of Giovanna Caleffi Berneri was followed by a troubled period for the journal. The turnover of several editors and managers further exposed underlying issues such as the general pauperisation of Italian anarchist forces and the inability to cope effectively with the triumph of capitalist and state-centric logic in Italy and internationally. Despite the youth and workers' movement of the late 1960s bursting on to the Italian political and cultural scene, *Volontà* remained inward-looking and removed from the pervasive and innovative ferment that shook Italian society. Paradoxically, in 1969, when the student and workers' protest that exploded across the Western world signalled a renewed interest in libertarian and anarchist ideas and an increasing number of young people approached the anarchist movement, the journal reduced publication from monthly to bimonthly. This exposed an ongoing political crisis and a regression to questions of identity, often entrenched in defence of a purer, more traditional and less hybrid thought, unwilling to be contaminated by other cultural influences, even when these were close to those traditionally considered anarchist. Even more significantly, the leading social revolts of this period – the birth of new forms of organisation from below, the Vietnam War, the explosion of movements like those of Provos and the hippies, along with all the new social realities moving in an egalitarian and anti-authoritarian direction – found only marginal space in the pages of *Volontà*. Similarly, the dramatic Piazza Fontana bombing in Milan on 12 December 1969, the strategy of tension, the 'accidental' death of Giuseppe Pinelli, and the period of neo-fascist and state terrorism occupied only minimal space in its pages (See Chapter 1).

The efforts of the editors seem to have been directed more at illustrating the differences between anarchism and Marxism on a theoretical and doctrinal level. In an era in which many left-wing extra-parliamentary groups that adhered to Marxism were active, the journal highlighted the contradictions between doctrinal and authoritarian (Marxist) thought and those movementist and libertarian components marginally represented in Marxist groups. This was an important endeavour at the time, but certainly not to the extent of diverting attention from the protest and rebellion movements and their libertarian tendencies. Such diffidence towards contestation movements reveals the editors' inability and unreadiness to seize the positive and libertarian aspects emerging from the new situation, and, above all, their dramatic isolation from those experiences.

The journal became marginal even to the Italian anarchist movement: subscriptions fell, and readership declined significantly. It is only with the last issue of 1976 that *Volontà* rose again. A new editorial group completely renewed the journal, reconnecting with its origins. This role fell to members of the anarchist group 'Franco Serantini' of Valdobbiadene (Treviso), who were active in the Gruppi Anarchici Federati (Federated Anarchist Groups, hereafter GAF), and were already experienced at running *A/Rivista Anarchica*,[2] a monthly anarchist journal, as well as hosting a series of editorial and cultural conferences and seminars that attracted international attention. This shift was completed with the editorial staff passing from Valdobbiadene to the Milan-based Gruppo Anarchico Bandiera Nera (Anarchist Black Flag Group) in 1980, an arrangement that lasted until 1996 (Berti 2016).

A Workshop of Anarchist Research (1980–1996)

From its first issue in 1980, *Volontà* became a quarterly, with a new graphic design and more international contributors. From 1987 there were three issues a year, mainly monographs.

The journal defined itself as 'a workshop of anarchist research' [*laboratorio di ricerche anarchiche*]. *Workshop* because of the liveliness and plurality of approaches, a live process of cultural experimentation driven by intellectual curiosity. *Research* because it favoured exploration over declaration. *Anarchist* insofar as the general frame of reference and identification with anarchist thought remained central.

---

[2] *A/Rivista Anarchica* was a monthly anarchist journal founded in Milan in 1971 by anarchist militants close to the GAF, in particular those belonging to the anarchist circle Ponte della Ghisolfa, of which Giuseppe Pinelli was a key figure. After the 1969 bombing of Piazza Fontana and the death of Pinelli, anarchists felt the need to have a coherent platform on which to narrate their counter-histories of the unfolding events. Paolo Finzi (1951–2020), who was a young militant of the circle and considered Pinelli to be his 'anarchist master', was one of the founders of *A/Rivista Anarchica* and acted as the director from 1972 to his death in 2020.

The editorial piece in the first issue of 1980 clearly explained the editorial changeover with respect to the years of decline, and the choice to publish quarterly. It reads:

> For many years, V. has been looking out for its own identity. To be sure, not an ideological one: that is and has always been out of the question. It is looking for what we can call an editorial identity, for its role in anarchist publishing ... Our choice in this regard, which only reinforces the choice of the last two years, is to make it an instrument for updating and deepening anarchist culture. This, in our opinion, means trying to produce a journal that is loyal to the historical-ideological heritage of anarchism and is open to the contributions of contemporary libertarian thought, is enriched by engaging with the most interesting strands of the social sciences. Anarchism is not a glorious but obsolete tradition: it is a live and fertile ensemble of analyses, experiences and intuitions. It is a rich 'capital' of past theoretical and practical labour, which can be put to use only through sustained theoretical and practical labour. (*Volontà* 1980: 3)

The editors believed that Italy was in need of such a journal, one whose core editorial line was the combination of established anarchist theory with libertarian praxis. This challenge was addressed not only to the anarchist movement, but also to a growing cultural space which, perhaps unconsciously, was rediscovering libertarian approaches and anti-authoritarian themes. The lack of a critical space like that offered by *Volontà* – at least in the minds of its editors – would have left an entire heterogeneous, spontaneous and plural movement without any anarchist cultural reference, thus favouring the extension of the Marxist (majority) and liberal-socialist (minority) hegemonies in Italian progressive and left-wing culture. This was the cultural and political project behind the editorial line: an all-out challenge to renew anarchist thought and action. The end of the brief but intense experience of *Interrogations* (an international magazine of anarchist research founded by Louis Mercier Vega, produced in four languages between December 1974 and June 1979) freed the energies of some Italian and international anarchists who found a new space for cultural production and research in *Volontà* (see Chapter 1). The aim was, above all, to keep anarchist thought alive through an honest, open, ideologically unregimented dialogue with those elements of the social sciences which could best be crossbred with an anarchist culture in constant evolution. This was a considerable but necessary effort to guide the transition from a declarative to a pragmatically open anarchism, one that was, at the same time, strongly anchored to its core values (Codello 2009).

Figure 13.1 Covers of *Volontà* designed by Fabio Santin from 1980 to 1985.

Benjamin Beit-Hallahmi / Murray Bookchin /
Reba Çamuroglu / Ernest Gellner / Luciano
Lanza / Alberto Melucci / Edgar Morin / Mira
Oklobdzija / Guy Scarpetta / Arturo Schwarz /
Jirina Siklová / Colin Ward

● **NOSTRA PATRIA**
● **E' IL MONDO INTERO**

VOLONTÀ

Fernando Ainsa / Marcello Bernardi / Sandra
Bonfiglioli / Cornelius Castoriadis / Eduardo
Colombo / André Gorz / Leopold Khor / Francesco
Maiello / Elena Petrassi / Pietro M. Toesca /

● **I TEMPI**
● **DELLA LIBERTA'**

VOLONTÀ
laboratorio
di ricerche
anarchiche

trimestrale
anno XLIX - n. 1 del 6/1995
sped. in abb. postale / 50% - Milano
tasse perçue

Giorgio Agamben / Juan Martinez Alier / Massimo
Alvito / Franco Bunčuga / Giancarlo De Carlo /
Carlo Doglio / Heidi Freifrau / Paul e Percival
Goodman / Franco La Cecla / Richard Levine /
Louis Mannie Lionni / Alberto Magnaghi / Dunia
Mittner / Fabrizio Paone / Pietro M. Toesca /
Nicoletta Vallorani / Colin Ward / Piero Zanini

● **LA CITTA'**
● **E' NUDA**

VOLONTÀ
laboratorio
di ricerche
anarchiche

trimestrale
anno XLIX - n. 2-3 del 10/1995
sped. in abb. postale / 50% - Milano
tasse perçue

Pietro Adamo / Nico Berti / Amedeo Bertolo /
Francesco Codello / Eduardo Colombo / Ronald
Creagh / Rossella Di Leo / Tomás Ibañez / Luciano
Lanza / René Lourau / Kirkpatrick Sale / Salvo
Vaccaro

● **LE RAGIONI**
● **DELL'ANARCHIA**

VOLONTÀ
laboratorio
di ricerche
anarchiche

trimestrale
anno L - n. 3/4 del 12/1996
elèuthera

Figure 13.2 Covers of *Volontà* designed by Ferro Piludu from 1991 to 1996. The final issue (bottom right) features Piludu's Da Vinci/anarchy image, which was, for decades, the logo of the CSL.

The tension between the fundamental ideas of anarchism and the necessity of renewal is well synthesised by Nico Berti (1975), who emblematically titled one of his essays in *Interrogations* 'anarchism *in* history, yet *against* history' (see Chapter 11).

The context in which this libertarian research unfolded was characterised by the failure of the recent attempts to transform society and the subsequent triumph of consumer capitalism. The ideas developed were an important attempt to address this new social and cultural situation, after the profound crisis affecting all the protest movements born out of 1968 and the pervasive disillusionment about the real possibility of radical change, affecting even the most engaged militants (see Chapter 2, note 3).

This situation posed several challenges, not least because anarchist research was prone to the risk of indulging in abstract theorising, severed by concrete experimentation. Yet the need to find new ground on which to start the work of a libertarian cultural reconstruction was more urgent than ever. The more traditional wing of the anarchist movement increasingly took refuge in self-identitarianism, often unable to grasp the new challenges that a more complex and hedonistic society poses to radical thought.

Volontà's editors seized the opportunity to privilege a more pragmatic and pluralist libertarian dimension over traditional anarchism – without denying the latter, but rather trying to enhance and deepen it.

The international anarchist conference 'Venice 1984' represented a starting point, or rather a *re*-starting point, bringing together the contributions of world anarchism in an extraordinary discussion that marked a decisive passage – also taking place in *Volontà* – between an inward-looking anarchism and a libertarianism anchored in a *new anarchism* (see Bertolo, Chapters 2 and 4).

From Revolution as Event to Revolution as Process: The Social Imaginary and Anarchist Utopias

A priority for the new editorial team was to initiate a genuine and lucid discussion on the concept of revolution without illusions.

The editors were all active anarchist militants and many of them were members of the GAF. The GAF were the most culturally and politically innovative anarchist organisation from the late 1960s until the end of the 1970s. A numerical minority, compared with the other two Italian Federations (FAI and GIA),[3]

---

[3] The Federazione Anarchica Italiana (Italian Anarchist Federation), or FAI, was founded in Carrara in 1945, significantly inspired by Errico Malatesta's 'Anarchist Programme'

the GAF developed a new organisational model which was based on the federation of affinity groups rather than a synthesis federation, like the FAI and GIA. This structure strengthened both personal relationships and collective thinking, also two of the defining traits of *Volontà* in this era. In particular, this structure allowed the production of collective thinking and research beyond individual disciplinary boundaries. The shared years of revolutionary militancy forged a community of research that echoed throughout the editorial work.

These anarchist activists had all gone through the most intense period for Italian and European anarchism and, throughout the 1970s, gave birth to numerous initiatives, whether cultural or strictly militant. They were driven by the shared idea that classical anarchism should be renewed, but also the shared belief – not blind faith – that the struggles and agitations they were actively involved in were likely to lead to a revolutionary transformation of society. To be sure, the journal's themes were often the result of a series of interdisciplinary seminars which were organised according to two essential criteria: to be the result of collective thinking, and to focus on some strategic conceptual knots for the renewal of anarchist thought and libertarian action. The defeat and authoritarian/Stalinist drift of the armed struggle, the collapse of the protest movements, and the social hangover caused by the ability of the capitalist system to plagiarise the socio-popular imaginary made it even more difficult – for critical and dissatisfied militants like those of *Volontà* – to be *against* history (that of domination and exploitation) and yet anchored in social reality.

Efforts therefore focused on pursuing a third way between identitarian insularity and pragmatism as an end in itself. Reflecting on the concept and viability of revolution took on a renewed strategic significance. Collective research hence attempted to define the relationship between historical time and revolutionary time, in a context where the social imaginary was increasingly dominated and colonised by a subtler and more insidious authoritarian ideology, and the anarchist movement weakened. The analysis of the rising techno-bureaucracy as a new ruling class, carried out by both the GAF and *Interrogations* (see Chapter 1), needed to be expanded, and the old 'reformism versus revolution' debate of the socialist left (generically understood) was to be overcome.

Volontà hosted numerous interventions around the debate on revolution (not always explicitly, often intersecting with other topics), including a special issue on the topic in 1985 (no. 1). The journal outlined a vision of radical change that is

(see Richards 2015). During the 9th Congress of the FAI in 1965, a split led to the formation of the Gruppi di Iniziativa Anarchica (Groups for Anarchist Initiative), or GIA, who were critical of the anarcho-syndicalist roots of the FAI.

close to Élisée Reclus's (2013) theory of the relationship between revolution and evolution. The idea was to overcome the classical idea of revolution as an *event* in favour of conceiving it as a series of accelerations, interspersed with hidden periods of erosion, that is, more of a *process*, a sustained conflictual dynamic made of an infinite series of small transformations, rather than a cathartic outcome. It is no coincidence that during these years the journal published some fundamental contributions, such as those from Colin Ward, Cornelius Castoriadis, Murray Bookchin, Tomás Ibáñez, Eduardo Colombo, John Clark, Marianne Enckell, Carlos Semprun Maura, Claude Lefort, René Lourau, Pierre Clastres and Noam Chomsky, together with those of Amedeo Bertolo, Nico Berti, Roberto Ambrosoli, Luciano Lanza and Rossella Di Leo, among others. The debate, here always understood as *research*, did not aim at ending the interrogation with a conclusive answer, but rather at producing a continuous form of interrogation, a true embodiment of the collective thought discussed earlier.

A central concern for the editors was the fact that radical change always requires a profound shift in the social and individual imaginary. To this end, various contributions addressed the issue of building a strong anarchist imaginary. This means grasping its utopian function, its radical and subversive force, capable of destabilising established habits and paradigms of domination. As Bertolo (Chapter 8, p. 145) put it:

> A deep transformation of basic social structures – a 'revolution', whatever one might mean by that – also requires a deep transformation of psychological structures, and both of these transformations can only take place under the pressure of an extremely strong emotional charge, a strong and passionate will for transformation that spreads out across leading social agents . . . but also through more sizeable popular milieu . . . This implies that there has to be a sufficient spread of an imaginary that is not only lucidly rational but also emotionally rich.

From this perspective, it goes without saying that the debate triggered by Murray Bookchin (1995) between social anarchism and lifestyle anarchism was resolved by overcoming a forced contradiction between the two poles of the question. In fact, from a careful reading of its editorial line, *Volontà* was always unwilling to accept overly schematic dual oppositions, trying to suggest and, where possible, practise an open reading of reality. This meant tenaciously advancing the search for a third (fourth, fifth, etc.) way to avoid the reduction of socio-cultural realities to dual oppositions (Hegelian-Marxist after all), instrumental to the logic of domination.

Hence, it is apparent that there is 'no *single* anarchist system that might represent humanity's point of arrival, whether near or far. The anarchist utopia contains a *space of freedom* to be explored, a space in which to experiment with infinite and chiefly anarchist social forms, a space of freedom in which to weave diversity and equality in infinite forms' (see Chapter 8, p. 148). This effort to escape from dominant ideologies, and to free anarchist thought from the influences of Marxism especially, renewed the pragmatic gaze that characterised the anarchism of many of the thinkers published in *Volontà*. To use the words of Colin Ward (1996: 52): 'The anarchist alternative is that of fragmentation, fission rather than fusion, diversity rather than unity, a mass of societies rather than a mass society.'

To build a libertarian society it was necessary to be aware that

> The roots of domination do not lie in *nature* but in culture, not in '*things*' but in the imaginary. Individual and collective rebellion against domination is thus possible only if *one conceives it as possible*, if one conceives to be possible all that the unconscious State and State rationality tell us is impossible, only if the non-place of the libertarian and egalitarian utopia denies the place of hierarchical ideology. (Bertolo, Chapter 8, p. 150)

To overturn the social imaginary in an anti-authoritarian direction means founding a subversive, radically transformative and instituting imaginary.

> Utopia lives entirely in the break it establishes with what exists. When utopia enters historical time, it challenges the whole political institutionalisation at place, whose existence is denied by the very possibility of a utopian alterity. At that moment, such a break is called revolution. But revolution is not the end of history, it is only a moment of its continuity in which a qualitative change disrupts social institutions. (translated from Colombo 1981: 29)

Change, according to the analyses published in *Volontà*, is inevitably revolutionary when it goes in a libertarian and non-authoritarian direction. It is radically different from the existent, it is gradual, it is cultural because it threatens established habits and certainties, but it is also social and concrete because it needs continual ruptures, both symbolic and factual.

> Radical transformation is possible only with the occurrence of an anomalous situation that entails a succession of accelerated qualitative transformations, which are able to anesthetise the reproduction of fear of freedom and radically alter the collective imaginary. (translated from Lanza 1981: 15)

The debate went on incessantly, as the problem of revolution was a fundamental historical and ideological point in this historical phase of anarchism in Italy and beyond. The divide deepened between those concerned with a rediscovery of the founding authors of anarchist thought and important concrete experiences (e.g. the Spanish Revolution of 1936) and those advocating for a gradual but more radical change and break with tradition.

This discussion endured because the style of confrontation was characterised by a dialogic (and not dialectical) effort. The 'I win, you lose' logic is replaced by a 'workshop of anarchist research'.

The Meaning of Domination and the Problem of Freedom: Beyond Democracy

Throughout the 1980s the journal was concerned with the anarchist definition of the concepts of authority, power and domination, how these terms were embodied in the social, political, cultural, economic and relational reality, how they were expressed, and most of all: what is anarchist freedom? How is it different from its Marxist and liberal conceptualisations?

In 1983, two special issues of *Volontà* (nos. 2 and 3) were devoted to the problem of Power and its implications for anarchist theory. Firstly, conceptual clarity was considered indispensable from an epistemological point of view. In an illuminating essay, Amedeo Bertolo distinguishes between authority, power and domination and their meanings in light of anarchist interpretation (see Chapter 4). Authority and power have two different meanings: authority can be a freely recognised competence (authoritativeness), as opposed to a role determined by an established hierarchy; power as 'power to do' (an expression of anarchist freedom), as opposed to 'power to make others do', that is, 'domination' (the institutionalised exercise of force). This distinction removes any suspicion of 'conceptual naivety', often unjustly attributed to anarchism.

The unequal possession of power is the basis of any authoritarian society. Domination intersects both the right and the left, and only anarchism can break this pattern of interpersonal, economic, political, cultural and social relationships. The polysemy of power is the neutral border between freedom and domination. In fact, 'being able to do' – 'power to do, ability to do' (*poter fare*) – is an expression of extreme freedom (not just individual freedom, but social freedom), but 'power to make others do' (*poter far fare*) is the violent exercise of privilege and is, therefore, the denial of freedom in that it is the antithesis of equality (see Bertolo, Chapter 4). Anarchy does not mean anomie, but a conscious and responsible choice of freely defined norms, accepted and modifiable at any time.

This is not an abstract idea of dissent but guarantees the conditions in which it is possible to realise alternatives according to the pluralistic conception of social life that characterises this kind of anarchism. It should be remembered that the constant point of reference of the journal's editors was the Bakuninian conception of freedom, according to which my freedom does not end where yours begins (the liberal conception), but my freedom cannot be fulfilled if you are not equally free (anarchist social freedom).[4]

Freedom in its eternal struggle against domination can concretely express itself only if we are to take seriously the problem of 'voluntary servitude', dramatically pervasive in contemporary society.[5] Eduardo Colombo analysed the general paradigm of obedience, regarded as the precondition of the existence and reproducibility of domination. Once this is assimilated into the collective imaginary, a 'voluntary' servitude governs the actions of individuals and the whole of society, so that understanding the mechanisms through which obedience and passivity penetrate human beings becomes strategically important. Colombo (1983: 81), through his psychoanalytic training, analysed the 'constitution of power at the symbolic level of significance and its phantasmal and institutional reproduction'. John Clark (1994) and Eugène Enriquez (1980) focused on the same topic, with different viewpoints, but still aiming to dig into the foundations on which domination is based and obedience is exercised. Rossella Di Leo (see Chapter 10) introduced another foundational aspect of power and domination, namely that expressed in gender relations. Di Leo's anthropological gaze leads her to reject mainstream feminism's monocausal explanations to focus on a specific relation of domination (sexual asymmetry) as paradigmatic of overarching structures of authoritarian relationships more broadly.

Finally, we should note the analysis of Tomás Ibáñez (see Chapter 3). Drawing from Michel Foucault, he argues that a society without power cannot exist. It is not possible to have an anomic community devoid of social ties and without decision-making processes that are valid for everyone. It is therefore necessary

---

[4] Codello is referencing Bakunin's (1980: 237) declaration in the early 1870s that 'I am truly free only when all human beings, men and women, are equally free'.

[5] The idea of 'voluntary servitude' is taken from Étienne de La Boétie's *Discourse on Voluntary Servitude*. Published clandestinely in sixteenth-century France, it focuses on the puzzle of how and why the mass of people acquiesce to political domination when the authority of rulers is reliant only on the complicity of the ruled. Whilst clearly foreshadowing later anarchist ideas, the political legacy of La Boétie's *Discourse* is more ambivalent; the most easily available edition today, for example, is available courtesy of the Mises Institute, a bastion of 'free' market libertarianism and vulgar neoconservatism.

to develop a libertarian conception of power, since this intersects horizontal relationships as well as (obviously) vertical ones. Ibáñez refers here to power as a concrete and guaranteed expression of doing (being able to do), while he reiterates his radical opposition to the metamorphosis of this power into domination (power to make others do).

Anarchism is doomed to impotence if it does not define power as a set of rules freely produced and accepted by all, including the decision-making process and its application. In this debate, an emphasis on anarchist freedom as freedom *of* rather than freedom *from* prevails. This means to choose the positive (of experimental concreteness) over the negative. There is wide agreement over the limitations attached to the liberal stance on the division of power: the matter is not about reducing and balancing power, but rather transforming it (or, better, ending its transformation into domination).*

The editorial team of *Volontà* knew all too well that an engagement with the key relationship between the political and the social, and the limits of democracy, was necessary at this point. An original and innovative approach to these themes could highlight some unresolved issues in the anarchist vulgate too. Such was the challenge posed by Nico Berti (1989), who argued that politics is a science and practice that manages the tensions produced by reality in favour of those who engage in it. No society, even a libertarian one, can ignore politics, and classical anarchism, according to Berti, has not been able to produce its own politics. In condemning the historical forms of the political, anarchism has limited itself to considering the social as its only legitimate field. By denying politics, because of an inability to create its own, anarchist thought and practice had surrendered to impotence. Berti draws from theory – published in *Volontà* – developed by Cornelius Castoriadis (1989), Miguel Abensour (1989), Claude Lefort (1989), Thom Holterman (1987) and Alain Thèvenet (1994), all attempting in different ways to incorporate the political into the social. In his own later work, Berti further explores the idea that classical anarchist thought neutralises the role of politics through the social. As the history of anarchist socialism shows, this resulted in all-round failure and the marginalisation of anarchism. To overcome this situation, anarchism must develop its own political theory and praxis. What could a political theory of post-classical anarchism look like? What are the implications and contradictions that this entails? This was the great challenge for everyone involved.

---

* *Volontà* also dedicated two monographic issues to the theme of freedom: *I tempi della libertà*, *Volontà*, Milan, 1995, n. 1, and *I due volti della libertà*, *Volontà*, Milan, 1995, n. 4.

The initial answers came from Colombo (1989) and Bookchin (1989); the first recognised that the specificity of politics lies in its intentionality and self-referentiality. However, as the French Revolution showed, the political and the social cannot be separated. The political demand of 1789 and the social demand of 1793 could not be met in a revolutionary continuum. On the other hand, Bookchin believes that what is commonly referred to as politics is nothing more than a technology of State organisation. However, politics does not exhaust itself in this function: on the contrary, its physical milieu has almost always been the city. It is in the perennial conflict between the city (understood as a community) and the State that we can find clues on how to rebuild social politics.

At this point, the discussion inevitably turns to attempts to sketch a political vision of anarchism by critiquing actual democracy and identifying alternative libertarian ways of organising social life.

Anarchist thinkers have always denounced the fallacy (in terms of true freedom and authentic equality) of the democratic system. Classical anarchist thinkers (from Pierre-Joseph Proudhon to Errico Malatesta) emphasised that anarchy and democracy were different and, in some respects, irreconcilable concepts. This is hardly surprising in the period spanning the nineteenth century and the first half of the twentieth century (even earlier in the United States). The rise of dictatorships across Europe, starting with Fascism and Nazism, highlighted the need to revisit the anarchy/democracy divide and to better understand the evolution of democracy under conditions of globalisation and financial capitalism (see Codello 2015). *Volontà* devotes several articles and special issues to these themes, grappling with the question of whether anarchism is democratic or not. According to the editors, the answer could only be twofold: anarchism encompasses democracy yet wants to overcome it. The anarchist proposal for social organisation supersedes the rules of democracy; it opens up a space beyond the political, to be understood as an autonomous category from the social.

According to Bertolo (translated from 1994: 27):

democracy and anarchy are not reducible to one another but (under certain conditions) neither are they antithetical, that anarchy is both the most complete form of democracy but also its irreducible exceedance . . . A quantitative and qualitative beyond . . . Thus, anarchists' political conception is, must be, more democracy, as well as something else. If not, it is a within [rather than a beyond]. To be sure, anarchists believe that it is both more and different . . . Anarchy can be conceived as an extreme form of democracy, as well as a different form of constructing the political space. Perhaps, even as something lying beyond the political space itself.

Tomás Ibáñez poses the interesting question: when we talk about democracy, are we referring to normative or actual democracy? 'Actual democracy does not respect any of the principles of normative democracy, which, after all, constitutes a reasonable, if not acceptable model' (translated from Ibáñez 1994: 66). The same applies to anarchism, so what matters is to measure its degree of concreteness and applicability and to develop robust critical and self-critical thinking. Other contributions grasped the deeper meaning of this debate in the comparative judgement of democratic and totalitarian regimes, recognising liberal democracy as 'the lesser evil', without renouncing the idea of a 'beyond' democracy ['Democracy and Beyond' is the title of the 1994 issue of *Volontà*]. However, an unsettling concern emerged: such an observation could obliterate the revolutionary nature of anarchism, and the anarchist identity could be lost. Here identity returns to the fore, although not explicitly, representing a constant challenge for the journal's cultural project, that is, to renew anarchist thought without disavowing its difference from both liberalism and Marxism (see, for example, La Torre 1980; Alemany 1981, 1982; Chomsky 1982; Di Leo (Chapter 12); Clark 1994; Vaccaro 1994).

Following the debate on the relationship between democracy, liberalism and anarchist thought, *Volontà* published a series of articles aimed at outlining some guidelines for anarchist political thought. In those years, the editorial team was characterised by a more pragmatic perspective, aimed at thinking through a gradualist and experimental anarchism. The team was, for the most part, made of the same people who had organised a meeting to mark the centenary of Bakunin's death in 1976, the 'International Conference of Studies on the New Masters' in 1978 (see Chapter 1; Codello 1979; Venza 1979), and the conference on autogestion and its theoretical and practical implications in 1979.

Political anarchism can be defined by autogestion. But this is only one of its possible forms. Federalism, libertarian municipalism and direct democracy give substance both to the concept of autogestion and to the anarchist political perspective. Through the analysis and enhancement of these concepts, the journal took an experimental and innovative turn with respect to the traditional and classic visions of anarchism.*

Important in this sense were the contributions of Murray Bookchin and João Freire. Freire took a pragmatic and experimental direction, theorising proper

---

* See, in particular, issue 3 of *Volontà* in 1989, *Autogestione. Utopia riformista o strategia rivoluzionaria?* [Autogestion: Reformist utopia or revolutionary strategy?], which was dedicated to historical and contemporary experiences of libertarian social organisation.

stages in a path of gradualist change in order to find immediate and viable answers for a possible anarchist politics. He acknowledges that the absence of an imposed authority does not necessarily lead to the affirmation of authentic libertarian values. The idea of a libertarian society must be developed bearing in mind that conflict cannot be eliminated, but it can be regulated through constant negotiation via the method of consensus. Society is to be designed in a highly organised and participatory fashion, regulated by agreements and contracts with a variety of protagonists, levels and articulations, not by general, abstract or imposed laws. This programme must be conceived within a framework of regulatory principles that enhance autonomy over heteronomy, cooperation over competition, guided by strong values such as freedom and solidarity in close relation to one another. Libertarian self-organisation and decision-making (indispensable in any society) inevitably also include delegation, which must in turn be characterised by revocability, effective and real control, and limited and specific mandates. The community dimension is key for libertarian social organisation: beyond a certain dimension, no anti-authoritarian organisation is possible. Ultimately, according to Freire, 'rather than expanding forms of counter-powers, which limit the field of action of institutional powers, it is a question of fuelling anti-power processes that strengthen and reinforce societal logic against the logic of the state' (translated from Freire 1983: 21). In various contributions, Bookchin introduced the ideas of communitarianism, direct democracy, federalism and libertarian municipalism, all organisational models closely consistent with an ecological and libertarian society (see Bookchin 1987, 1991). The journal managed to merge these issues with a properly anarchist internationalist dimension.*

Bookchin stressed the role of communitarianism as an alternative to statism. In his opinion, anarchists should focus on concrete action on the ground, rather than engaging with sterile, generic protests against the State. Only in this way can new social configurations emerge as alternatives to the dominant system. Thus, federalism, municipalism, autogestion and solutions that favour direct and participatory action could constitute the political path of a renewed anarchism. To overcome the hierarchical logic of statism and centralisation, it is necessary to give life to concrete forms of experimentation that can be defined as direct democracy. Bookchin's ideas are well known, and do not need further

---

* Such a dimension is well captured by the title chosen for the 1990 *Volontà*, issues 2–3, devoted to these themes: *Nostra patria è il mondo intero* [Our country is the entire world], a refrain taken from the anarchist song written by the anarchist Pietro Gori (1865–1911) in 1895.

discussion here. It suffices to say that it was *Volontà* that introduced the thought of the American libertarian ecologist to Italy in the early 1990s.

From Theory to Praxis

Classic themes and arguments around human and social life found ample space in many issues of *Volontà* and stimulated wide-ranging research to cross-contaminate anarchist ideas with libertarian theories and experiences from different disciplinary fields. The editors constantly sought inspiration, questions, ideas and validation in order to test anarchist ideas through praxis and offer a truly plural and innovative viewpoint.

A case in point is the attention given to economics, an unusual topic for anarchist theory. Anarchism (or rather *anarchisms*) had classically dealt with the economic issue by dividing itself between those who saw communism as the most suitable option for an anarchist society, those who deemed collectivism and mutualism more suitable to guarantee individual freedom and social sharing, and those who accepted the utility of guaranteeing individual possession only so long as it avoided any form of exploitation. Communism, collectivism, mutualism and libertarian individualism (certainly not anarcho-capitalism) have always been thought of as regulating principles of a libertarian economy. With this understanding, and the firm belief that these strategies must all be scrutinised and not resolved by a one-fits-all solution, *Volontà* disrupted the dominant debate and paved the way for new critiques and ways of understanding the economic.

The most interesting and innovative contributions came from Luciano Lanza (see Chapters 6 and 7 in this volume), who made a Herculean effort to escape the dualism of liberalism-communism, envisaging a libertarian society that combined individual freedom and a 'libertarian market' with genuine equality of living conditions, while guaranteeing a form of 'entrepreneurship' without exploitation.

Lanza argues that the economy is a theoretical and practical manifestation of domination in its historically determined forms, and therefore does not have its own foundational values, nor its own related representation of humanity and the world. As opposed to domination, present in every known society, the economic (understood as a world in itself, as an objective reality, as a science that responds to itself) can be found in Western societies starting from a very specific point in history. Yet, the economic is a representation of reality that has profoundly changed the social imaginary, and hence society. It is a myth that filled an historical social void determining, as a signifier, the actions of human beings. Although it appears as an immortal myth, it is actually fragile and, as such, can be modified. In fact,

> bigger or smaller groups of producer-consumers do not compete with the capitalist market, but become independent by creating non-economic [*a-eco-nomiche*] logics, which can lead to significant disruptions because they make temporary autonomous zones visible. Such zones abide to a new logic that no longer foresees groups of producers-consumers, but something different, yet to be included in the vocabulary of the economic. (translated fromLanza 1996: 240)

The economic, too, is therefore nothing more than a perception of reality, which in turn creates the reality we live in. A libertarian society is characterised by the refusal to maintain an autonomous economic sphere, as the economic must not have its own specific scope but must rather conform to other institutions (of kinship, community, etc.). Escaping the economic means escaping current society, which is *the* economic society. The dominant rationality is an economic one, encompassing all, including the political. The aim is difficult but not impossible: to promote a society which no longer pivots around economic values, where the economy is a means for human life, not its ultimate end. Within this framework, it is clear that the economic has a plurality of forms, all linked to the specific context of the communities in which they develop. Anarchism therefore moves 'beyond the economic' (Chapter 7) while proclaiming its harmfulness.

These topics were vividly debated in *Volontà*, whose pages hosted a variety of seminal contributions for which thinking of a society 'beyond the economic' meant to also address its eco-compatibility. Ecology became a crucial issue for *Volontà*'s editors at a time when environmental theories featured in the political debate but their libertarian dimension was underexplored. The main ideas discussed in the journal had Murray Bookchin's anarchist social ecology as a key point of reference.

Several of Bookchin's articles were published in *Volontà* between 1980 and 1994, signalling the need to complement classical anarchist thought (especially that of Reclus and Kropotkin) with a new ecological vision able to combine the environmentalist and libertarian dimensions, the inseparable link between ecology and libertarian social organisation. An alternative way of thinking emerged, distinct from both institutionalised/reformist Green parties and deep ecology's fundamentalism. Such thinking was guided by the idea that real ecological change can only be achieved through radical transformation in power relations and social inequalities.

Various authors contributed to the debate with a pluralist outlook (John Clark, Roberto Ambrosoli, Paul Feyerabend, Janet Biehl, Franco La Cecla, Jean Baudrillard and Wolfgang Sachs, to mention a few).* A debate on social ecology could not be separated from a discussion on human nature, and the relationship between culture and nature. Readers were offered perspectives rejecting both human nature as essence (essentialism) and culture as something existing outside (separable from) its relationship with nature.

The relationship between universalism and relativism, the profound nature of epistemology (Morin and Laborit 1982), the meaning and limits of science, and the dangers of fundamentalism in every area of life and social thought (Ambrosoli 1982) were also vividly discussed.

Volontà also paid particular attention to concrete issues, by narrating historical and contemporary experimentations, and by getting back to thinkers – not only anarchists – whose insights could lead to actual libertarian development. So, the city, housing, urban planning and social geography were discussed in important contributions which made the journal a privileged, and in some respects unique, place for debate at the European level.**

The same can be said for libertarian education and the critique of traditional school systems. Themes that ran through the anarchist tradition were developed by combining classical authors' fundamental questions with analyses and narration of contemporary experiences on the ground.*** Last but not least, several articles and issues were devoted to gender and libertarian feminism.****

---

* Two special issues appeared on the topic of ecology and anarchism: *Pensare l'ecologia* in 1987 (nos. 2–3) and *Pornoecologia: la natura e la sua immagine* in 1992 (no. 2).

** See, for example, issue no. 2 of *Volontà* in 1986, which appeared under the title 'The Idea of Living' (*L'idea di abitare*). Nos. 1–2 in 1989 included essays by Ivan Illich, Colin Ward, John Turner and Giancarlo De Carlo; no. 4 in 1992 was titled 'Boundless Geography' (*Geografia senza confini*), with contributions from Colin Ward and Claude Raffestin especially; nos. 2–3 in 1995, 'The City Is Naked' (*La città è nuda*), featured essays by Colin Ward, Giancarlo De Carlo, Carlo Doglio, Franco Bunčuga and Pietro M. Toesca.

*** See, for example, 'Education and Freedom' (*Educazione e libertà*), in issue no. 1, 1987; 'The Child between Authority and Freedom' (*Il bambino fra autorità e Libertà*) in issue no. 3, 1993 (see, in particular, the contributions by Ivan Illich, Marcello Bernardi and Lamberto Borghi); and Codello (1996) on libertarian education.

**** See, for example, the various articles in no. 4, 1982; no. 1, 1983; nos. 1–2, 1988 (especially the various essays by Rossella Di Leo and Marianne Enckell).

Reasons for Anarchy: The Anarchism of *Volontà*

It is not possible here to do justice to the variety of issues covered by the journal in these crucial years.* We can certainly say that *Volontà* made a difference by moving freely between topics, ideas, experiments and philosophies, always casting a critical eye on Power. This may seem obvious for an anarchist journal, but it is less so when we consider the multiplicity of themes that were explored in a pragmatic way without ever losing their 'anarchist compass'.

The last issue of *Volontà* appeared in 1996, marking fifty years of the journal's publication, and bore the emblematic title 'The Reasons for Anarchy'. Emblematic because, at the end of the journal's rounded exploration of libertarian culture, the reasons for thinking as anarchists clearly emerge. A long journey in several directions that did not mark out a final path, without a sense of conclusion or return. It was a 'disoriented' journey that had radically challenged many certainties while preserving all that remained valid. It was a cultural operation also made up of life, experimentation, initiatives, struggles; a true artisan workshop of remarkable finesse.

In its pages we can find insights and choices that may be taken for granted by (some of) today's anarchists but were anything but obvious at the time. *Volontà's* anarchism anticipated a series of important questions and strategic themes that would become key to anarchist thought. But even more importantly, the journal was an important tussle within a broader cultural and political strategy that was being explored by Italian and international anarchist militants.

This extraordinary cultural operation was concerned with the unity of thought and action, reasoning and feeling, ethics and secularism. *Volontà* combined international collaborations and multidisciplinarity with a plurality of interpretations, research and debates. These were the elements of an authentic artisan workshop, which enhanced collective thinking and established a close link between social anarchism and anarchism as an existential practice (or, as Bookchin would put it, a 'lifestyle'). At a time when the anarchist movement was

---

* To give you a flavour of this, here are the titles of some of the monographic issues not mentioned: 'The Libertarian Dimension of 1968' (*La dimensione libertaria del Sessantotto*) in 1988, no. 3; 'Un/making Art' (*Dis/fare l'arte*) in 1988, no. 4; 'Drugs: The Vice of Prohibiting' (*Droga: il vizio di proibire*) in 1991, no. 1; 'Notes of Revolt' (*Note di rivolta*) in 1993, nos. 1–2; *Penne all'arrabbiata* in 1993, nos. 3–4; 'Crime and Punishment' (*Delitto e castigo*) in 1994, no. 1; 'Unveiled Fundamentalisms' (*Fondamentalismi senza veli*) in 1996, no. 1; 'Spain, 1936: Utopia Is History' (*Spagna 1936: l'utopia è storia*) in 1996, no. 2. There was even an issue dedicated to psychoanalysis (1985, no. 2)!

in crisis, in which there was a high degree of cultural and social disorientation, the journal was able to hold a straight course while immersing itself in a problematic and contradictory reality.

In those difficult years, *Volontà* gave priority to the libertarian, anti-authoritarian dimensions of relational and social living, giving new lifeblood to anarchist thought and allowing it to test the coherence of its utopian (but indispensable) vision. *Volontà*'s last issue took stock of its publishing experience in a collection of essays that tried once again to reaffirm, after years of research, the validity of collective anarchist thinking and libertarian social practices. It was clear to the editors that anarchist thought, given up for dead many times, showed an unsuspected vitality. Indeed, it influenced numerous sectors of culture and social life, at times unknowingly, in other circumstances explicitly.

The experience and the cultural project of *Volontà* has continued to animate many initiatives and triggered further innovative research. Its legacy lives through the work of the CSL and its publishing house, elèuthera, and the Ateneo degli Imperfetti [University of the Imperfects] in Marghera (Venice). It is a political project that envisages a new social organisation that moves from the simple to the complex without the need for hierarchical institutions, capable of representing an adequate alternative to the mortal crisis of Marxism and the deadly spread of liberalism.

Volontà, as the expression of an Italian anarchist editorial and political group, understood before others that 1968 and 1969 had posed challenging, crucial questions to both theory and practice, thus representing a new opportunity to be seized for the renewal of anarchist thought. The choice of establishing a dialogue with the broader libertarian fringe, as materially embodied in behaviours, relationships, experiences, thoughts and reflections, allowed the journal to radically innovate the classic dimension of anarchist theory and to devise a new expression of anarchism itself.

Above all, *Volontà* understood the fundamental importance of international research. Anarchism is by vocation international and internationalist; it can never be enclosed in a provincial and self-referential dimension, unless it wants to perish.

References

Abensour, Miguel (1989), 'I paradossi dell'eroismo rivoluzionario', *Volontà* 4: 115–34.
Alemany, Josep (1981), 'Il tempo dei campi di concentramento', *Volontà* 4: 18–52.

Alemany, Josep (1982), 'Anarchismo e liberalismo', *Volontà* 3: 105–9.

Ambrosoli, Roberto (1982), 'Volontà e natura umana', *Volontà* 4: 19–32.

Anonymous (1980), 'Editoriale', *Volontà* 1: 2–3.

Bakunin, Michael (1980), 'God and the State', in *Bakunin on Anarchism*, ed. Sam Dolgoff, Montreal: Black Rose Books, pp. 225–42.

Berneri Family Archive (2012), 'Giovanna Caleffi Berneri e la cultura eretica di sinistra nel secondo dopoguerra', Reggio Emilia: Aurelio Chessa.

Berti, Nico (1975), 'L'anarchismo: nella storia ma contro la storia', *Interrogations* 2: 93–119.

Berti, Nico (1989), 'Alla radice del problema', *Volontà* 4: 105–14.

Berti, Nico (2016), *Contro la storia. Cinquant'anni di anarchismo in Italia (1962–2012)*, Milan: Biblion Edizioni.

Bertolo, Amedeo (1983), 'Lasciamo il pessimismo per i tempi migliori', *Volontà* 2: 3–13.

Bertolo, Amedeo (1994), 'Al di là della democrazia. L'anarchia', *Volontà* 4: 9–32.

Bertolo, Amedeo (2019), 'La funzione utopica nell'immaginario anarchico', in Amedeo Bertolo (ed.), *Anarchici e orgogliosi di esserlo*, Milan: elèuthera, pp. 177–86.

Bookchin, Murray (1987), *The Rise of Urbanisation and the Decline of Citizienship*, San Francisco: Sierra Club Books.

Bookchin, Murray (1989), 'Società, politica, Stato', *Volontà* 4: 39–58.

Bookchin, Murray (1991), 'The Left That Was: A Personal Reflection', *Left Green Perspectives* 22.

Bookchin, Murray (1995), *Social Anarchism or Lifestyle Anarchism: An Unbridgeable Chasm*, Edinburgh: AK Press.

Castoriadis, Cornelius (1989), 'Potere, politica, autonomia', *Volontà* 4: 28–40.

Chomsky, Noam (1982), 'Il tempo dei campi di concentramento', *Volontà* 1: 91–101.

Clark, John (1994), 'Ripensare la società', *Volontà* 4: 93–116.

Codello, Francesco (1979), 'La valutazione a schede nella scuola italiana', *Volontà* 1: 7–18.

Codello, Francesco (1996), 'L'educazione libertaria', *Volontà* 3–4: 243–70.

Codello, Francesco (2009), *Gli anarchismi*, Lugano: La Baronata.

Codello, Francesco (2015), 'Democrazia e anarchia', in Luciano Lanza (ed.), *La pratica della libertà e i suoi limiti*, Milan: Mimesis-Libertaria, pp. 127–44.

Colombo, Eduardo (1981), 'L'utopia contro l'escatologia', *Volontà* 3: 15–30.

Colombo, Eduardo (1983), 'Dell'obbedienza, il potere e la sua riproduzione', *Volontà* 2: 79–113.

Colombo, Eduardo (1989), 'Della polis e dello spazio sociale plebeo', *Volontà* 4: 7–38.

De Maria, Carlo (ed.) (2010), *Giovanna Caleffi Berneri. Un seme sotto la neve*, Reggio Emilia: Berneri Family-Aurelio Chessa Archive.

De Maria, Carlo (2019), *Una famiglia anarchica. La vita dei Berneri tra affetti, impegno ed esilio nell'Europa del Novecento*, Rome: Viella.

Enriquez, Eugène (1980), 'Le forme interiorizzate della repressione', *Volontà* 2: 63–8.

Freire, João (1983), 'Idee per una alternativa politica dell'anarchismo', *Volontà* 2: 12–27.

Holterman, Thom (1987), 'Oltre la democrazia: la sociocrazia', *Volontà* 4: 153–67.

Ibáñez, Tomás (1994), 'L'incredibile leggerezza dei democratici', *Volontà* 4: 57–70.

Lanza, Luciano (1981), 'La rivoluzione e la sua immagine', *Volontà* 1: 4–17.

Lanza, Luciano (1996), 'Il mito economia', *Volontà* 3–4: 231–42.

Lanza, Luciano [1997] (2004), *Secrets and Bombs: Piazza Fontana 1969*, Hastings: Christie Books.

La Torre, Massimo (1980), 'Discutendo di democrazia', *Volontà* 2: 17–36.

Lefort, Claude (1989), 'Democrazia e rappresentazione', *Volontà* 4: 135–52.

Morin, Edgar, and Henri Laborit (1982), 'Conversazioni. La natura dell'uomo', ed. Luciano Lanza, *Volontà* 4: 33–7.

Reclus, Élisée (2013), 'Evolution, Revolution and the Anarchist Idea', in John Clark and Camille Martin (eds), *Anarchy, Geography, Modernity: Selected Writings of Elisée Reclus*, Oakland: PM Press, pp. 138–55.

Richards, Vernon (ed.) (2015), *Life and Ideas: The Anarchist Writings of Errico Malatesta*, Oakland: PM Press.

Sensini, Paolo (2004), 'Pio Turroni', in *Dizionario biografico degli anarchici italiani*, Pisa: BFS Edizioni, vol. 2, 635–8; available at <https://www.bfscollezionidigitali.org/entita/14856-turroni-pio?i=1> (last accessed 10 June 2021).

Thèvenet, Alain (1994), 'Una politica anarchica?', *Volontà* 4: 71–92.

Vaccaro, Salvo (1994), 'L'implosione statuale', *Volontà* 4: 151–74.

Various Authors (2012), *Giovanna Caleffi Berneri e la cultura eretica di sinistra nel secondo dopoguerra*, Reggio Emilia: Berneri Family-Aurelio Chessa Archive.

Venza, Claudio (1979), 'Forze armate italiane e nuova politica del PCI. Appunti bibliografici', *Volontà* 1: 19–37.

Ward, Colin (1996), *Anarchy in Action*, London: Freedom Press.

Author Biographies

Giampietro 'Nico' Berti (Bassano del Grappa, Vicenza, Italy, 1943) joined the anarchist movement at a young age, coming into contact with Amedeo Bertolo and the Milanese group Gioventù Libertaria [Libertarian Youth] in the early 1960s. Shortly after, in 1965, he contributed to the birth of the Federated Anarchist Youth Groups (GGAF) which became the Federated Anarchist Groups (GAF) in 1970. In 1969 he co-founded with Elis Fraccaro the Nestor Makhno group in Venice-Marghera, also affiliated to the GAF.

In 1971 he co-founded the monthly magazine *A/Rivista Anarchica*, with Amedeo Bertolo, Rossella Di Leo, Luciano Lanza, Fausta Bizzozzero, Roberto Ambrosoli and Paolo Finzi, and in 1976 he was among the promoters of the Centro Studi Libertari/Giuseppe Pinelli Archive (CSL) in Milan, participating in all of its main initiatives and contributing in particular to the international conferences organised over the decades in Venice, from the conference of Bakuninian Studies in 1976 to the conference on 'Authoritarian tendencies and libertarian tensions in contemporary societies' organised as part of Venice 1984.

In the editorial field, he collaborated with the international quarterly *Interrogations* (1974–1979) and served as a member of the editorial team of the journal *Volontà* from 1980 to its closure in 1996. Subsequently he was part of the editorial committee of the periodical *Libertaria*. He also collaborated with the anarchist publisher Antistato (1975–1985), and then since 1986 with elèuthera.

He was a professor of contemporary history at the University of Padua (and between 1998 and 2002 also at the University of Trieste), where he taught on the history of political parties and ideologies of the twentieth century. His research interests revolve around the history of ideas between the nineteenth and twentieth centuries. With respect to anarchism, his main publications (in

Italian) include *Francesco Saverio Merlino: From Socialist Anarchism to Liberal Socialism, 1856–1930* (1993); *An Exorbitant Idea of Freedom: Introduction to Anarchist Thought* (1994); *Anarchist Thinking: From the Eighteenth to the Twentieth Century* (1998); *Errico Malatesta and the Italian and International Anarchist Movement 1872–1932* (2003); and *Freedom without Revolution: Anarchism between the Defeat of Communism and the Victory of Capitalism* (2012). His latest book, *Against History: Fifty Years of Anarchism in Italy* (2016), is devoted to the history of the Federated Anarchist Groups (GAF) and to the many cultural and editorial initiatives carried out over the decades. He was also the national coordinator of the *Biographical Dictionary of Italian Anarchists* (2003–2004).

Amedeo Bertolo (Milan, Italy, 1941 – Milan, 2016) was born to a Friulian family, and by a curious twist of fate grew up in the same public housing project where Giuseppe Pinelli and Pietro Valpreda also lived, though he would only meet them years later. From his father, a mosaicist with whom he worked for a year, Amedeo learned to create designs whose realisation, tile after tile, required time, patience and determination.

He was accepted to the Department of Agriculture at the University of Milan ('I chose it because it was the shortest registration line,' he admitted), where he remained after his graduation as a professor of agricultural economics (this perhaps explains the recurring agronomic metaphors in his texts, such as the one on anarchism and alcohol content; see Chapter 2).

His public life began well before his engagement with academia, in 1962, with a booming event: the first political kidnapping of the post-war period. Amedeo, together with a group of young anti-fascists, kidnapped Isu Elías, the Spanish Vice Consul to Milan. The act was carried out in order to save the life of Jorge Conill Valls, a Spanish anarchist condemned to death by Franco's regime (a verdict that would later be changed to life in prison).

From this moment his existential journey as a militant began, leading to the formation, towards the end of the 1960s, of the GAF. One of three national anarchist federations which were active at the time, the GAF were unique for they were composed largely of youths and were organised in affinity groups.

The GAF years were also marked by the Italian State's 'strategy of tension' (see Chapter 1). Amedeo was one of the protagonists of the counter-information activities carried out by the Crocenera circle, which he and Giuseppe Pinelli had founded in 1968. Amedeo and Pinelli met through the Bandiera Nera, an anarchist group based in Milan, at the anarchist circle Ponte della Ghisolfa, also in Milan. A year later came the Piazza Fontana bombing, falsely attributed to anarchists by important State officials, and then Pinelli's violent death, tossed from a window at Milan's police headquarters. These events marked the height of anti-anarchist propaganda, dismantled in the months that followed by a formidable counter-information campaign (the Crocenera, for example, published a book entitled *The Boss' Bombs: People's Trial of the Italian State and the Milan Bombing Investigators*). A solitary campaign at first – 'Hysterical Press Conference at Circolo Ponte della Ghisolfa' ran one major headline – it soon became widespread.

This was a powerful experience for Amedeo that came to an end with the GAF's dissolution in January 1978, an event foreshadowing the transition from the idea of a movement-party to the idea of a movement-community. It was out of this shift that an extended 'brotherhood' was born, one destined to endure.

Yet the 1960s were not just assassinations, subterfuge, sham trials and 'State slaughters' [*stragi di stato*]. They were also years of revamped libertarian creativity that led to 1968. It is no coincidence that midway through the decade, young European anarchists invented a symbol destined to match the new anarchic imagination: the circle-A. Thanks to its simple iconography, the symbol would quickly conquer walls all over the world. The circle-A was conceptualised in Paris – Tomás Ibáñez used the symbol for the first time in the newsletter *Jeunes Libertaires* – but its 'graphic debut' was made in Milan, where Amedeo, with the help of an upside-down glass, carved it on the stencil for the first mimeographs made by the anarchist group Gioventù Libertaria. This same group opened the first club named after Wilhelm Reich, an obvious nod to the sexual revolution. They also organised the international libertarian Provotariat in Milan, inspired by the cultural provocations being performed by the Provos movement in the Netherlands.

Amedeo's militancy was coupled with an intense editorial activity; ancillary at first, it slowly became his priority. While he only released three slim editions of the periodic *Materialismo e Libertà* [Materialism and Freedom] in the 1960s, in 1971 Bertolo co-founded the monthly journal *A/Rivista Anarchica*. The money that gave life to what was until 2020 the best-selling anarchist journal in Italy was initially intended for another project: an anarchist commune in the Siena countryside. But the idea had trouble taking off amidst the tumultuous events of 1968–1969, and the funds were diverted to a journal 'of struggle and reflection' more in line with the times. Reinventing himself as a journalist and graphic designer, Amedeo worked for *A/Rivista Anarchica* until 1974, when he began collaborating with two other publications: the international quarterly *Interrogations* (1974–1979) and *Volontà*, which he co-edited from 1980 until its closure in 1996.

With the Centro Studi Libertari, which he co-founded in 1976 in Milan, he organised and participated in dozens of conferences, seminars, round tables and debates, mostly in Italy but also abroad, in a continuous effort to keep up with libertarian thought and experimentation emerging in different fields across the world. While this undertaking may have had its peak in 1984 with the international anarchist meeting 'Venice 1984', Bertolo continued organising anarchist-related events for many years to come.

Over the years, his attention moved increasingly from periodicals to books. He first joined the publishing house Antistato (1975–1985) which picked up the work initiated by Pio Turroni's legendary Gruppo Editore L'Antistato (1949–1975). In 1986, he co-founded elèuthera with Rossella Di Leo, his militant and life partner, giving birth to yet another collective adventure that has lasted over thirty years and continues today.

He died in Milan on 22 November 2016.

Francesco Codello (Valdobbiadene, Treviso, Italy, 1953) was drawn to libertarian ideas at the end of the 1960s above all through the thought of Leo Tolstoy. In the early 1970s he fully adhered to anarchist ideas and founded the anarchist group 'Franco Serantini' in Valdobbiadene, which later joined the Federated Anarchist Groups (GAF). The group is very active on the ground, engaging with workers in the main factories and in schools, disseminating anarchist publications, and participating in the struggles, and also by carrying out large-scale campaigns of counter-information and anti-fascist militancy.

He actively took part in the various international anarchist conferences held in Venice throughout the 1970s ('Bakunin Hundred Years Later', 1976; 'The New Masters', 1978; 'Autogestion', 1979) and in the Triveneto coordination of various anarchist groups until the early 1980s. He was part of the editorial team of the anarchist journal *Volontà* from 1978 to 1982 and then of *Libertaria* (first journal and then yearbook, 1999–2018) and frequent contributor to the monthly magazine *A/Rivista Anarchica* (1971–2020). He has been a member of the Centro Studi Libertari /Giuseppe Pinelli Archive in Milan since its foundation in 1976.

He has written numerous articles and essays on anarchism, education, history and political and social current affairs, published in Italian and European journals. In 2008 he founded the Libertarian Education Network, an organisation that collects numerous experiences of libertarian schools in Italy and promotes meetings, seminars, conferences on educational issues and comparisons between various existing experiences. Since its foundation (2005) he has been a member of the EUDEC (European Democratic Education Conference) and participated in numerous meetings and seminars on anti-authoritarian education in Europe, Brazil and Israel. He is a founding member and activist of the Ateneo degli Imperfetti in Marghera (Venice) since 2000. The Ateneo promotes meetings, conferences, debates, seminars and conferences on anarchism and in particular on how a libertarian vision permeates different disciplines of study and research today.

He graduated in pedagogy and later in philosophy. He was a primary school teacher and then a school principal. He is currently an independent researcher and a collaborator of self-managed and libertarian organisations. He has held hundreds of seminars in various Italian cities. In addition to several contributions in collective books, he has authored the following volumes (in Italian): *Education and Anarchism* (1995); *Good Education: Libertarian Experiences and Anarchist Theories in Europe from Godwin to Neill* (2005); *Vase, Clay or Flower?* (2005); *Neither Obey nor Command* (2009); *Anarchisms: A Brief Introduction* (2009); *Free to Learn* (with Irene Stella, 2011); *The Human Condition* (2017); and *The Bell No Longer Rings* (2019). He was also editor of Colin Ward's anthology *The Incidental Education* (2018) and Leo Tolstoy's anthology *The Refusal to Obey* (2019).

Currently, he serves as editor of the Milan-based publishing house elèuthera.

Eduardo Raul Colombo (Quilmes, Argentina, 1929 – Paris, France, 2018) was a physician and psychoanalyst, and very early on began the anarchist militancy that would constitute the salient feature of his entire existential path.

Already in the 1940s, whilst still a student, he joined the FORA (Federación Obrera Regional Argentina), participating in its anarcho-syndicalist struggles throughout the country, even during the recurring periods of dictatorship that marked Argentina's history. He also started collaborating with the most important Argentine anarchist periodical, *La protesta*, later assuming editorial responsibility.

After graduating in medicine, he became a professor of social psychology at the universities of first La Plata and later Buenos Aires. He was expelled from the university after the 1966 military coup at the hands of General Onganía. In 1967 he took over the direction of the magazine *Psiquiatría Social*, but in 1970 he was forced to flee to Paris, together with his partner Heloisa Castellanos and their two children, Laura and Mateo. Despite the initial difficulties encountered in reintegrating into work, he soon established himself as a psychoanalyst, a profession that continued until the end of his days, always with a Freudian, strongly anti-Lacanian orientation. Even before re-establishing his career path, he began a sustained and intense collaboration with European anarchist movements, particularly in France, Spain and Italy.

In the early 1970s, he joined the Informations et Correspondances Ouvrières (ICO) group, which used to publish the bulletin of the same name. When this latter terminated its activity, he co-founded the periodical *Lanterne noire* (1974–1978) together with various anarchist militants from the Mouvement du 22 Mars and the editorial staff of Noir et Rouge (1955–1970).

In the meantime, his collaboration with the Italian movement strengthened, in particular with the group around the Centro Studi Libertari/Giuseppe Pinelli Archive in Milan. He took part in their first international conference organised in 1976 to mark the centenary of the death of Bakunin. Both Eduardo and Heloisa joined the editorial group of *Volontà* in 1980 until the closure of the journal in 1996.

Eduardo also engaged in an intense activity as an essayist that led him to write about twenty political books (translated into various languages), accompanied by a more strictly psychoanalytic production.

As a member of the French CNT [Confédération Nationale du Travail], he edited the CNT-RP editions for a period and above all he was one of the founders, in 1997, of the French anarchist journal *Réfractions*, of which he remained one of the main editors until his death.

After a short illness, he died in Paris on 13 March 2018. The funeral ceremony held at the Père-Lachaise cemetery on 19 March saw a large participation of anarchists from various countries, especially from the Latin world, who recognised him as one of the more consistent and refined anarchist thinkers of the last decades.

Rossella Di Leo (Catania, Italy, 1951) became an anarchist in the wake of the 1968 student protests that broke out all over the world. She left her native Sicily at the end of 1970 and moved to Milan, the city of origin of her maternal family, to study political science at the University of Milan in the hottest years of protest. In Milan, she continued her anarchist militancy, becoming close to the area of the Federated Anarchist Groups (GAF), who were particularly active at the time in the counter-information campaign following the Piazza Fontana massacre in December 1969 and the killing of Giuseppe Pinelli, who was one of the GAF's best-known exponents.

Her path soon intersected with that of Amedeo Bertolo, who became her militant and life partner, to the point that their biographies from 1971 onwards largely coincide. Alongside political activism, which was very intense throughout the 1970s, since 1971 she has been engaging in an equally intense editorial and cultural activity, which is still a fundamental part of her life. Her editorial journey, initially as a journalist, began with the birth of the monthly journal *A/*

Rivista Anarchica (February 1971), continued with the international quarterly *Interrogations*, founded in Paris in 1974 by Louis Mercier Vega, and finally landed at *Volontà*, which was based in Milan from 1980 until its closure in 1996. Since 1976 she has been a driving force behind the cultural activities of the Centro Studi Libertari/Giuseppe Pinelli Archive, which in its forty-five years of life has organised hundreds of conferences, workshops and seminars, often international in scope, aimed at keeping alive the historical memory of anarchism and renewing contemporary anarchist thought, including the 'Venice 1984' international anarchist meeting. However, her greatest commitment has always been in the field of publishing, from the beginnings in 1975 with the Antistato publishing house to the anarchist publisher elèuthera, co-founded with Amedeo Bertolo in 1986, which to date remains her core activity.

Tomás Ibáñez (Zaragoza, Spain, 1944) was smuggled from his native Spain to France by his mother in 1947 to escape the Franco regime. His schooling took place in Toulouse, Marseille and Paris. He obtained the License of Psychology at the University of Paris in 1967. He worked at the Laboratory of Social Psychology of the Sorbonne from 1968 to 1973 and returned to Spain in 1973. He obtained his doctorate in 1980 at the Autonomous University of Barcelona, where he was later appointed professor of social psychology, and he taught there until his retirement in 2007. He also served as vice-rector of the same university between 1994 and 1999. He has published some thirty books and book chapters and a hundred articles, with a critical orientation towards the mainstream of the discipline. See, for example, in English, 'Social Psychology and the Rhetoric of Truth' (1991) in *Theory and Psychology* and *Critical Social Psychology* (SAGE, 1997).

He began his anarchist militancy in 1960 by participating in the creation of the group of Jeunes Libertaires of Marseille, then in September 1963 he moved to Paris, where he was one of the promoters of the creation of the Liaison des Étudiants Anarchistes and of the Comité de Liaison des Jeunes Anarchistes. He is at the origin of the creation of the Circle-A, proposed as a symbol of anarchism in April 1964. He was a militant simultaneously with the Anarchist Federation, the Libertarian Youth, the Iberian Federation of Libertarian Youth and the Anarchist Youth Group, playing an active part in the fight against the Franco dictatorship. With the participation of the militants of the Gruppi Anarchici Federati (GAF), he was one of the organisers of the first European Meeting of Young Anarchists in Paris in April 1966. He was arrested during the events of May '68, and his condition of political refugee turned the decree of expulsion from France into house arrest outside Paris. During those years he published around twenty articles, in the *Bulletin des Jeunes Libertaires, Le Monde Libertaire* and *Action Libertaire*.

Returning to Spain in 1973, after the death of the dictator, he actively participated in the reconstruction of the CNT and the libertarian movement as well as in initiatives of a libertarian nature such as the creation of the journal *Archipielago*. He has participated in numerous international libertarian conferences and since 1973 has published nearly a hundred articles and twenty books and book chapters, some of which have been translated into other languages, such as, in English, *Anarchism Is Movement* (Freedom Press, 2019) and, in Italian, *Il libero pensiero* (elèuthera, 2007). He is currently a member of *Réfractions* in France and *Libre Pensamiento* in Spain.

Luciano Lanza (Milan, Italy, 1945) began working as an accountant for a famous Milanese firm in the mid-1960s, where he remained employed for a dozen years. At the same time, he began his political militancy by joining first the Sacco and Vanzetti Circle and later the Bandiera Nera [Black Flag] group, and the Federated Anarchist Groups (GAF). From that moment, he took part in all the main events that mark the history of the GAF, one of the three national anarchist federations active in that period. In particular, he was active in the counter-information campaign that marked the turbulent historical period known as the 'strategy of tension', during which repeated terrorist attacks were carried out by neo-fascist groups with the connivance of certain sectors of the Italian secret services. Years later, in 1997, he devoted a book-investigation – *Bombs and Secrets* – to that crucial period of Italian history.

In 1977 he left the profession of accountancy and became a bookseller, opening the Utopia bookshop in Milan, which rapidly became a point of reference for the Milanese anarchist milieu. After a few years, he embarked on a career as an economic journalist, working for top Italian newspapers and in particular for the weekly *Il Mondo*, where he also served as editor-in-chief. He co-founded and took part in various editorial and cultural initiatives set up by the GAF, namely the journals *A/Rivista Anarchica* and *Interrogations*, the Centro Studi Libertari/ Giuseppe Pinelli Archive and, above all, the journal *Volontà*, of which he had editorial responsibility until its closure in 1996. In 1999 he founded the quarterly journal *Libertaria*, which was published until 2017.

Index